D0894126

Inattentional Blindness

MIT Press/Bradford Books Series in Cognitive Psychology
Stephen E. Palmer, editor

Inattentional Blindness

Arien Mack and Irvin Rock

A Bradford Book
The MIT Press
Cambridge, Massachusetts
London, England

© 1998 Massachusetts Institute of Technology

All rights reserved. No part of this book may be reproduced in any form by any elec-
tronic or mechanical means (including photocopying, recording, or information storage
and retrieval) without permission in writing from the publisher.

This book was set in Palatino by Graphic Composition, Inc., Athens, Georgia.

Printed and bound in the United States of America.

Library of Congress Cataloging-in-Publication Data

Mack, Arien.
    Inattentional blindness / Arien Mack and Irvin Rock.
        p.   cm.
    "A Bradford book".
    Includes bibliographical references and index.
    ISBN 0-262-13339-3 (alk. paper)
        1. Visual perception.   2. Attention.   3. Visual discrimination.
I. Rock, Irvin.   II. Title.
BF241.M26   1998
    152.7'33—dc21   97-28254
                                                                    CIP

Contents

Series Foreword

The series on Cognitive Psychology presents a collection of definitive books on cognition viewed from a psychological perspective. It includes undergraduate and graduate textbooks, major reference works, and research monographs on the cutting edge of psychological knowledge, and on occasion, as the situation warrants, a few edited volumes. Books in the series concern a wide variety of topics in cognition, including perception, attention, imagery, memory, learning, categorization, language, problem solving, thinking, and cognitive development. Although the primary emphasis is on presenting psychological theories and findings, most volumes in the series have an interdisciplinary flavor, attempting to develop important connections between cognitive psychology and the related fields of anthropology, computer science, education, linguistics, neuroscience and philosophy.

Stephen E. Palmer

In memory of my beloved daughter, Lisa P. Mack

Preface

This book is a narrative description of research designed to explore perception without attention that began in 1988 and initially was carried out in our two widely separated laboratories—one at the Graduate Faculty of the New School for Social Research, and the other at the University of California, Berkeley. With the exception of the first and last chapters, the book is a chronological history of this research project. Thus the reader can follow the trail that led to the final conclusions, and can consider the reasons why initial explanations and hypotheses were either discarded or revised and how new questions arose along the way.

The research brought to light some dramatic and surprising findings, and although many questions remain, some things of importance have been learned. The single most important lesson is that there seems to be *no conscious perception without attention*. Given the explosion of work in the last decade on preattentive perception, this is a provocative claim. Nevertheless, it is one to which we were ineluctably drawn by these findings; we hope, by the end of this book, the reader will be as well.

Although this book deals with material and questions that have been the subject of much research and discussion in the field, we have made no effort to summarize or refer to all the relevant literature. Rather we have chosen to cite representative examples of bodies of work and apologize to those whose research we have failed to mention. Just to be perfectly clear, this book neither attempts to provide a theory of attention, nor to relate the findings reported to possible brain structures. This latter strategy, even though increasingly prevalent in the literature, seems to me (and on this point my coauthor would have been in full agreement) not only premature but frequently misleading.

The book does not contain the very detailed accounts of stimuli and procedures normally found in professional journals. However, we do try to provide enough information so that it is possible to understand what each of the experiments was like. Even so, the book contains a considerable amount of data and detail, the inclusion of which seemed essential to our purpose. However, wherever possible details about the stimulus displays and the procedures used appear in a smaller font slightly indented, making it easier for readers who prefer to ignore this level of description to do so by simply skipping over these passages. In addition, many of the displays are schematically represented, often with an indication of the most important results obtained, which at times may repeat what is in the text itself. This redundancy is also intended to make it easier to grasp the essentials of what was done and what was found.

The first and last chapters are meant to serve as bookends for the chapters that fall in between them. The first chapter provides a summary of the main research findings and the last summarizes the conclusions drawn from the findings. The rest offer detailed accounts of the many experiments, their outcomes, and the reasoning that led from one experiment to the next.

The research began as a collaboration, as did the writing of this book. Unfortunately, the collaboration came to an unexpected and untimely end. In December 1994 Irvin Rock learned that he had pancreatic cancer. During the precious few, very difficult and painful months between this dreadful diagnosis and his death on July 18, 1995, he continued to work, more than seemed humanly possible, and we tried to continue our discussions about the book. Nevertheless, at the time of his death the book was not yet finished and research was still in progress. There were, however, at least partial, preliminary drafts of all but the last two chapters.

Irvin Rock's death was an irreparable loss. He was my teacher, my collaborator, and one of my closest friends. And this book suffered as well. Had he lived, some of the conclusions and explanations surely would have been different and probably wiser. The book therefore does not represent a full collaboration, and I know there are things that I have written with which he would have disagreed. In his absence, however, I saw no alternative to the approach I took, which was to provide explanations of the results and draw conclusion from them that seemed coherent and reasonably well supported by the data. This sometimes meant modifying or eliminating some text he had written. I regretted this, but I consoled myself with the knowledge that frequently what I was deleting was material that had been written before all the results were in.

One conclusion I am fairly sure would have made my coauthor uncomfortable—which we had just begun to talk about when he became too ill to pursue it—was that the meaning of a stimulus is one of the main, if not the main determinant of whether it succeeds in capturing attention under conditions of inattention. I think he may have found this so difficult to accept because it seemed to him to be an "extra-perceptual" explanation of perception. And while his own account of perception—which is most clearly stated in his book, *The Logic of Perception*—relies on assumptions about the rational and problem-solving character of the perceptual system, nevertheless, for him, the determining factors were internal to the perceptual system. I believe he thought that it is one thing to assert, as he did, that the perceptual system is rule governed, that the rules are rational in nature, that it is inferential, and that its goal is to answer questions about what objects or events the sensory input is most likely to represent, but quite another to argue that what determines the content of perceptual consciousness is the meaningfulness of the processed information. This gives a decisive role to nonperceptual processes because meaningfulness is frequently based on semantic rather than formal considerations. In truth, awarding meaning so important a role in an account of the connection between perception and attention is only marginally more comfortable for me, if only because there is no clear measure that permits the ranking of meaningfulness. Nevertheless, the concept does seem to explain a substantial amount of the data, which is why it figures so prominently here despite the reasons militating against it. It seems to provide the most comprehensive account of our results.

There are undoubtedly other things that have been asserted in this book to which my coauthor would have objected as well. For example, he could not easily accept the notion that, at least under conditions of inattention, the object or stimulus that captures attention is likely to be an unconscious percept. Had he lived these issues would have been thoroughly discussed and some consensus arrived at, for this is how we dealt with our disagreements at each earlier step in our collaboration.

Unfortunately, Irvin Rock did not live to read and revise the last chapter in which an effort is made to pull together and explain all the findings. Of course, this means that only I am responsible for its errors. There were also a considerable number of significant additions and deletions to every other chapter, and all of those that had been drafted while he was alive were revised after his death. This means that I may be responsible for many of the errors that appear in these chapters as well.

Acknowledgments

Many people contributed to this project. Of these the most essential were the graduate students and research assistants at the New School for Social Research and the University of California at Berkeley without whom the research simply would not have been done. Their participation began with the programming of the experiments and designing of the stimuli, and extended to performing the experiments and collaborating in the analysis and explanation of the results. Indeed, the only misgivings we had about our decision to write a book about this work rather than to report it in a series of research and review articles was that it would deprive our young collaborators of the recognition they deserved. Had we written articles, their names would have appeared among the list of authors, providing some of them with not one but a number of publication credits. We have tried to make up for this by indicating in the text in which laboratory particular experiments were done and by whom, but this does not adequately convey the extent of their contribution.

There were a group of assistants whose contributions, however, can not be adequately acknowledged by a mere footnote. In this group are Willann Stone, Teresa Hartmann, Jack Hoppenstand, and Michael Silverman at the New School for Social Research, and Christopher Linnett, Tony Ro, Harris Ingle, and Diane Beck at the University of California, Berkeley. Willann Stone was an active collaborator in the early days of the research and extended our understanding of the relevance this work might have for children suffering from an Attention Deficit Disorder. Teresa Hartmann joined the New School perception laboratory not long after the research began and remained throughout the writing of this book. She participated in almost every aspect of the project and probably—more than anyone else—was essential to it. She not only designed and performed many of the important experiments done at the New School, she drafted the originals of most of the figures and tables in this book as well. Jack Hoppenstand designed and ran all the auditory experiments, worked diligently to improve the graphic representations of our data, and most important, thought long and hard about the conclusions that seemed might follow from our results. Michael Silverman not only ran his share of the experiments, but extended our research in an important new direction that is likely to link it to new research areas.

In Berkeley Tony Ro and Christopher Linnett designed much of the research done there and helped clarify many difficult issues. Harris Ingle and Diane Beck, also at Berkeley, were essential resources during the period in which the book was being written, when it was no longer possible to discuss the Berkeley work with Irvin Rock. Without them and without Ethan Newby and Dan Kuang, who did the last research on this project done at Berkeley, it would not have been possible to complete or coherently describe this work.

I would also like to thank the staff at the San Francisco Exploratorium and the New Jersey Liberty Science Center for generously allowing us to run our experiments in their institutions. Our need for subjects was virtually insatiable and both institutions provided us with access to an endless supply. Thanks are due as well to the thousands of people who participated as subjects.

Two other people were extremely important both during the research and writing phases of this work. Stephen Palmer and Bill Prinzmetal, both of whom are on the Berkeley Psychology faculty, were always ready to talk about our findings and to provide invariably thoughtful comments and advice. Both of them read the original drafts of each chapter and their comments surely helped me to avoid many potential errors. They also shared with me the pain of watching the progression of Irvin Rock's illness and stood by me and this work after his death. I will forever be grateful to them. No one could replace him as a colleague and collaborator, but Steve Palmer came as close as anyone could.

The entire research project was generously supported by the National Institutes of Mental Health, and I am particularly grateful to Howard Kurzman for his understanding during the period of Irvin Rock's illness and after his death. Thanks are due as well to Amy Pearce Brand, our editor at MIT Press, and to Guenevere Nelson-Melby, who did an heroic job of copyediting the book manuscript. Finally I would like to acknowledge my debt to the Graduate Faculty of the New School where I have taught since 1966. This institution has given me the freedom to do my research in perception, to edit *Social Research,* and has supported me in all the other things that I have been lucky enough to be able to do as a faculty member there.

Chapter 1

An Overview

Motivation for the Research

What is the relationship between attention and perception? How much, if anything, of our visual world do we perceive when we are not attending to it? Are there only some kinds of things we see when we are not attending? If there are, do they fall into particular categories? Do we see them because they have captured our attention or because our perception of them is independent of our attention?

Most people have the impression that they simply see what is there and do so merely by opening their eyes and looking. Of course, we may look more closely at some things than at others, which is what we ordinarily mean by "paying attention," but it probably seems to many people as if we see nearly everything in our field of view.

However, many have experiences that seem to contradict the belief that, to one degree or another, we perceive everything in view and that our attention merely permits us to see some things in more detail than others. Almost everyone at one time or another has had the experience of looking without seeing and of seeing what is not there. The experience of looking without seeing is most likely to occur during moments of intense concentration or absorption. During these moments, even though our eyes are open and the objects before us are imaged on our retinas, we seem to perceive very little, if anything. For example, most people who drive have experienced these brief moments of not seeing, that is, of "functional blindness," which produce astonishment and alarm when awareness returns. Similar moments of "sighted blindness" can occur during particularly absorbing conversations or in moments of deep thought. Why do we have these experiences if perceiving only requires opening our eyes?

There is an opposite experience that also raises questions about the relation between perception and attention. When we are intently awaiting something, we often see and hear things that are not there. For example, many people have had the experience of hearing footsteps or seeing someone who is anxiously awaited even though the person is not there, and there are no footsteps. On these occasions, it is as if our intense expectation and riveted attention create or at least distort a perceptual object. Here, instead of not seeing (or hearing) what is there when we are distracted, we are seeing (or hearing) what is not there, or perhaps more accurately, misperceiving what may actually be there, but which we are anxiously awaiting. Both experiences appear to implicate attention in the act of perceiving. This kind of experience was eloquently described by William James.

> When waiting for the distant clock to strike, our mind is so filled with its image that at every moment we think we hear the longed-for or dreaded sound. So of an awaited footstep. Every stir in the wood is for the hunter his game; for the fugitive his pursuers. Every bonnet in the street is momentarily taken by the lover to enshroud the head of his idol. (1981, 419)

Grouping and Attention

The body of research we describe here is concerned with the relationship between visual perception and attention. Our initial motivation for studying this relationship developed from two independent but related sources. One was our interest in perceptual organization and the question of whether, as has generally been believed on the basis of principles first uncovered by the Gestalt psychologists, that the organization of the visual field into separate objects occurs automatically, at an early stage in the processing of visual information, or at some later stage, possibly after attention has been engaged. We already had reason to doubt that the grouping of the visual field on the basis of these principles is as early and spontaneous as most theorists believed. These doubts stemmed from the results of research done by one of us (IR) and his coworkers on the question of whether grouping by proximity or by similarity of lightness or shape is based on the retinal (proximal) attributes of units or rather on their perceived attributes.

This research established that these kinds of grouping in fact do not occur at the earliest stages of visual processing but, rather, occur later, after the processing that underlies perceptual constancy has been accomplished.[1] Because constancy processing generally depends upon available information about distance and/or surface lightness, constancy can occur only after this information has been taken into account. Thus, changing the relative retinal proximity of an array of elements from one in which the vertical elements are closer together than are the horizontal elements, to one in which the horizontal elements are closer, by slanting the array in depth, does not change the perceived grouping of the elements into vertical columns as long as

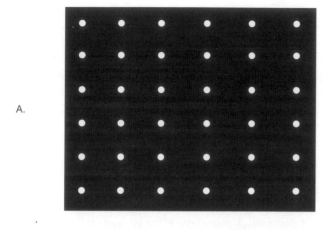

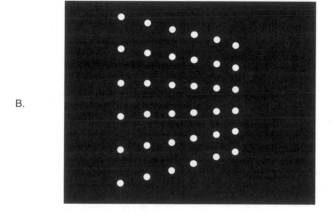

Figure 1.1
Grouping of elements by proximity.
A. Pattern of lights as they appear in frontal plane.
B. Same pattern as it appears when rotated in depth.

sensory information about slant in depth is available (Rock and Brosgole 1964) (figure 1.1). Thus the grouping of elements in a scene on the
basis of their closeness is not a function proximity on the retina, but of
their *perceived* proximity.[2] Consequently, grouping cannot occur automatically at the lowest level of perceptual processing, and this leaves
open the possibility that it might fail to occur without attention.

However, although there is good reason to doubt that grouping
based on Gestalt principles is an early achievement of visual processing, there seemed to be a compelling reason to believe that at least

one product of organization, namely the formation of the elementary units that provide the basis for grouping, was an early achievement of the visual system and therefore occurred without attention. As others have previously noted (Treisman 1982; Neisser 1967), attention is inherently intentional. It must be directed to some *thing*, and whatever that thing is, it must exist prior to the activation of attention, for only then is there something to which we can turn our attention. A surprising consequence of the research this book describes is that this view, which at the outset appeared to have the force of logic, was contradicted by the results.

Pop Out and Attention

The second source of our initial motivation for investigating the relation between perception and attention stemmed from concern with the methods most researchers have used to decide whether a perceptual process requires attention or instead is preattentive. Prior research into the relation between perception and attention has been based on a method that not only fails to eliminate attention, but in fact depends upon it. In all this research observers are required to perform some sort of visual search task. For example, they may be asked to report, as quickly as possible, whether a particular target—say a red circle—is present in a visual array consisting of green circles (see Treisman and Gelade 1980; Treisman 1988). In a variation of this design, subjects are not given a predefined target but rather are asked to report only whether an odd object is present in an array that is either homogenous or contains a single odd object (for example, see Julesz 1981). These arrays generally consist of a variable number of nontarget objects that are called "distractors." The relationship between the time it takes the subject to report the presence or absence of the target and the number of distractor elements is considered to be the indicator of whether the target stimulus is processed without attention. If, on trials in which a target is present an increase in the number of distractor elements causes no corresponding increase in the time it takes to report the target, the target stimulus is said to be processed "preattentively" (i.e., without attention). Or, if the time to report the presence of the target increases as the number of distractors increase, the stimulus is said to require focused attentional processing (see, for example, Treisman and Gelade 1980).

The reasoning here seems quite straightforward. If a target "pops out" (i.e., if the number of distractors does not affect how quickly it is seen), then it would seem that its perception does not require a serial search through each item in the array. If, however, the time to report that target increases with the number of distractors, then it seems equally plausible to conclude that the target does require searching through the array sequentially. Arrays in which targets pop out are said to be processed in parallel (i.e., all the objects are thought to be processed simultaneously), whereas arrays in which objects fail to pop out are believed to require serial processing. It was initially believed that the targets that pop out compose the set of basic or primitive features of perception, which are distinguished by the fact that they are perceived without attention, whereas the combination of these features into more complex objects requires serial processing and focused attention. (See Treisman 1985.)

Another less widely used technique for identifying the primitive features of perception thought to be perceived without attention entails presenting visual arrays very briefly, for example, for 50 msec. or less. Here too the subjects are given a search task. They are asked to report whether a target, which can either be a single object or a patch of segregated texture (Julesz 1981), is present in the array. If the observers are able to detect the target in these multielement arrays more or less effortlessly in the brief time allowed, the conclusion is drawn that it is detected without attention. The reasoning here also seems quite straightforward. If the target is detected when the entire array is presented very briefly, it cannot depend upon either a sequential search involving either a series of eye fixations that require significantly more time to execute than is provided in these experiments, or a sequential shifting of attention without changes in fixation, which also would require considerable more time to effect.

This very brief summary of the experimental methods widely used for studying preattentive perception should make clear why these methods do not successfully eliminate the possible contribution of attention. In every case the observers are engaging in a visual search which, by definition, is an activity requiring attention. To look and try to find something is to attend to the array in which it might be present and to *intend* to see it. How then can one conclude that attention has been eliminated? Thus doubts about these methods of studying perception without attention were part of the motivation for this research. To study perception without attention a new method is required that effectively eliminates it. Any method that involves deliberate search is, therefore, ruled out in advance.

The Inattention Paradigm

Because no adequate method was available, a new one had to be devised. It had to guarantee that the observer would neither be expecting nor looking for the object of interest, but would be looking in the general area in which it was to be presented. We also thought it might be necessary to engage the subject's attention with another task, because without some distraction task, it seemed possible that by default attention might settle on the only object present. The method we devised, a version of which has been used in most of the research, meets these criteria.[3]

Observers were asked to report the longer arm of a cross briefly presented on the screen of a personal computer usually viewed from a distance of 76 cm. The cross that served as the distraction stimulus or, rather, as the object of the distraction task, was centered either at fixation or in the parafovea within 2.3 degrees of fixation. One of the arms of the cross was horizontal and the other was vertical. The cross dimensions changed from trial to trial, with the length of a cross arm ranging from 2.7 degrees to 4.5 degrees, and the length differences between the arms of the cross ranging from 0.1 degree to 1.8 degrees.[4] In all the early experiments the cross was centered at fixation. Only later was it centered in the parafovea. The cross was presented on the screen of a computer for 200 msec., which is less time than it generally takes to move the eyes from one location in space to another, that is, to make a saccadic eye movement. Thus we could be reasonably certain that the observers were not changing their fixation during the time the cross was visible.[5]

In most cases, as soon as the cross disappeared, a pattern mask appeared for 1500 msec. that covered the entire area of the visible screen, a circular area about 8.9 degrees in diameter (10.6 cm) in which the cross was displayed. The mask was meant to eliminate any processing of the visual display after it disappeared from the screen. Before each presentation of the cross, a fixation mark was displayed at the center of the screen, and the subjects were asked to keep their eyes focused on it until the mask appeared. When the mask disappeared, subjects reported which line of the cross seemed longer. This procedure was followed on the first two or three trials (figure 1.2a). On the third or fourth trial, a *critical stimulus* was presented in a quadrant of the cross within 2.3 degrees of fixation (figure 1.2b). (In experiments in which the cross was located in the parafovea, this stimulus was most often presented at fixation (figure 1.3). What qualified this stimulus as critical was the fact that it was presented to subjects quite close to fixation (or at fixation) while their attention was engaged by the cross task and they were neither searching for nor expecting it.

Immediately following the trial in which the critical stimulus was presented, the subjects were asked whether they had seen anything on the screen other than the cross figure, that is, anything that had not been present on previous trials. This question was asked throughout the research, even though it had the potential of increasing the likeli-

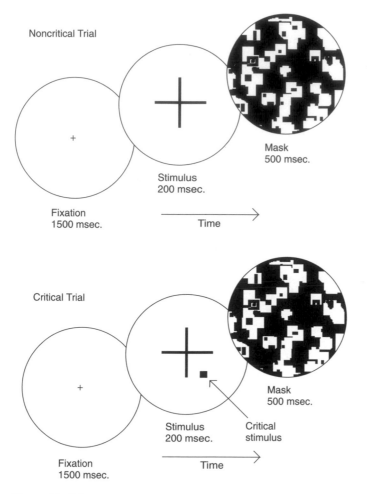

Figure 1.2a & b
Critical stimulus in parafovea: noncritical and critical trial display.

hood of positive responses when nothing else had actually been seen.[6] The answer to this question provides the data about what is perceived without attention. If the subjects reported seeing something, they were asked to identify it either by describing it or by selecting it from a set of alternatives presented to them in a recognition test. In many experiments, even if subjects had not seen the critical stimulus, they were asked to select it from a set of alternatives. We reasoned that if many subjects who reported seeing nothing new on the trial in which the critical stimulus was presented (hereafter called the "critical trial") guessed correctly, it would indicate that the stimulus in fact either had been "perceived" without awareness or was perceived and quickly forgotten, despite the subject's report to the contrary.

An important feature of the inattention method is that it permits only one critical trial per subject, although subjects were given a few more trials thereafter for reasons to be made clear shortly. This feature of the inattention paradigm is crucial because once subjects have been asked about something on the screen other than the cross (and possibly seen it as well), it is likely that they now will be actively looking for something else and thus no longer view the critical stimulus under conditions of inattention. Two consequences of this limit of one inattention trial per subject are that each experiment requires a large number of subjects, and each new experiment demands a new, naive group of subjects. However, fortunately each subject takes only a few minutes to test. Approximately 5,000 subjects were tested in our two laboratories during a period of seven years.

Following the three or four trials that constituted the inattention condition of the experiment, other trials were run which differed only in the instructions to the observer. In the New School for Social Research laboratory (hereafter the New School laboratory), the next set of trials were explicit divided attention trials in which subjects were asked to report the longer line of the cross while at the same time reporting the presence of anything else on the screen. Again, the critical stimulus was presented with the cross on the third of these divided attention trials. In the laboratory at the University of California at Berkeley (hereafter the Berkeley laboratory), the subjects were given an additional four trials, on the third of which the critical stimulus was again presented; they were again asked after this trial whether they had seen anything in addition to the cross. This was an implicit divided attention trial, because subjects now probably had reason to expect another stimulus and to be questioned about it. The divided attention trials provide information about the subjects' ability to see both the longer line of the cross and the critical stimulus and thus tell us whether both are perceptible *with* attention.

The last trials (one in the Berkeley laboratory, three in the New School laboratory) served as the full attention control trials. At this point subjects were told to continue to maintain fixation on the central mark, to ignore the cross, and to report only what else they saw on the screen when the cross was present. On the last trial in the Berkeley laboratory, the cross and critical stimulus were presented together. In the New School laboratory, the critical stimulus was presented along with the cross only on the third trial of the final, control triad of trials. In the first and second of these trials only the cross was present. (Table 1.1 summarizes the general procedure followed in the two different

Table 1.1
Procedures: New School and Berkeley Experiments.

New School conditions:

Inattention trials:
(Report distraction task only)
1. Distraction task
2. Distraction task
3. Distraction task and critical stimuli

Explicit divided attention trials:
(Report both distraction task and presence of something else)
1. Distraction task
2. Distraction task
3. Distraction task and critical stimuli

Full attention trials:
(Ignore distraction task; report only the presence of something else)
1. Distraction task
2. Distraction task
3. Distraction stimulus and critical stimuli

Berkeley conditions:

Inattention trials:
(Report distraction task only)
1. Distraction task
2. Distraction task
3. Distraction task
4. Distraction task and critical stimuli

Implicit divided attention trials:
(No new instructions)
1. Distraction task
2. Distraction task
3. Distraction task
4. Distraction task and critical stimuli

Full attention trials:
(Ignore distraction task; report only the presence of something else)
1. Distraction stimulus and critical stimuli

laboratories.) The control trial was important in establishing the perceptibility of the critical stimulus under conditions of brief, masked, and often parafoveal (rather than foveal) presentation when attention was allowed. Throughout our experiments subjects virtually always succeeded in seeing and correctly identifying the critical stimulus and its location in the control trials. It is important to note that the location of the critical stimulus was randomly varied from one quadrant of the cross to another in experiments in which the cross was centered at fixation and the critical stimulus appeared in the parafovea, so that its position was never predictable. In contrast, when the critical stimulus was presented at fixation and the cross appeared in the parafovea, it was the location of the cross that varied from trial to trial.

The comparison of greatest interest is between reports of the critical stimulus on the inattention trial and those on the full attention control trial because this indicates what, if anything, is contributed by attention. If there is no difference, that is, if the perception of the critical stimulus on the inattention trial is indistinguishable from its perception on the full attention control trial, then it is clear that attention is not required for its perception. Conversely, if the perception of the critical stimulus on the inattention trial differs significantly from its perception on the control trial, then attention *is* required for its perception. If, on the inattention trial, the critical stimulus is either not seen at all or is detected without being correctly identified, whereas on the control trial it is both seen and identified, then attention clearly is implicated in its perception.

In the case of experiments on grouping and pop out in which an entire array served as the critical stimulus, the array was not confined either to a quadrant of the cross or to fixation, so the exact procedure used in these experiments differs somewhat and is described in detail in chapter 2.

Subjects

Even though we tested approximately 5,000 subjects in the course of this research, they tended to share several general characteristics. For the most part, subjects were recruited from the student populations at the New School or the University of California at Berkeley, and so they tended to be of normal student age—between 17 and 35—and fairly evenly divided between men and women. Our insatiable need for naive subjects caused us to run some experiments at the Exploratorium in San Francisco and in the Liberty Science Center in New Jersey because they offered access to large and previously untapped subject pools. These subjects were visitors to the museums and tended to be somewhat older than the students, but very few were older than 45. All subjects had either normal or corrected to normal eyesight.

Because most of the experiments were extremely brief, it was possible to ask subjects at the Exploratorium and the Liberty Science Center to participate out of a sense of curiosity. Subjects at the New School and Berkeley, however, were modestly rewarded. At the New School subjects were given the option of receiving $2 for their time or entering a lottery in which they had a one in fifty chance of winning $100. Most participants chose the lottery. Subjects tested in Berkeley were offered candy bars as a token of our appreciation—a reward that when tried, failed to satisfy their New School counterparts.

Summary of Findings

The story of this research, perhaps like all research stories, is one of surprises and changing hypotheses. We began with one prediction about what our results would look like and why, and ended with quite a different set of results and interpretations. This book relates the story of this research journey. In this chapter we begin by giving the reader an overview of where we began and where we ended up. The subsequent chapters provide fuller descriptions of what we found and what we believe it means.

We began with the problem of grouping first described by the Gestalt psychologists (Mack et al. 1992). They recognized that the parsing of the visual array into objects was not dictated simply by the presence of the image on the retina, and therefore must be the result of activities carried out by the perceptual system. In their view, the operations that yielded grouping were spontaneous and automatic, (autochthonous, to use their term) and were a function of how the brain processes operate. Although the Gestalt view of the brain has been superseded, the view that grouping occurs spontaneously at an early stage of visual processing is very much alive (Treisman 1982; Neisser 1967; Julesz 1984). Because we doubted the Gestalt account of these grouping processes, which made them independent of attention and based them on retinal stimulation, our research began with a set of experiments designed to explore grouping under conditions of inattention. The Gestalt grouping arrays constituted the critical stimuli in these experiments.

Our doubts about the independence of grouping from attention were confirmed overwhelmingly. Texture segregation failed to be perceived without attention even when based on a vertical-horizontal difference in the orientation of elements, which is known to be one of the most effective segregators. In addition, grouping by proximity, similarity of lightness, and common fate also failed to be perceived without attention. In contrast, with attention directed to the grouping patterns, grouping and texture segregation were generally perceived.[7] In these experiments the grouping patterns consisted of small elements that filled the area surrounding the cross and even though the subjects did not perceive the grouping without attention, they were aware of the multiple elements. We now believe that this was because large displays of elements filling so much of the field attract attention.

Attention and Object Properties

In parallel with our experiments on grouping, another set of experiments (Rock et al. 1992a) explored whether various properties of perceptual objects are perceived without attention. Because we began with the belief that there must be features of objects that exist prior to attention, if only because attention must have an object, it seemed important to determine what these preattentive features were. The properties chosen for examination were: the presence and location of an individual element, color, numerosity, motion, flicker, and shape. These, rather than other properties, were chosen because they seemed likely candidates for early preattentive processing and were assumed to be so by other investigators (Treisman 1986; Yantis and Jonides 1990; Yantis 1993; Folk, Remington, and Wright 1994; Jonides and Yantis 1988; Theeuwes 1991; Theeuwes 1992). For example, color, motion, and very simple shapes were found to pop out and were thus thought to be independent of attention (Treisman 1988). The perception of location, which has been the subject of dispute between those who think it is perceived without attention and those who think it is not (Treisman and Gelade 1980), seemed to us a property that might be perceived without attention. We came to this conclusion because it provides the basis for the execution of saccadic eye movements and because it seems to be the basis for the deployment of attention and so ought to be independent of it.[8]

These experiments examining various properties of perceptual objects yielded results different from those of the experiments on grouping. In these experiments, the critical stimulus was a single, small object (with the exception of the numerosity experiments). It was presented in a quadrant of the cross within about 2.0 degrees of its center, which coincided with fixation. When the property under examination was color, the critical stimulus was a small, brightly colored square. When the property was location, the critical stimulus was the same small square in black. In the case of numerosity, multiple small black squares served as the critical stimulus. With motion the critical stimulus was a small black bar or square that moved stroboscopically from one quadrant to another. In the case of shape, the critical stimulus was a solid black or colored, simple geometric shape, either a circle, square, diamond, or cross. When flicker was explored, the critical stimulus was repetitively pulsed on and off during the time it was present on the screen.

With the exception of shape, each of these stimuli were perceived under conditions of inattention by about 75% of the observers, which is a percentage that is not only significantly greater than chance, but is also not significantly different from the results obtained in the full attention control condition. At this point in our research, we took these results to mean that motion, location, color, and at least the gross perception of numerosity were perceived without attention. Because the perception of shape failed under conditions of inattention, however, we concluded that it required attention, particularly because subjects in the divided and full attention control conditions had no difficulty reporting it. It should be noted that about 75% of the subjects detected the presence, color, and location of the critical shape stimulus in the inattention condition, even though they were unable to identify its shape. The interim conclusion we reached was that the perception of shape, unlike the perception of motion, color, location, and numerosity, requires attention.

Inattentional Blindness

A puzzling and surprising aspect of all the experiments examining the perception of a small number of critical stimuli under conditions of inattention was that, on average, 25% of the observers *failed* to detect their presence. In answer to the question "Did you see anything on the screen on this trial that had not been there on previous trials?" about 25% of the observers answered "no" and, when queried further, continued to assert that they had seen only the cross. Furthermore, when asked to pick out the critical stimulus from an array of alternatives, their performance did not differ from chance. This was true whether the stimulus was a moving bar, a black or colored small square, or some colored, geometric form. In contrast, virtually no subject failed to perceive the critical stimulus in the control condition, and most perceived it on the divided attention trial. The consistency of this result made it difficult to ignore, and before long it was clear that it was a highly predictable, robust phenomenon, which was potentially of great theoretical significance. Because this inability to perceive, this *sighted blindness,* seemed to be caused by the fact that subjects were not attending to the stimulus but instead were attending to something else, namely the cross, we labeled this phenomenon *inattentional blindness* (IB). A suprathreshold stimulus present for 200 msec. within 2 degrees of fixation was not detected when the subjects were not expecting it and were attending to some other object. IB was a startling, and to our knowledge, heretofore unrecognized and unstudied phenomenon.

The discovery of this phenomenon and the finding that IB was often much greater than 25% not only altered the direction of the research but led to a drastically revised hypothesis. The discovery of IB raised serious questions about whether in fact anything at all is perceived without attention and ultimately led us to adopt the working hypothesis that *there is no perception without attention.* We will attempt to justify and support this hypothesis as we examine the evidence in the remainder of this book, but it is essential to bear in mind at the outset that the term *perception* here refers to explicit conscious awareness and is to be distinguished from what is referred to as subliminal, unconscious, or implicit *perception,* that is, perception without awareness. Thus the hypothesis that we believe the evidence presented in this book supports is that there is no *conscious* perception without attention.

Early Results Reinterpreted

The discovery of IB and the adoption of this new hypothesis provoked a reinterpretation of our original results. At the outset we believed that the experiments examining the fate of various perceptual properties under conditions of inattention would reveal which ones were perceived without attention. We were certain that one or more of these properties would be perceived because, as we have noted, we believed that attention demanded a preexisting perceptual object. Since we found that color, numerosity, motion, flicker, and location were properties of objects that subjects generally reported under conditions of inattention in our original experiments, we had concluded that at least these properties were perceived without attention. However, once one concludes that there is *no* perception without attention, it of course follows that anything that is perceived must be perceived because attention is engaged. If some critical stimulus is perceived in our inattentive condition, it must be because it has captured or attracted attention. Thus these early data were reinterpreted to mean that numerosity, location, color, and motion were properties of a stimulus that could capture attention. However, even this proposition did not survive the final analysis.

Having discovered IB, we changed the focus of the research from an exploration of the aspects of objects that are perceived without attention to an exploration of IB and a search for what properties of a stimulus attract attention. The set of questions that emerged were all related to achieving a fuller understanding of this phenomenon. Could the degree of IB be increased? Was it possible to demonstrate more conclusively that IB was an inattentional phenomenon that could be increased or decreased by manipulating attention? If nothing is perceived without attention, what sorts of objects capture attention? What is the fate of stimuli that are not perceived under conditions of inattention? Do they simply drop out at some early stage in the processing of visual information or are they processed more fully, yet not consciously perceived? These and other questions set our research agenda.

Inattention Blindness at Fixation

The concept of IB emerged from the recurrent finding that about 25% of the subjects in our many early experiments failed to detect the presence of the critical stimulus when it was a single object or a set of objects presented within 2.3 degrees of fixation in a quadrant of the cross when the cross was centered at fixation. However, its full strength was most powerfully revealed by the finding that IB is much greater for stimuli presented *at* fixation. Early experiments revealed that a colored spot that is seen about 75% of the time when it is presented parafoveally in a quadrant of the cross may be seen only 15% of the time if it is presented at fixation when the cross is located parafoveally. This will no doubt surprise the reader, as it initially did us.

We originally switched the positions of the cross and critical stimulus in order to determine whether the 25% of the subjects who failed to see the critical stimulus under conditions of inattention when it was about 2 degrees from fixation did so because fixation is privileged with respect to perceiving. Thus we thought that by placing the critical stimulus at fixation and centering the cross about 2 degrees from fixation in one of the positions previously occupied by the critical stimulus, IB might be completely eliminated. We never expected that the opposite would occur. We assumed that with the critical stimulus imaged on the fovea while attention was directed to the cross centered in the parafovea, any failure to detect or identify the critical stimulus *had* to be a function of inattention (see figure 1.3).

The reasonable expectation, of course, was that this change would eliminate IB, for how could an observer fail to detect a suprathreshold stimulus presented for 200 msec. at fixation? Moreover, even though it is well known that attention can be separated from fixation, that is,

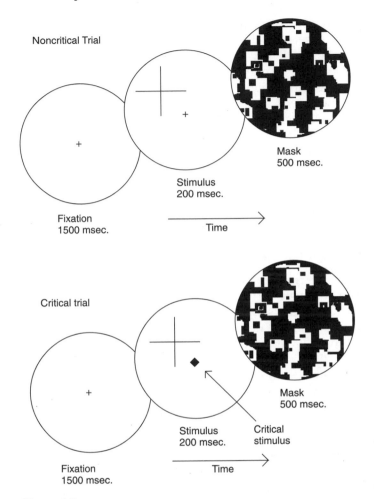

Figures 1.3
Critical stimulus at fixation: noncritical and critical stimulus displays.

with some effort we can attend to a region other than the one fixated, it nevertheless seemed likely that some residue of attention might invariably remain attached to an object at fixation. This was another reason to expect IB to decrease for objects at fixation. Oddly, even though it has long been known that attention can be separated from fixation, it seems that no one has ever investigated whether it is possible to completely resist the impulse to attend to an object at fixation. It not only seemed reasonable to assume that placing the critical stimulus at fixation would increase the frequency with which it was seen, but also would increase the frequency with which it was correctly identified.

Exactly the opposite occurred! Not only did the observers *not* identify the critical stimulus more often, but the amount of IB more than doubled. When the critical stimulus was a simple geometric shape, either solid black or outlined, identical to those that had served as critical stimuli earlier, between 60% and 80% of the observers *failed* to detect it. Subjects repeatedly (in separate experiments) reported that they had not seen anything other than the cross on the critical trial even though a completely familiar, high-contrast, geometric shape subtending at least 0.6 degree of visual angle had been present at fixation for 200 msec. This result, quantitatively far greater than the original results from which the discovery of IB emerged, vividly illuminated the causal connection between perceiving and attending. The hypothesis that without attention there is no perception now seemed strongly supported by the data.

Inhibition of Attention

Evidence that IB is greater at fixation suggested that attention could be actively inhibited from operating on input from some particular spatial location, and this was confirmed in a series of experiments. If we assume that attention normally is paid to objects at fixation, which seems highly likely, then when a visual task requires attending to an object placed at some distance from fixation, attention to objects at fixation might have to be actively inhibited. This then could explain why IB is so much greater when the inattention stimulus is present at fixation. In the original procedure, with the cross centered at fixation and the critical stimulus appearing in a parafoveal region defined by a quadrant of the cross, there is no reason for the subjects to inhibit attention to any particular region surrounding the cross.[9]

This inhibition of attention was verified in a series of experiments described in chapter 4. In one of these experiments it was possible, by presenting a small black square in each of the four quadrants of the cross, to create as much IB for a critical stimulus located in the parafovea as for the same stimulus at fixation. These squares were located in each of the positions in which the critical stimulus could appear. On the critical inattention trial, the critical stimulus replaced one of these squares. The rationale for this variation was that because the four squares were always present and were clearly irrelevant to the subject's task, the subject might tacitly learn to not pay attention to them, that is, to inhibit attention to them just as we presumed he or she did with the region around fixation. If so, the results should show a significant increase in the frequency of IB for the critical stimulus; this was precisely what occurred. This result suggests that subjects tacitly learn to inhibit attention from particular spatial locations, and that this leads to a significant increase in IB.[10]

IB and Attentional Focus

If IB results from the failure of a stimulus to attract attention, then it should be possible to manipulate the frequency of IB by manipulating the area to which attention is paid and its relation to the critical stimulus. For example, decreasing the area of attentional focus should lead to an increase in IB for objects outside that focus, even if their position relative to fixation remains unchanged. This hypothesis was supported by a series of experiments.

These experiments and others described in chapter 4 provide strong additional support for the view that there is no perception without attention. When the inattention stimulus falls outside the area to which attention is paid, it is much less likely to be seen. Moreover, if, for whatever reason, the observer inhibits attention to a particular spatial location (for example, the area at and around fixation), this too will decrease the likelihood that the critical stimulus will be seen. As will become clear, with both these factors operating, IB is virtually 100%.

IB and Salient Stimuli

The accumulating and compelling evidence of IB and of its relation to attention engendered a question about whether there might be some visual stimuli that would capture attention reliably even under conditions in which other stimuli went undetected. If perception requires attention, and attention, when otherwise engaged, must be captured before perception can occur, then it seems highly likely that a stimulus that is important might be a candidate for such capture. Because one's name seemed like such a stimulus, it seemed a reasonable tool with which to begin exploring this conjecture. In addition, it is known that one's name is one of the few stimuli most likely to be heard when it is presented to the unattended ear in a selective listening experiment (Moray 1959). We wondered whether there was a visual analogue to this effect. Somewhat surprisingly, given the visual complexity of a name, we found that there was. Observers almost invariably see their own names under conditions of inattention when it is presented at fixation and attention is directed to the cross task or even to a lexical distraction task. Under the same exact conditions, a highly familiar word like *Time* yields strong IB, as does someone else's name, a brightly colored spot, or a shape.

Even more surprising than the "own name effect" was the finding that observers are largely blind to a stimulus that is almost identical to their own names with the only difference being that the first vowel is replaced by another vowel; for example the name *Jack* is transformed to *Jeck*. This finding clearly points to a high level of analysis of the critical stimulus even when it is not consciously perceived.

There are a few other stimuli that we discovered will also capture attention under conditions of inattention. They seem to share with one's own name the characteristic of having high signal value and a high degree of familiarity. One of these is a cartoon-like happy face that generally is seen and identified under conditions of inattention. Just as a mildly doctored version of one's own name is not likely to be seen, a scrambled or sad version of the face generally will not be seen without attention. Presenting this altered version under exactly the same conditions as the happy face produces frequent IB.

Other Stimuli

Up to this point we have summarized only the evidence revealing that there are at least a few meaningful stimuli that can attract attention under conditions of inattention and that are thus consciously perceived. It is our assumption that the perception of these stimuli that are presented at fixation entails the overcoming of the inhibition that otherwise would be likely to lead to IB. But our data also indicate that there is at least one other factor that may facilitate the capture of attention.

Size

One of these is size. We have some evidence, reviewed in chapter 7, that a black disc subtending an angle of 1 degree or more will be seen most of the time under conditions of inattention, even when located at fixation, whereas a similar but smaller disc, for example, one which is only 0.6 degree in diameter, will be perceived infrequently. Because these stimuli differ only in size, size would appear to be the critical difference.[11] Moreover, multi-element displays covering a large area, like those used in the exploration of grouping, also are perceived under conditions of inattention, even though the grouping is not. This too implies that large size is an attribute that can capture attention. Because in both of these cases, attention seems to be attracted by a physical characteristic of the stimulus—namely its size—any general explanation of what is likely to capture attention under conditions of inattention must take this into account.

Familiarity

The fact that one's own name and a happy face icon are likely to be seen under conditions of inattention suggests the possibility that the familiarity of a stimulus by itself might be a factor in the capture of attention, since both one's name and a happy face icon are not only meaningful, they are also highly familiar. However, a direct exploration of this issue failed to yield any clear evidence that this was so. Familiarity by itself does not seem to be responsible for the capture of attention.

Deep Processing

The discovery that there are complex stimuli such as names and faces that are able to overcome the inhibition of attention at fixation suggests that stimuli that suffer IB may be processed extensively by the perceptual system. If, for example, a happy face or one's name is perceived while a scrambled face and slightly altered name is not, then it seems reasonable to assume that the bottleneck or filter that is responsible for limiting the contents of perception is located at a late stage of processing. (Bear in mind that it is not that these modified stimuli are not correctly identified, which might not be surprising given their novelty, but rather that their very presence goes undetected.) How else can one explain why *Jack* is seen by Jack, but *Jeck* goes undetected as if it were not present at all?

The hypothesis generated by these findings and others like them is that retinal input from stimuli that are not the focus of attention is subjected to extensive processing and, only those objects to which attention is either voluntarily directed or that capture attention at a late stage of processing are perceived. It is as if attention provides the key that unlocks the door dividing unconscious from conscious perception. Without this key, there is no awareness of the stimulus.

This hypothesis shares many of its features with the account of the role of attention in perception known as the *late selection theory* (Deutsch and Deutsch 1963). This theory stands in opposition to the *theory of early selection* (Broadbent 1958; Treisman 1969) that locates the bottleneck or filter at an early stage in the processing of visual input. According to this theory the reason why one's own name is perceived even when not attended is because it, unlike most other stimuli, has an extremely low perceptual threshold, so that only the coarsest kind of information is required for it to be perceived (Treisman 1969). The early selection theory, however, has no ready explanation for the finding that an apparently trivial modification in a stimulus has such profound perceptual effects. The coarse information that is deemed to be sufficient for recognition when presented on the unattended channel should get through the early attentional filter and ought to lead to at least false recognition. In contrast, a late selection theory has no difficulty with these results, and in fact takes them as evidence of its validity. If attention is captured at a high level of processing, then it is reasonable to assume that only a "valid" instance of the stimulus will succeed in capturing attention.

The balance shifts towards an early selection theory when it comes to accounting for the fact that size matters in the capture of attention, although this might not be true if it is perceived rather than retinal size that is the important factor. In either case, our results appear to support a flexible selection theory, that is, one that allows for selection on the basis of either high- or low-level attributes of stimuli depending on the nature of the stimulus. It may be that the system operates to minimize effort and so will select on the basis of a low-level attribute like size if possible but, if not, will process the input more deeply, as seems to be the case with lexical stimuli.[12]

Evidence from Priming Studies

The hypothesis that even unattended stimuli are processed extensively received additional support from priming experiments described in chapter 8. These experiments were designed to determine whether stimuli to which subjects either were inattentionally blind or failed to see accurately nevertheless were tacitly perceived and encoded. The question the priming experiments explored was whether stimuli that are undetected demonstrably influence a subject's performance on a subsequent task.

Lexical stimuli were chosen as the critical stimuli for the priming studies because they were the kinds of stimuli primarily used in studies of priming (see, for example, Schacter 1987). Evidence of priming was sought by means of a stem completion task that followed immediately upon the completion of the critical inattention trial, that is, after the subjects had reported their observations. In the stem completion task, subjects were given the first few letters of the critical stimulus word and asked to complete this "stem" with the first word or words that occurred to them. If observers who were blind to the critical word stimulus presented on the inattention trial, offered the word as a stem completion significantly more often than subjects not previously exposed to it, this constituted evidence of tacit high-level processing and encoding of the stimulus. This is precisely what the priming experiments revealed. These results added strong support to a late selection theory of perceptual processing and were taken as evidence that un-attended and unperceived stimuli may be processed to the seman-tic level.[13] It is only at this late stage that they either capture or fail to capture attention and are consequently either perceived or go undetected.

The Role of Expectation

There is a certain ambiguity about our method concerning what aspect or aspects of it are essential in creating the condition of inattention that leads to IB or other kinds of inadequate perception. One aspect of the method is the requirement to attend to a difficult task, such as the judgment of the longer line in the cross figure. But that aspect alone has been emphasized by many other investigators seeking to ascertain the effect of inattention. The other aspect of our method is the creation of a mental state in which nothing other than the cross is expected on a trial. This lack of expectation eliminates any intention to process the critical stimulus. It is logically possible that the lack of expectation alone can lead to IB and other failures of perception. This question is addressed in chapter 9.

Perception or Memory

There is also the question of whether IB and the failure to describe a stimulus correctly, for example to identify its shape or grouping, are failures of perception or of immediate memory. This question has arisen repeatedly in cognitive psychology and is very difficult to re-solve. It is possible that the critical stimulus that unexpectedly occurs is fleetingly perceived, but not encoded in such a way as to survive over the next several seconds until the subject is asked "Did you see anything else on that trial besides the cross?" To address this question we developed a method that we believe is sensitive to it. The basic idea was to present a second stimulus, identical to the critical one, and in close temporal contiguity with the critical one, but under conditions where it would be consciously perceived. If the critical stimulus is per-ceived in addition to this second one, then the subject should either have the experience of duality, that is, of two stimuli, or the experience of apparent motion, from the critical stimulus to the additional one or vice versa. We address this question in chapter 9.

The Perseveration of IB

In the experiment just referred to in which a second stimulus was pre-sented after the first, critical stimulus disappeared from the screen, we found a startling amount of blindness for this second stimulus. Because this stimulus was presented following the 200 msec. presentation of the critical stimulus and was a discrete event, we expected it to be consciously perceived. To our surprise, however, we found that many subjects failed to see it. A series of experiments were carried out to explore this *perseveration effect*. We found that the second stimulus could remain on the display screen for a surprisingly long interval following the offset of the cross, in other words, following the actual trial, without being perceived. IB occurred here even though there was no longer any task to which the subject had to continue to attend. We interpret this effect to mean that the state of inattention to anything but the cross was maintained over time. These findings are also described in chapter 9.

Conspicuity

We also investigated the question of the role of conspicuity of the critical stimulus. In most (but not all) of our experiments, the critical stimulus is a single circumscribed entity. It appears on a relatively homogeneous background (except for the presence of the cross) so that under conditions of attention one might regard it as conspicuous. If, as we believe, the sequence of events is one in which the critical stimulus either does or does not attract attention, then it ought to follow that its conspicuousness would be relevant to such attraction. Therefore we performed a few experiments in which we created "visual noise" in the background to lower conspicuity. Chapter 3 details these experiments.

Auditory Deafness and Tactile Insensitivity

Because there seemed some anecdotal reasons to believe that analogues to IB might occur in other sensory modalities, we designed a few experiments (described in chapter 10) to explore this possibility. Although we did not study these modalities in any systematic way, we did find clear evidence of both auditory deafness and tactile numbness in situations in which the subjects were attending to some other task involving the same sensory modality. Subjects reported that they did not hear a tone or a word that was presented to one ear while they carried out a version of a shadowing task with stimulation in the other ear. Similarly, subjects were unaware of a puff of air delivered to one forearm while they were attempting to report what letter was being written upon the other. In both these cases, subjects had no difficulty localizing and describing the unexperienced stimulus under conditions of both full and divided attention. These data, which must be considered preliminary, suggest that attention may be necessary for perception in all sensory modalities.

Unresolved Questions

The research described in this book is incomplete. It raises more questions than it answers and the explanations we provide are not fully adequate. Nevertheless, we chose to describe it now rather than wait for a fuller understanding, because that understanding may not be achieved, at least not in the near future, and the phenomenon of inattentional blindness seems sufficiently important so that interest in it ought not depend on the particular theory employed to explain it.

The apparent inconsistencies in some of our results pose questions to any attempted explanation. These will be taken up in some detail in the concluding chapter but some forewarning may be useful. Although the majority of the evidence this research has yielded appears to support a late selection theory of attention, some aspects of the data are not obviously compatible with it—one of which already has been mentioned. The fact that there are cases in which the critical inattention stimulus is detected but not identified (e.g., a shape) or not fully identified, presents a problem for a theory of late selection. If all retinal input is processed to a high level, then why should anything be detected, if it is not identified? In experiments in which a familiar, colored, geometric shape appears in a quadrant of a cross centered at fixation, many instances occur in which the subjects correctly report the color of the stimulus and its quadrant location but fail to identify its shape. If retinal input is processed to the level of recognition and perhaps meaning, why this failure of shape perception? There are also other troubling cases in which the critical stimulus is detected—that is, the subjects report they have seen something that was not present on earlier trials—but they are unable to identify it. If it is detected, an occurrence that, according to the theory of late selection, entails the involvement of attention at the late level of processing, why is its identity not perceived? In subsequent discussions an attempt is made to account for these apparent counterinstances to our proposed explanation, but it seems appropriate to alert the reader early to the fact that the data to be presented are not completely consistent and that there remain problems in need of resolution.

It is probably not too soon, however, to give the reader a summary of how the theory of late selection will be adapted to make provision for these sorts of problematic data. If the critical stimulus falls within the zone of attention, the probability that it will receive some benefit from attentional processing seems high. If, however, the critical stimulus has no particular intrinsic signal value and is irrelevant to the subject's assigned task, then perhaps the attentional warrant that permits a stimulus to pass from implicit to explicit perception is minimal, so that only its presence or its bare bone features are perceived. If the same stimulus were to fall outside the zone of attention, then it is far more likely that even its presence will go undetected, because it does not have the benefit of even minimal attentional processing. This is in fact what happens. Thus it seems possible that the failure to identify a detected stimulus need not be read as evidence contrary to a theory of deep processing and late selection. We discuss this later.

Definitions

Thus far we have used the term *attention* and its subcategories of *captured* and *voluntary* attention, *levels of processing, consciousness* and even *perception* as if they had widely agreed-upon meanings, which anyone familiar with the literature on this topic knows is not the case. *Attention,* of course, is at the heart of our research and is among the most difficult of our key terms to define, even though in some sense William James may have been correct when he wrote that "everyone knows what attention is." He continues, "It is the taking possession of the mind, in clear and vivid form, of one out of what seem several simultaneously possible objects or trains of thought. Focalization, concentration, of consciousness are of its essence" (1983, 381). For the most part we will simply try to be clear about what we mean by it rather than engage in a discussion of its deep philosophical meaning. Although saying what one means by attention is never easy, a few words are in order at the outset.

The vast literature on attention makes it clear that it is not a unitary process. At the very least it has both a capacity and spatial aspect (Kahneman 1973) and is directly related to expectation, set, and intention. It may be voluntary or involuntary and may have as its objects sensory objects or ideas. Many metaphors have been used to describe it, for example: a spotlight (Posner 1978), a zoom lens (Eriksen and Murphy 1987), or a filter (Broadbent 1958). They are useful, as any good metaphor is, but are not definitive. In this book, the term *attention* is used to refer to the process that brings a stimulus into consciousness. It is, in other words, the process that permits us to notice something.[14] Our use of the term is most closely allied to what in the literature is called *selective attention.* Given this interpretation, however, an obvious question is whether conscious perception is anything more than attention? A discussion of this question is postponed until the concluding chapter.

Attention can be voluntary and entail the intention to notice and sometimes the expectation that some particular thing may be present. It may also be involuntary, in which case it does not entail intention or expectation, but rather, its operation is elicited by some stimulus event. Thus in one case (voluntary attention) the activation of attentional processes must precede the eliciting stimulus event, and in the other (captured attention) it must follow. The process of capturing attention is sometimes thought to be automatic but, whether it is, it is at least passive.

Consciousness, like *attention*, has been a recurrent and slippery subject of philosophical discourse and no deep discussion will be attempted in these pages. We simply mean, by consciousness (if one can mean anything simple by consciousness), the phenomenal awareness of something; we mean by conscious or explicit perception the awareness of visual objects. Implicit or unconscious perception, on the other hand, is perception without awareness. Because it is not conscious, the only evidence that it has occurred is indirect and comes from subsequent actions or perceptions that reveal its influence. However, a plausible definition is that the nonconscious percept has the content usually present in conscious perception: what is unconscious has the possibility of becoming conscious (Searle 1992).

Levels of processing is a term embedded in a theory of perception that asserts that the retinal input is transformed into information by a hierarchical sequence of processing stages that culminate in the act of perception. An early or low-level stage in this process is generally considered to entail parallel processing of the input and to be independent of attention, whereas a late stage occurs toward the end of the processing chain and generally implicates attention, sequential processing, and semantic content. High or late levels of processing are normally associated with more complex cognitive processing. The remainder of this book elaborates the findings, theories and problems raised in this chapter.

Chapter 2

Texture Segregation, Grouping, Pop Out, and Attention

Grouping and Level of Processing

One of the goals of our research was to determine what acts of perception can occur without attention. We thought that if there were any such acts, the organization of the visual field would certainly be among them. Since the pioneering work of the Gestalt psychologists made clear that we never perceive without perceiving segregated objects (the single exception occurs when we look at a completely homogenous field), and that this segregation is not simply accounted for by the retinal input, many contemporary investigators have assumed that the processes responsible for this operate automatically and outside the domain of attention (for example, Neisser 1967; Treisman 1982; Beck 1982; Julesz 1984). Although the evidence presented in this chapter and throughout this book challenges this assumption, there is obvious force to the argument that some segregation of the retinal input ought to precede the activation of attention, if only to provide it with an object.

Prior to the research this chapter presents, however, there already were grounds for doubting whether grouping processes operate early and automatically with no contribution from attention. The standard illustrations of grouping by similarity or proximity devised by the Gestalt psychologists, which continue to be used in textbook descriptions of perceptual organization, show an array of elements that appear either as columns or rows by virtue of their proximity or color similarity (see figure 2.1). Another kind of organization of the visual field into parts is referred to as *texture segregation,* which is usually considered a contemporary instance of grouping by similarity in which small elements—often lines in the same orientation—appear segregated from a group of identical elements with a different orientation (figure 2.1). Because classical grouping by both proximity and similarity have been shown to be a function of perceived rather than retinal stimulus characteristics, and this is at least partly true for texture segregation based on orientation differences as well, it is no longer possible to assume

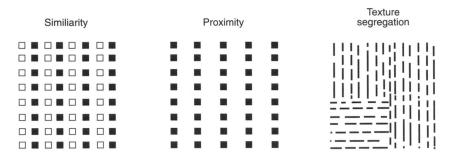

Figure 2.1a, b, c
Examples of gestalt grouping by similarity, proximity, and texture segregation.

that grouping is solely an early achievement of visual processing. (The evidence for this can be found in Rock and Brosgole 1964; Rock et al. 1992b; Olson and Attneave 1970; and Palmer, Neff, and Beck 1996.) In addition, there is also evidence that form perception—which is implicated in organization—depends on attention (Rock, Schauer, and Halper 1976; Rock and Gutman 1981). It therefore seems relevant to ask whether grouping and texture segregation can occur in the absence of attention.

There is one previous attempt to answer this question directly (Köhler and Adams 1958). Subjects were presented with pictures of novel outline shapes drawn on sheets of transparent material that were superimposed upon pictures of classical proximity patterns made up of small regular elements, which, by virtue of grouping, appeared either as rows or columns of dots. Both the novel shapes and the grouping arrays were simultaneously visible. Subjects were asked to attend to the shapes and to assign aesthetic ratings to them. Subsequently subjects were queried about the underlying dot patterns. The reasoning here was that if grouping occurs without attention, subjects should report it when describing the dot patterns, even though these underlying patterns were only the backgrounds on which the novel shapes to which the subjects were asked to attend appeared.

Despite the fact that the design of this experiment might not have completely eliminated attention to the dot arrays (the presence of which were surely perceived by the subjects because they were present for as long as it took subjects to respond), the reported results nevertheless reveal the influence of attention. The investigators found a significant difference between the degree of proximity that yielded reports of grouping in the inattention condition and the attention control condition. With attention directed to the grouping pattern, a much smaller proximity ratio yielded reports of grouping than without attention. In other words, when subjects were attending to the overlaid figures, reports of grouping of the background dots into rows or columns required a much greater difference between the horizontal and vertical distances separating them. However, the fact that grouping was perceived in the inattention condition, even if it was weaker and required stronger proximity tokens, suggests that it may be independent of attention, although attention may have a supplementary, facilitory effect. Whatever the meaning of these results, the importance of the question this experiment attempted to answer was a compelling reason for further investigation.

The Perception of Texture Segregation

Using our inattention method,[1] we attempted to determine whether the perception of various kinds of grouping requires attention.

> In these experiments, unless otherwise indicated, the first three trials constituted the inattention condition, followed by the three trials constituting the divided attention condition, and concluding with the three trials constituting the full attention, control condition. These conditions differed from each other only by virtue of the instructions given to the subjects (Mack et al. 1992).[2] We presented the subjects with the task of reporting whether the vertical or horizontal arm of a briefly presented cross centered at fixation was longer. The dimensions of the cross varied from 4.8 degrees to 2.6 degrees and the differences between the vertical and horizontal lengths ranged from 0.3 degree to 1.7 degrees. (See note 4, chapter 1, for the dimensions of each of the crosses.) In the group of experiments that examined texture segregation, the black cross was embedded in a field of clearly visible, small, black line elements that varied in length from 0.3 to 1.7 degrees and filled the circular area described by the arms of the cross (figure 2.2). Approximately the same number of elements were present in each of the quadrants of the cross. On the trials prior to the critical trial (the third trial in each triad of trials), all the elements had the same orientation. They were either all vertical or all horizontal. On the critical trial texture segregation was introduced by rotating the elements in one quadrant of the cross by 90 degrees. (For example, if all the elements had been vertical, the rotated elements were horizontal, as in figure 2.2.) A vertical-horizontal orientation difference was chosen because it has been shown to be among the most perceptually salient feature differences (Beck 1966, and Beck 1967). The cross and line elements were visible for 200 msec. and, unlike most other experiments we performed, no mask was used in an effort to try to increase the possibility that the texture segregation would be perceived without attention. (If texture segregation is perceived without attention,

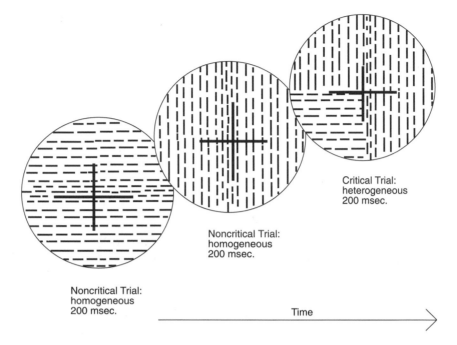

Critical Trial:
heterogeneous
200 msec.

Noncritical Trial:
homogeneous
200 msec.

Noncritical Trial:
homogeneous
200 msec.

Time

Figure 2.2
Texture segregation, displays: noncritical and critical trials.

subjects should perceive the odd quadrant on the critical trial in the
inattention condition.)

On the critical inattention trial, immediately after the subjects reported which cross line was longer, they were asked whether the pattern
in one of the quadrants appeared to differ from that in the other three
and if so, they were asked to locate it. Even when subjects were unsure
of their answers, they were asked to guess. The same questions were
asked of the subjects in the divided attention condition, except that in
this condition subjects also were asked in advance to report both the
longer cross line and the texture segregation if it appeared. In the full
attention control condition the subjects' only task was to report texture
segregation when they perceived it.

Because the cross task was intended to be attentionally demanding,
it was important that it not be too easy. The data from this and every
other of the many experiments in which judging the longer line of the
cross served as the attention distraction task confirmed its appropriate-
ness. (See figure 3.2 for a representative summary of cross judgment
data obtained over 8 trials.) Subjects' performance on this task generally improved over the first few trials so that their performance on the

critical inattention trial was generally better than on the preceding trials. (Subjects were generally about 60%–70% correct on the first trial and 70%–80% correct on the third, critical inattention trial.) This is important because if the subjects had performed less well on the critical trial, it might have indicated that they were dividing their attention between the cross and the critical stimulus and therefore that the critical stimulus was not being observed under conditions of inattention.

Only 45% of the subjects reported that they perceived an odd quadrant on the critical inattention trial, and only 25% of these subjects correctly identified its location. (Assuming that there was no difference in the probability of guessing whether an odd quadrant was present, the probability that they would guess that one had been present was 50%. Similarly, if subjects were no more likely to guess that the odd section of the array was located in one quadrant rather than another, the likelihood that they would guess any particular quadrant was 25%.) Because neither of these results differed from what could be expected by chance, it seems clear that texture segregation was not being perceived without attention. In contrast, on the critical trial in the full attention control condition, 95% of the subjects reported texture segregation and 90% correctly located the odd quadrant.

In order to eliminate the possibility that the difference between the control and inattention conditions was a matter of sheer practice, we reversed the order of conditions, placing the three full attention trials first. Thus in the first three trials the subjects were instructed to ignore the cross and report on the array surrounding it, which on the third trial contained an odd quadrant. This condition was then followed by the inattention condition in which the subjects now were told that their *only* task was to report the longer arm of the cross. The last condition in this version of the experiment was the divided attention condition. Despite this change, only 55% of the subjects reported seeing an odd quadrant on the critical inattention trial, and of these subjects only 10% correctly identified its location. Moreover, texture segregation was not perceived in the inattention condition, even though reversing the order of conditions necessarily called attention to the texture segregation, so that one might have expected subjects to be on the lookout for it in the inattention condition. In contrast, 100% of the subjects perceived the segregation on the critical trial in the full attention condition that now came first, and 80% identified its location correctly. Thus practice was irrelevant. Results from the critical trial in the divided attention condition make it clear that subjects were perfectly capable of accurately perceiving both the longer cross line *and* the texture segregation when explicitly asked to do so. The clear conclusion that can be drawn from these results is that texture segregation is not perceived without attention.[3] Later we came to believe that this is so because texture segregation fails to capture attention, at least when attention is otherwise engaged.

Grouping by Proximity and Similarity

An analogous set of experiments examined the more classical cases of the grouping of dot patterns by proximity or similarity and produced equally compelling evidence that these kinds of grouping are not perceived without attention.

> In the experiments on grouping by proximity the elements surrounding the cross were small black squares (0.37 degree on a side) that were evenly spaced on every trial except the critical ones. On these trials the interelement separation was 0.43 degree. On the critical trials in which grouping into rows or columns by proximity was introduced, the separation between elements in one direction was either about twice that in the other (0.48 degree versus 0.86 degree) or almost four times greater (0.25 degree versus 0.96 degree). The greater proximity difference was introduced upon finding that the smaller difference did not lead to the perception of grouping on the critical trial in the inattention condition. In contrast to the texture segregation experiments, in many of these experiments a pattern mask followed each trial. On the critical inattention trial, immediately after the subjects made their line length responses, they were asked whether the pattern surrounding the cross appeared to be evenly spaced or arranged into vertical columns or horizontal rows. (figure 2.3).

As in the texture segregation experiments, it made no difference whether the full attention condition was first or last, even though when it was first it called attention to the grouping. Subjects failed to perceive the grouping unless they were explicitly asked to attend to it in advance. In the full attention condition 100% of the subjects reported the grouping when it came first and 70% did so when it came last. In contrast only 10% of the subjects reported it on the critical trial in the inattention condition when it came first and only 20% did so when it came last. If we assume that the three possible responses to the question of whether subjects had perceived any particular organization to the elements surrounding the cross, (namely, vertical, horizontal, or evenly spaced) were equally likely, pure guessing ought to have yielded a 33% correct response rate. Of course, the three kinds of responses in fact may not have been equally likely, because subjects who were guessing might have had a preference for reporting that the elements were evenly spaced, especially since on the initial trials they had been. In fact, "equally spaced" was the most frequently given re-

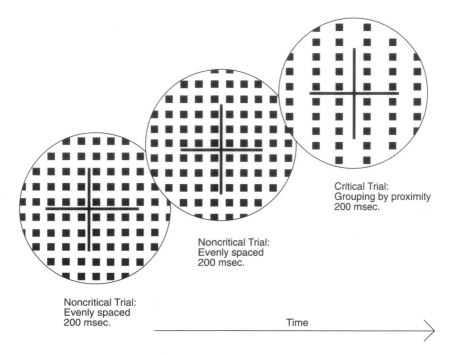

Figure 2.3
Proximity grouping displays: noncritical and critical trials.

sponse in this condition. The presence or absence of a mask also proved to make no difference, because when it was removed, subjects continued to fail to report the grouping in the inattention condition.[4]

Grouping by lightness similarity fared no better under conditions of inattention. In these arrays rows or columns were created by alternating black and white square elements. In the trials prior to the critical one, the small black and white elements were randomly arrayed and yielded no clear grouping. On the critical trial when the alternation was horizontal, the array appeared as rows; when it was vertical, it appeared as columns (figure 2.4). Because there were no differences between the perception of grouping by similarity of lightness and grouping by proximity, the results were combined for analysis. Under conditions of inattention, subjects simply did not perceive the grouping, although with full attention or divided attention the grouping was reported. However, unlike the results from the experiments on texture segregation, subjects who correctly reported the grouping in the divided attention condition made significantly more errors in reporting the longer line of the cross, suggesting that it may be more difficult to perceive both the proximity or similarity grouping *and* the longer line

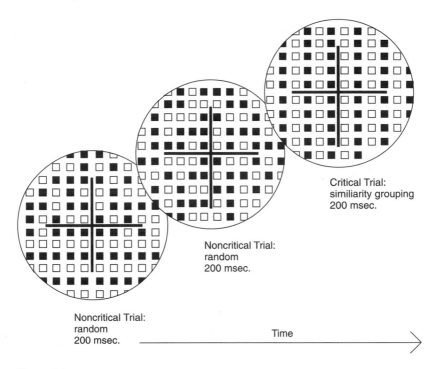

Critical Trial:
similiarity grouping
200 msec.

Noncritical Trial:
random
200 msec.

Noncritical Trial:
random
200 msec.

Time

Figure 2.4
Similarity grouping displays: noncritical and critical trials.

in the brief period in which they were displayed. This result would appear to underscore the conclusion that these kinds of grouping, which for so long have been assumed to occur automatically, that is, preattentively, in fact require the active engagement of attention. Most subjects reported the appropriate grouping in the full attention control trial.

This conclusion was reinforced by several experiments in which we attempted to determine whether subjects spontaneously report grouping into rows or columns in dot arrays like the ones used in our inattention experiments. We were prompted to examine this question because we wanted to know whether the failure to report row or column grouping in the inattention experiments might not mean that subjects had failed to see it, but only that they had not deemed it relevant or appropriate to report. We did, of course, explicitly ask about row and column grouping after the array disappeared in the inattention condition, but there seemed to be some small chance that because it might not have seemed important it may have been instantly forgotten.

A very large group of subjects (about 100) were asked to look at a series of twelve patterns made up of small square elements. These patterns were grouped either into rows or columns by lightness or proximity or were evenly spaced and identically colored with no particular grouping. The critical stimuli used in the inattention studies were always included, and each pattern was shown on the computer screen for 200 msec., duplicating the exposure time in the main experiment. This series was shown three times, and after each pattern was shown subjects were asked to describe what they saw. For the first two series no special mention was made about rows or columns. However, if subjects had not reported them by the end of the second presentation, in the third series they were explicitly asked whether they perceived them.

By the third presentation of the series of patterns all subjects correctly described the grouping, but some of these subjects failed to do so spontaneously and only did so when they were explicitly asked. This would seem to indicate that although subjects may have perceived the grouping, they may not have thought to report it, which in turn suggests that the grouping of these arrays is not a very salient property. This conclusion is somewhat surprising given the ubiquity of these kinds of displays which are often used in perception textbooks as illustrations of "spontaneous" grouping.

Having determined that grouping even if perceived might not be reported, we tried to increase the likelihood that it would be reported if perceived in the main experiment. We did this by testing a group of subjects in the inattention experiment immediately after they participated in the just described experiment in which every subject described the appropriate row or column groupings even for the grouping pattern that later served as the critical stimulus on the inattention trial of the main experiment. We reasoned that if these subjects, like the others we tested earlier, also failed to report grouping under conditions of inattention, this most likely meant that they actually had failed to perceive it and not that they had simply failed to report it. Because they had just participated in an experiment in which the grouping in the critical stimulus displays had been explicitly called to their attention, it seemed unlikely that they would not report it if they perceived it.

Even with this modification of procedure the performance of these subjects was no different on the critical inattention trial than the performance of all the prior subjects who had never been shown the grouping arrays or had been questioned about grouping before testing. Thus the failure to report the grouping under conditions of inattention seems to be due to a true failure of perception rather than of memory or reporting.

The final experiment in this series served as a control experiment and looked at the perception of actual vertical and horizontal bars under the same conditions used for examining grouping by proximity and similarity. Because the perception of oriented bars does not entail grouping, at least grouping of the classical kind in which separate elements are grouped with one another, it was necessary to establish that their perception occurred without attention. Otherwise, the failure to find that rows or columns of individual elements grouped by proximity or similarity were not perceived could not be attributed to the failure to perceive grouping but simply to the failure to perceive oriented bars.

> The vertical or horizontal bars were created by simply filling in the horizontal or vertical spaces between the black and white elements used in the similarity display or between the black squares in the array of homogeneous elements (figure 2.5). These bar patterns were present on the critical trial. On the preceding trials the pattern surrounding the cross consisted of black evenly spaced squares or randomly arrayed black and white squares.

A significant majority of the subjects (60%) correctly reported the bars on the inattention trial. Of course, the fact that 40% failed to do so is somewhat surprising, but probably can be accounted for by the fact that the presence of the background elements on the trials preceding the critical one led subjects to actively inhibit attention from the background or simply to ignore it. Another factor to consider is that the perception of the solid bars also requires perceptual organization, but of a different kind. Such organization has recently been hypothesized to be based on the principle of uniform connectedness (Palmer and Rock 1994), and it seems likely, given the results reported in this book, that even this kind of perceptual organization requires some degree of attention to be perceived. Despite these conjectures, it is important not to lose sight of the fact that the bars were reported by a significant number of subjects, which was not the case when the perception of rows or columns required the grouping of individual elements by proximity or similarity.

The conclusion that grouping by proximity and similarity are not perceived under conditions of inattention is consistent with the findings demonstrating that these kinds of grouping rely on postretinal, constancy operations (see, for example Rock and Brosgole 1964; Rock et al. 1992b). Findings reported by Palmer, Neff, and Beck (1996) also demonstrate that similarity grouping is not based on retinal shape but rather on the amodally completed perceived shape, thus also implying that higher order processes are involved in grouping.[5]

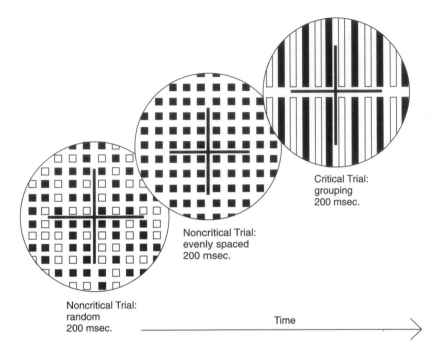

Critical Trial:
grouping
200 msec.

Noncritical Trial:
evenly spaced
200 msec.

Noncritical Trial:
random
200 msec.

Time

Figure 2.5
Control bar pattern displays: noncritical and critical trials.

Grouping by Common Fate[6]

Even though there was no evidence of static kinds of grouping without attention, it nevertheless seemed possible that grouping based on motion might occur. The reasoning that allowed us to think it might be possible was grounded in several considerations. First, the fact that the motion of a single element sometimes is perceived under conditions of inattention (Mack et al. 1991) suggests that under some conditions motion may be capable of capturing attention.[7] Second, grouping based on the coherent motion of elements has been shown to dominate grouping based on element proximity in an array in which they were made to conflict (Driver and Baylis 1989). The same experiments yielded additional data illustrating the strength of grouping by common motion, suggesting to the investigators that the perception of this kind of grouping might be mandatory. Finally, other investigators have assumed that common fate yields a form of texture segregation that occurs preattentively (Beck 1972; Julesz 1981; Treisman 1982).

Grouping by common motion was first described by Wertheimer in his classic article "Principles of Perceptual Organization" (1923) where he refers to it as the principle of "common fate." Elements in an array that move in the same way appear to form a perceptual unit or figure that stands out from its background. If the elements are simply a number of stationary random dots, then, if the motion is stopped, the perception of grouping is eliminated, demonstrating that it is the common motion alone that creates the grouping. Johansson (1950), in his important work on event perception, makes significant use of grouping by common fate in his vector analysis theory, which asserts that the perceptual system automatically performs a vector analysis of all the motion in the visual field. Vectors of common motion are grouped together to provide the perceptual background against which the unique, unshared motion vector stands out as figure. Although the question of whether attention is a precondition for vector analysis was never explicitly raised, it seems safe to infer that it was not deemed necessary since this process was taken to be automatic. Thus for these various reasons it seemed appropriate to examine grouping by common fate under conditions of inattention.[8]

The major set of experiments in this series involved 80 subjects and shared many of the features of the experiments on orientation-based texture segregation and grouping by proximity and similarity.

> The cross centered at fixation served as the object of the distraction task. Three or four bar elements (0.2 × 1.4 degrees) were arrayed in each of the quadrants of the cross (see figure 2.6). On the two trials prior to the critical trial the bars were present but stationary (figure 2.6). The critical trial introduced grouping by common fate (figure 2.7). All motion was stroboscopic and consisted of three 0.7 degree displacement steps with a 0 msec. interstimulus interval. Elements were present in each of their four locations for 50 msec. Thus the motion display was present for the entire standard 200 msec. viewing interval. (Earlier work described in the next chapter determined that if the critical stimulus is a single bar displacing under these same conditions, it is seen as moving by a majority of subjects under conditions of inattention.) Three different instances of grouping by common fate were examined. In one instance grouping by common fate was defined by the coherent motion of the bars in one quadrant—for example in one case they moved to the right—while the bars in the other three quadrants remained stationary (motion versus no motion). In another instance the motion of the elements in one quadrant was orthogonal to the motion of the elements in the three other quadrants. For example, one quadrant of elements moved to the right while all the other elements moved down (grouping by an orthogonal motion difference). In the third instance the motion of the elements in one quadrant was coherent (for example, to the right or downward), while the elements in the other three quadrants moved randomly (coherent versus random motion) (see figure 2.7). All presentations except for the coher-

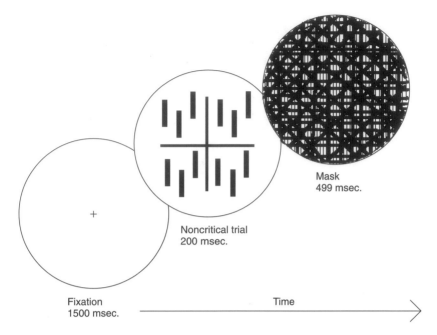

Figure 2.6
Noncritical common fate display.

ent versus random motion were masked, and each subject was tested
under inattention, and divided and full attention conditions, in that order, except in the case of coherent versus random motion, when, in order
to potentiate the perception of grouping, the order of testing was reversed and began with the full attention control. In this latter case there
was only a single trial in the inattention condition, which came last after
the full attention and divided attention trials.

The only case that yielded results that might be interpreted as indicating the perception of grouping under conditions of inattention was
that of motion versus no motion. Seventeen of the 20 subjects tested
in this condition (85%) reported seeing a difference on the critical trial,
and although these subjects correctly described the difference, that is,
they reported that some elements moved, only 9 of them were able to
correctly locate the quadrant in which the motion occurred. What this
result fails to tell us, however, is whether the perception of a difference
simply reflects the fact that subjects were aware that on the critical
trial some elements moved and others did not or, rather, reflects the
perception of a group formed by the coherent motion of a set of bars.
If the difference the subjects reported seeing was merely that at least

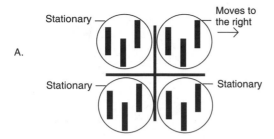

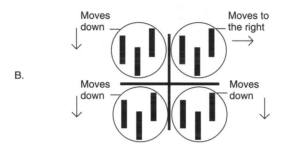

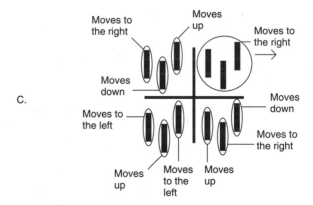

Figure 2.7
Critical common fate displays.
A. Stationary versus coherently moving elements.
B. Coherent orthogonal motion in two directions.
C. Coherent versus random motion of elements.

one bar moved and others did not, it would not be evidence of grouping by common fate, because it would not be evidence that the subjects had perceived the moving bars as forming a unit distinct from the stationary background. What this result undoubtedly does mean is that motion does appear to capture attention or pop out when it occurs in an otherwise motionless field. This is consistent with the finding that a single moving bar is perceived under conditions of inattention, because it too occurs in an otherwise motionless field.

Neither of the other two common motion conditions yielded any evidence of perceived grouping or motion segregation. Only 40% of the subjects reported seeing a difference among the quadrants on the critical inattention trial when common fate was based on an orthogonal motion difference and only 15% did so when the grouping was based on the difference between coherent and random motion.[9] Neither result provides evidence that grouping by common fate occurs without attention. In contrast, most subjects not only reported each instance of grouping with full attention, but also generally correctly reported its quadrant location.

These failures to perceive motion segregation occur despite the fact that evidence presented in chapter 3 demonstrates that the motion of a single element within a quadrant of the cross centered at fixation is generally perceived under conditions of inattention. The failure to perceive motion segregation is consistent with the failure to perceive other kinds of grouping, despite the fact that the presence of the elements making up the grouping or texture segregation patterns is detected. This failure, therefore, is a failure to see the difference between elements. Why this failure occurs is a matter of some interest. At the very least it suggests that the processing upon which grouping is based either does not occur under conditions of inattention or its products do not automatically reach the level of conscious awareness. Nothing we have done allows us to definitively decide which of these is the case, but, given the final account of our findings, it is the latter alternative that is the more compatible and therefore the more attractive. A fuller discussion of this problem is postponed until the concluding chapter.

Although motion segregation based on different vectors of motion was not perceived in the inattention condition, we have already noted that subjects were able to perceive segregation or at least a difference if it was based on motion versus no motion. We have no ready explanation for why this should be so, but we did explore the question of whether the motion of a single element in an array of stationary elements would be perceived to move under conditions of inattention (i.e., motion pop out). We thought that an answer to this question might help to clarify the meaning of this result for the following reason. If the motion of a single element in an array of stationary elements is detected without attention with about the same frequency as that with which subjects reported perceiving a motion difference in the arrays exploring common fate based on the difference between motion and no motion, it would suggest that the perception in the second case may be reducible to the perception in the first case.

> The experiments designed to address this question conformed to our standard format. The subjects were asked once again to report the longer arm of the cross that was centered at fixation. On the critical trial in the inattention condition elements appeared in the quadrants of the cross, one of which moved. In one group of these experiments, there were 16 elements, 4 per quadrant, 1 of which moved stroboscopically either vertically, horizontally or obliquely in three 0.2 or 0.7 degree discrete steps. The motion of the element was arranged so that it never crossed or covered any other element in the array. The elements were either bars (0.2 degree $\times$ 1.4 degrees, (figure 2.8a) or small squares (each side of which subtended 0.3 degree, (figure 2.8b). In some instances the moving element crossed fixation while in others its motion was confined to the parafovea but in no case did the moving element move beyond the notional circle defined by the arms of the cross. All trials were masked. A total of 73 subjects were tested.

Because the differences between the various versions of this experiment (for example, square or bar, 0.2 or 0.7 degree steps, etc.) did not significantly alter the outcomes, the results were combined for analysis. Only 3 of the 73 subjects failed to report seeing something different on the critical inattention trial, but, of course, this is to be expected given the fact that the array surrounding the cross consisted of 16 elements that appeared for the first time on this trial, and we already had established that the presence of multielement displays like these are detected under conditions of inattention. Therefore the question of more interest is how many of these 70 subjects perceived motion in the array. The answer is that only 29 (41%) of the subjects did so and only 16 (55%) of them correctly reported that only one element moved. When the motion was confined to a quadrant and did not cross fixation, 65% of the subjects who reported seeing motion identified the quadrant. In contrast, more than 80% of the subjects reported seeing a moving element in the divided attention trial, and all did so in the full attention control trial.

In another attempt to explore whether a single element would be seen to move in an array of stationary elements, we reduced the number of elements—which in this case were bars—to 4, 1 per quadrant. These elements again only appeared on the critical trial, and one of

A.

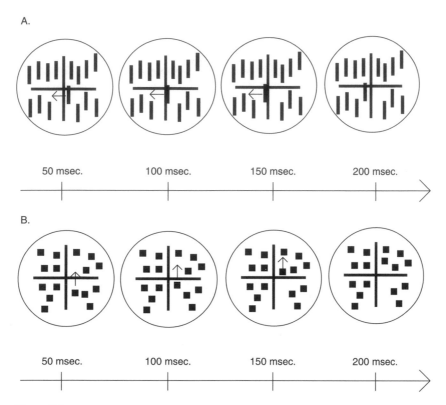

| 50 msec.   100 msec.   150 msec.   200 msec.

B.

Figure 2.8
A. Moving bar element display.
B. Moving small square element display.

them moved in 0.2 degree steps with motion confined to the parafovea. A mask was again used. Twenty new subjects were tested. Unsurprisingly all the subjects responded positively to the question of whether they had seen anything that had not been present on previous trials. Thus there was no IB for the array as a whole, which, of course, is expected because the pop out display again only appeared on the critical trial. (We did not ask subjects how many elements they saw, so we do not know whether they perceived all or only some of the elements, although other results described in chapter 3 suggest that most of them probably were perceived.) The important question is how many subjects reported seeing motion on the critical inattention trial, and the answer is that only 10 of the 20 did so (50%). All 10 of these subjects correctly located the quadrant in which the motion occurred, which would seem to indicate that they had actually perceived it and were not simply guessing. Thus, in this condition there is some evidence that element motion is perceived but the fact that half the subjects failed to perceive it is consistent with the other results just described.

If we compare the results from the motion segregation experiment in which the segregation was based on motion of all the bars in a quadrant and no motion of the bars in the other quadrants with those from the version of the experiment involving multiple stationary elements, only one of which moved, we find a clear difference. (This comparison is based on the version of the single element moving experiment that most closely resembled the common fate display, namely the version in which there were 16 bars, one of which moved in 0.7 degree steps.) When only a single element in the pattern moved, 6 subjects (33%) tested reported motion. In contrast, in the display that attempted to explore grouping by common fate, 17 of the 20 subjects (85%) tested perceived motion in the inattention condition. This difference is decidedly significant (X^2, $1df = 10.58$, $p < .01$) and indicates that subjects are more likely to perceive the motion/no motion difference when several rather than only a single element moves in a multielement display. Again, this may not be because the moving elements form a distinct group, but because when there are more than one element, the probability of detecting the motion of one of them increases.

An interesting aspect of our failure to find many subjects able to perceive the motion of a single element in a multielement stationary array is that these arrays ought to give rise to motion pop out if motion pop out were perceptible under conditions of inattention, because this is just the kind of an array that is used to investigate pop out. These results strongly suggest that motion pop out does not occur. The next set of experiments to be described were explicitly designed to explore the question of other kinds of pop out under conditions of inattention.

The Perception of Pop Out Without Attention[10]

The perception of pop out generally occurs when one distinctive thing (called the *target*) presented in a group of any number of other things (usually the same and called the *distractors*) is seen as odd or standing out. This may be because the identical elements form a perceptual group, which then serve as the background against which the odd or target element is seen as a figure. Alternatively, pop out may be based on the detection of local differences between one element and those that are in its immediate vicinity (Nothdurft 1992). Parallel analyses have been offered for texture segregation, namely that texture segregation is explained either on the basis of grouping of elements by similarity, or on the basis of the detection of local dissimilarities. (See

Northdurft 1992 for a clear discussion of this issue and for results supporting the second of these alternatives.) Whichever of these interpretations is correct, if we assume that one explanation accounts for both
phenomena, then it seems reasonable to predict that because we fail
to find much evidence of the perception of pattern segregation under
conditions of inattention, we should fail to find pop out as well. Of
course, such a failure would openly conflict with the claim that pop
out is the principle hallmark of preattentive vision. The theoretical pre-
sumption is that features that pop out are perceptual primitives, all of
which are processed quickly and in parallel (Treisman and Gelade
1980). Researchers engaged in studying pop out have assumed that
because it is based on parallel rather than serial processing, it is independent of attention, even though (as we have already noted) all pop
out experiments require subjects to actively search for the target and
consequently to attend to the entire array, which violates the assumption of independence from attention. Obviously the failure to find motion pop out that has just been described, already provides a partial
answer to the question of whether pop out occurs under conditions
of inattention.

> In these experiments, just as in the experiments examining grouping and
> texture segregation, the pop out array was presented within the circular
> area defined by the arms of the cross and conformed to our general
> method with the following differences. The screen color was switched
> from black to white to maximize contrast and had the desired effect of
> making the elements appear extremely bright. The fixation mark was a
> white 0.2 cm square (0.2 degree) placed at the center of the black screen,
> with the lines of the cross now white. There were 20 small circular 0.6
> cm (0.4 degree) elements, 5 in each quadrant of the cross, 1 of which was
> the target (figure 2.9). All elements were within 2.3 degrees of fixation.
>
> In the first experiment, for half the subjects the target was a red circle
> among green distractor circles, while for the other subjects the colors of
> target and distractors were reversed. Color was chosen as the distinctive
> feature for two reasons. First, because it is a feature which readily pops
> out, and second, because in experiments that preceded these we found
> that color was one of the features subjects did perceive under conditions
> of inattention. These experiments are described in the next chapter. (Sub-
> jects were screened for color blindness prior to their participation in the
> experiment.) On the critical trial in the inattention condition, which here
> was the fourth rather than third trial, immediately following reports of
> line length subjects were asked whether one of the elements around the
> cross was of a different color than the others. If they answered "yes"
> they were asked to choose from among six colors (red, green, blue, cyan,
> and magenta) in a recognition test and to indicate in which quadrant the
> differently colored element appeared.

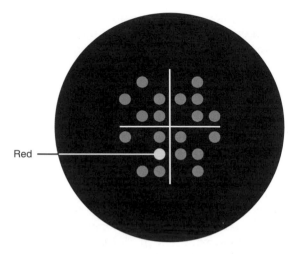

Figure 2.9
Color pop-out display: critical trial.

An important aspect of the procedure in this experiment was that the distractor elements, all of which were of one color (red or green), were present on every trial, thus duplicating the format of all the grouping experiments. On the critical trial one of the target elements was differently colored. As in the grouping experiments, subjects were not asked anything about the background pattern until immediately after the critical inattention trial. The decision to present the background array on the noncritical trials rather than to present it and the target only on the critical trial was made in order to minimize the possibility of surprise or shock. We thought this would be inevitable if, after several trials with only the cross present, there was a trial in which the cross was surrounded by multiple elements. It seemed possible that this shock might provide an alternative explanation for a failure to report pop out, which then could not be attributed to an absence of attention. Because no questions were asked about the background elements until after the critical trial, we reasoned that subjects would simply ignore them, that is, would not attend to them, and that this state of inattention would extend to the critical trial. This, of course, was exactly what we wanted to achieve because our purpose was to determine whether pop out occurred when attention was directed only to the cross.

Eight (44%) of the 18 subjects tested failed to see the circle of a different color. Another 5 subjects reported they had seen it, but incorrectly reported both its color and its location. One subject reported the color correctly and 3 reported the correct location. Only 1 subject who reported having seen the differently colored circle correctly reported both its color and location.[11] If we assume that these 6 subjects actually perceived pop out, then only 33% of all of the subjects perceived it. On the full attention control trial, all subjects reported seeing a different circle and 17 (94%) reported both the color and the quadrant location correctly. As usual there was no significant decrement in the subjects' cross task performance on the critical trial.

In a separate control experiment with 9 subjects, a catch trial array was substituted for the pop out array on the critical inattention trial, that is, there was no target and all the circle elements were either green or red. Five subjects (55%) reported seeing one circle that was different from all the others, indicating that there was a response bias to say "yes" in answer to the question "Was one of the circles different from the others?" Because the percent of subjects saying yes in the control catch trial condition was not significantly different from those saying yes in the experimental condition, an extreme interpretation of the results is that there is *no* genuine pop out in the experimental inattention condition. However, because a few subjects (5) who reported seeing a differently colored circle did correctly report either its color, its location, or both, a more reasonable interpretation is that a very small percentage of the subjects (33%) did achieve pop out. Nevertheless, the conclusion seems warranted that pop out failed to occur on the critical inattention trial, but almost always occurred on the full attention, control trial.

In a variation of this experiment in which every space within the circular region defined by the cross was filled (a total of 32 circles, 8 in each quadrant), there were *more* cases of pop out, roughly between 30–40%. However, by filling in every space, a very regular display was created (figure 2.10), one in which the distractors formed a background that appeared uniform. The target then appeared as a figure on a background of a different color. Therefore we are not inclined to give much weight to this particular finding and, in any event pop out was still quite poor compared to the control trial in which virtually all subjects reported the target as present and got both its color and quadrant location correct, and equally poor compared to the universality of pop out using color differences reported by most other investigators.

In the next experiment we combined color and shape using Xs and Os as the pattern elements. We reasoned that the combination of two features in the target that were different than the combined features of the distractors ought to make pop out very easy to achieve, if indeed,

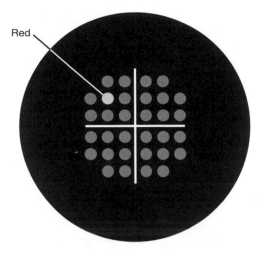

Figure 2.10
Regular color pop-out display: critical trial.

pop out can occur without attention. The target was, for example, the only red object or the only circle and only green object, and so on (figure 2.11).

> On the noncritical trials the background consisted of either of all Xs or all Os of one color, or all pluses or squares of one color, and subjects were instructed to ignore them as they had been in the previous experiment. Even though we had found in other experiments detailed in the next chapter that, by and large, specific shape is not perceived, these features still differed in component features such as straight versus curved contours and it is known from traditional experiments on search that Xs pop out among circle distractors and that the opposite also produces pop out. (Treisman and Souther 1985). On the critical inattention trial, the target was an X or an O in one color (e.g., green) and the distractors were the other shape in the other color (e.g., red).

The results on the inattention trial using the lenient criterion of also counting a plus as correct if the X had been the target or a square as correct if the circle had been the target were essentially the same as those from the original experiment. Forty-six percent of the subjects said that they saw the target. However, many of these subjects can be discounted because they failed to report its attributes or its location correctly and because we had already determined that there was a response bias to say yes (55%). In contrast, on the control trial all the subjects reported seeing the target and virtually all correctly reported its features and location.

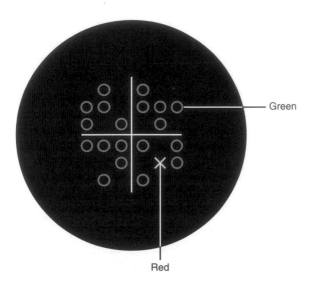

Figure 2.11
Pop-out display combining shape and color.

The next experiment was designed to clarify the role of the background elements on the noncritical trials. We had included these
elements on all trials to avoid the possibility that their surprise appearance on the critical trial might lead subjects to fail to report pop out
even if it occurred, or lead them to direct their attention to the background (which we sought to avoid). Of course, it was also possible that
the presence of the background on the trials prior to the critical one
led subjects to learn to ignore the background. We now wished to
determine whether the presence of the background had an affect on
the perception of pop out. Therefore, we repeated the first pop out
experiment using a red target and green distractor circles (or vice
versa), but this time they only appeared on the critical inattention trial.
Prior to the critical trial only the cross had appeared.[12]

Of the 18 new subjects tested in this experiment, all but 1 (94%) now
reported seeing a distinct target, but 2 of these subjects incorrectly
reported both its color and location. We therefore attributed the responses of these 2 subjects to the response bias to say yes and eliminated them from the group of subjects perceiving pop out. (In fact, in
a separate control experiment paralleling the inattention condition of
the main experiment with 9 other subjects presented with an array of
circles without a target, that is, a catch trial, 3 subjects (33%) said they
saw the target.) Of the remaining 15 subjects (83%) who reported
seeing something different in the experimental condition, all of them

correctly identified the color, the location, or both. In the control trial all subjects perceived the target and were correct about its color and location.[13] Furthermore over the seven-line judgment trials there were 93 (74%) correct line judgment reports out of a total 126, signifying that there was no significant decrement in correct line judgment reports on the critical inattention trial.

Therefore it is clear that the distractors play an important role, for when they are present on every trial, pop out does not occur under conditions of inattention. If the background array of objects is not present prior to the critical trial, then their surprise presence on the critical trial is likely to capture attention with the consequence that pop out is more likely to occur. On the other hand, if this array is present on the trials prior to the critical one and no questions are asked about it the subjects tacitly learn to ignore it and pop out does not occur. However, were pop out actually independent of attention this should not matter, because pop out should occur whether or not subjects have learned to ignore the background or to actively inhibit their attention from it.[14]

In the final experiment in this series we sought a middle ground, a condition in which subjects would not be surprised by the unexpected appearance of the background array on the critical trial because they had seen them on prior trials, and at the same time would not have learned to ignore the background either. This was accomplished by eliminating the circle background on some, but not all of the noncritical trials. In this way we sought to prevent the subjects from expecting them and from being prepared in advance to ignore them.

Thirteen of the 18 new subjects tested (72%) reported the target on the inattention trial, but 1 subject reported both the color and location incorrectly. Of the remaining 12 subjects, 6 reported both the color and location correctly while the other 6 subjects reported one or the other of these features correctly.

The results of this experiment thus fall between those from the experiments in which a background is present on *every* trial prior to the critical one and those in which *no* background occurs on any trial except the critical one. However, we are inclined to regard the first condition as the most appropriate because it would seem to guarantee that the subjects' attention is not attracted to the array of elements when they appear on the critical trial. As we note in subsequent chapters, any method that leads subjects to ignore, suppress, or inhibit a region of the field of view or certain objects in the field leads to one or another kind of perceptual failure. In the present case it leads to failure of pop out. In other cases, it leads to inattentional blindness.

The experiments described in this chapter demonstrate that inattention eliminates the perception of grouping, texture segregation, and pop out, even though subjects report having seen multiple elements. So at this point in the research it seemed that what is *not* achieved without attention may be the perception of the relationship of elements to each other or the apprehension of any difference among them. If this does not occur, then neither texture segregation nor pop out can be perceived.

In terms of the theory summarily spelled out in the first chapter, however, we interpret the fact that the elements around the cross are perceived at least in some global way in the inattention condition to mean that they have benefited from some minimal attention, probably because they fall within the area surrounding the cross to which attention is paid. (Evidence suggesting that this is the case is presented in chapter 4.) This area is approximately defined by the imaginary circle, the diameter of which is the longer arm of the cross. Because the multiple elements comprising the grouping and pop out arrays virtually fill this area, they are thus more likely to capture or receive some minimal attention than stimuli falling outside this region. The attention they receive, however, apparently is not sufficient to bring the grouping into consciousness. Put differently, the presence of these elements—of which there are many—does seem to capture some minimal attention by virtue of their location and numerosity, but the perception of the *relationship* among these elements is not consciously perceived.[15]

Conclusion

The experiments reported in this chapter reveal that common kinds of grouping and texture segregation do not appear to be perceived under conditions of inattention. In addition, an odd object in an otherwise homogenous array of objects is also not perceived, particularly if the conditions maximize the chance that the elements surrounding the cross will be ignored. The condition that is most effective in this regard is one in which a set of identical elements appear on the trials preceding the critical one.[16]

A question not answered by our results is whether it is even appropriate to describe the failure to perceive an odd object in an otherwise homogeneous array as a failure of pop out. Strictly speaking the current use of pop out refers to the fact that the time required to detect an odd object is independent of the number of objects surrounding it, in other words, it is a display size effect. Because, at least in the case of color pop out, we made no effort to systematically vary the number of background elements in the critical display our results may not be conclusive evidence of the failure of pop out without attention. However, if we simply take pop out to mean the immediate perception of a stimulus in a display containing many other similar elements, which has been one meaning of the term (Neisser 1967; Julesz 1981), then on this reading, we have clear evidence of a failure to perceive it without attention. Because the question of the correct definition either is arbitrary or is not resolved by the research described in this book, we can say nothing definitive about it and simply point out that the experiments just described do not necessarily bear on the issue of parallel versus serial processing that is typically revealed in experiments in which display size is manipulated. We do speculate about the relation between modes of processing, serial versus parallel, and their relation to attention and perception in the concluding chapter. But now we turn, in chapter 3, to the question of what is perceived under conditions of inattention given our findings that neither texture segregation nor grouping are perceived under these conditions.

Chapter 3
The Evidence for Inattentional Blindness

In this chapter we review some of our other earliest findings, describing the experiments more fully, and how we interpreted the results at that time.[1] In the previous chapter we described our experiments on grouping, texture segregation, and pop out, which were among the first experiments we performed with the new method, and we set forth the conclusions about perceptual organization that the results implied. Here we describe another set of very early experiments that were designed to answer this question, "If grouping on the basis of the Gestalt principle of organization is not perceived without attention, as virtually all investigators of perception have assumed, then what *is* perceived at an early preattentive stage?" It was in the process of performing these experiments that we first noticed that sometimes subjects failed to perceive the stimulus object or objects presented under what we took to be conditions of inattention. Our interest gradually shifted to this surprising finding and in this chapter we present the evidence that drove us to emphasize it. As noted, we called this total failure of perception under conditions of inattention, inattentional blindness (IB).

Experiments with Critical Object in Parafovea

A small square: In the first of these early experiments, we selected as the critical object a small black square, 0.2 cm on a side, subtending a visual angle of 0.15 degree that the subjects viewed from the standard viewing distance of 76 cm. Because these experiments were performed in the Berkeley laboratory, the critical stimulus was presented on the fourth rather than the third trial. It was located in one of the four quadrants created by the cross figure, and was centered on one of the imaginary 45 degree lines that bisect the 90 degree angle of a quadrant. It was approximately 2.0 degrees from the fixation mark and from the center of the cross. We thought that such a stimulus object probed the very basic level of perceptual processing because the question at issue was whether the mere presence of something can be detected without attention.

The procedure described below was followed with minor variations that are indicated at the appropriate moment in all the experiments described in this chapter.

> As noted in the previous chapter, the subject's task was to judge which arm of the cross was the longer one or (in these experiments) whether they were equal in length. Not only did this assigned task require attention, but it is safe to say that following several trials with this task alone (three in the present experiments), the subject had no expectation that anything else was to be presented. However, on the fourth trial something else was presented. In the first experiment it was the small square that was located in one of the quadrants. Following its presentation with the cross for 200 msec. and immediately following the subjects' responses to the cross, we explored their awareness of the small square by asking them whether they had seen anything that had not been present on the prior three trials. If they indicated that they had seen something new on this trial, we asked them what it was and in which quadrant it was located. The first four trials were followed by two more trials with only the cross present. These were the fifth and sixth trials. On the seventh and eighth trials, the small square was again presented in a randomly selected quadrant. We regarded the seventh trial as an implicit, divided attention trial, because the subject was now alerted to the possibility that something else besides the cross might be presented and thus might be set to perceive something else, in addition to the cross. (As already noted, this procedure was different than that used in the New School laboratory where subjects were explicitly asked to divide their attention between the cross task and anything else that appeared on the screen.) Prior to the eighth trial, which was the last, the subjects were told that they now did not have to perform the line length task and should merely fixate on the central fixation mark. We regarded this trial as a control in which attention was deployed to the small square. The control trial was important and necessary because it revealed the extent to which the parafoveally presented square would be perceived in the brief period when it was followed by a pattern mask and attention *was* allowed. Any difference in performance on the eighth trial and the fourth trial could then be attributed to the absence of attention on the fourth trial. We will not dwell on the results of the seventh, divided attention trial, except to say that, by and large, subjects did tend to perceive the critical object but not quite as often as on the eighth or control trial.

A mask that limited processing time to the 200 msec. of each trial appeared immediately after the cross on every trial. It was a grid of black horizontal and vertical lines as wide as the critical stimulus (the small square) completely covering the square and the lines of the cross. It remained on for 500 msec. Prior to each trial a fixation mark appeared for

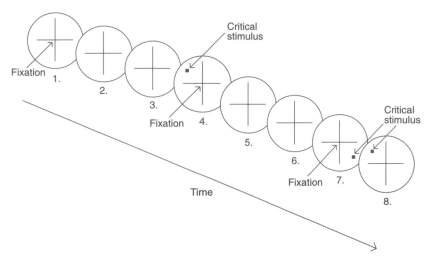

Figure 3.1
Sequence of events over eight trials.

1 second, centered on the screen and centered on the cross which followed. Figure 3.1 shows the sequence of events over the eight trials.

Before turning to the results concerning the small square, it is relevant to consider the accuracy with which the subjects performed the
cross task. These results are important because they are relevant to the
question of whether the surprise introduction of the critical stimulus
decreased accuracy of performance. Had this happened, it would have
indicated some division of attention.

In order to get a full picture of these results we combined the data
of several experiments in which a total of 136 subjects participated and
found that their average accuracy was 75%. The average performance
for each trial is given in figure 3.2.

Subjects improved their performance over the first three trials, after
which they maintained a level of around 70–80% correct. So the fact
that there was no decrement in performance on the trials in which the
critical stimulus was presented suggests either that no attention was
transferred from the cross to the critical stimulus or that it was, but
that by the fourth trial, subjects were able to maintain accurate performance on the cross task while also having their attention attracted to
the critical stimulus. Either of these interpretations is supported by the
results (also shown in figure 3.2) of 40 subjects who received seven
consecutive trials of line judgments of the cross only, that is, no test
stimulus was ever presented. The two curves are very similar. This

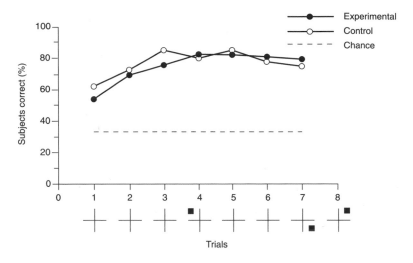

Figure 3.2
Line judgment accuracy.

finding suggests that performance on this task had reached a peak after three or four trials.

Nine of the 12 subjects reported seeing the small square, and all of them were able to identify the quadrant in which it appeared. The other 3 subjects (25%) said they had seen nothing more than the cross when asked immediately after giving their line judgment response to the cross. This was our first encounter with inattentional blindness although at this point we did not recognize it as such. Instead, we attributed it to the normal variability in results usually found in most perception experiments, and emphasized the fact that the majority of subjects did perceive the small square and its location. We interpreted this result to mean that attention was not required to perceive a connected region of uniform stimulation, an example of what Palmer and Rock (1994) referred to as the principle of uniform connectedness in perceptual organization. However, we were not sure what to make of the cases of IB.

Square in Several Quadrants
We then performed a series of experiments which we will summarize only briefly. In all of these the same method was used. In a second experiment the small square used in the first experiment was placed in more than one quadrant, that is, in either two, three or four quadrants, to determine if an object in more than one location could simultaneously be detected and located without attention. The placement

of each small square followed that of the first experiment, namely along the imaginary 45 degree line bisecting a quadrant and approximately 2 degrees from the fixation mark and center of the cross.

Of the 18 subjects who participated in this experiment, 13 reported seeing something on the inattention trial whereas 5 did not, representing an IB effect of 28%. Although this IB effect is similar quantitatively to the one found in the first experiment, it is surprising because there were more small square objects present over a more widely distributed area. Apparently some subjects failed to see any of these. In the control trial every subject reported the number of squares and their locations accurately.

As to the accuracy of perception on the inattention trial for the 13 subjects who did report seeing something else besides the cross, 9 reported the number of squares correctly and all but 1 of these subjects reported their locations correctly. The 4 subjects who correctly reported the number of squares were all from the group of subjects that had been shown three squares but reported seeing four. It is plausible to think of this outcome as a kind of symmetry or completion effect, or response bias. Having seen three items, one in each of three quadrants, these subjects might have assumed or believed they had seen a fourth, that is, one per quadrant. At this point in the research it therefore seemed that subjects could process information from more than one area of the display without attention, or, at least could do so without voluntary attention.

Numerosity

In a third experiment we sought to examine further the question of the perception of multiple elements without attention. This experiment addressed the question of whether all elements, regardless of number, are perceived without attention and whether they are all localized appropriately. One might think of this experiment as investigating the perception of numerosity without attention.

> We presented a cluster of small squares in one randomly chosen quadrant on the critical trials. There were either 1, 2, 3, 4, 8, or 16 small squares randomly arranged, with the restriction that each square had to fall in a location covered by the thick black lines of the mask. After the subjects reported on the orientation of the longer line of the cross figure and after answering the question as to whether they had perceived anything else besides the cross, they were given a recognition test. It consisted of the six possible clusters of squares, namely, 1, 2, 3, 4, 8, or 16, all in one quadrant (the correct one). In one variation the pattern of squares in the test was the same as the one presented on the critical trials, but, in another variation, the configuration of squares was different. This controlled for the possibility that subjects responded in the test on the basis

of similarity of configuration rather than on numerosity. It turned out that this did not matter. On the noncritical trials, that is, the first three, the fifth, and the sixth, nothing but the cross figure was presented. Experiments described in the previous chapter (which did not focus on the question of numerosity perception) revealed that the absence of any stimuli other than the cross on the first three (noncritical) trials—to which no response was required—was a very important feature of the procedure (see chapter 2, section on pop out). However, at the time this experiment on numerosity was performed we were not aware of this fact.

Of the 36 subjects, 5 (14%) were inattentionally blind, that is, they were unaware that anything else was presented on the fourth trial. This finding, of a smaller number of IB subjects than in most of our other experiments, was probably the result of the more massive stimulus, that, for half the inattention trials, was either 4, 8, or 16 squares.[2] Of the 31 subjects who reported seeing something else, 11 (35%) were exactly correct. On the control trial there were no cases of IB and the number of exactly correct responses was 14 of 36 (53%). Using a more lenient criterion for scoring a response as correct, namely one in which a response was considered correct if it was within plus or minus one step of the number of squares presented, 24 of the 31 subjects (77%) were correct on the inattention trial. On the control trial, virtually all subjects were correct by this criterion.

How should we evaluate these results? On the control trial there were few exactly correct responses. It is known that even with full attention, the perception (or report) of number of elements in a brief presentation is quite imprecise beyond about four elements and the results of our control trial bear this out (see, for example, Atkinson, Francis, and Campbell 1976), so we can hardly expect such perception to be precise *without* attention. Therefore our results suggest reasonably good performance on the inattention trial because it is not too much poorer than on the control trial, namely either 35% versus 53% for exact correctness or 77% versus 97% for the more lenient criterion. We conclude that subjects have an impression of numerosity without attention that correlates fairly well with the number of elements presented. Location of the quadrant in which the squares were presented was perceived correctly by virtually every subject on the inattention trial. Of course the criterion of correct quadrant is a crude one; we cannot tell with what precision the locations of each square was perceived without attention. Later experiments addressed this question.

Shape and Color
The next series of experiments concerned the question of whether the shape of the critical stimulus can be perceived under conditions of inattention. Previous research had indicated a negative answer to this

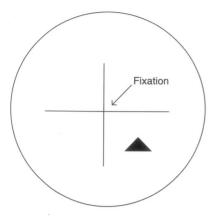

Figure 3.3
Display with critical shape in the parafovea.

question, but entirely different methods than ours were used (Butler and McKelvie 1985; Rock and Gutman 1981; Rock, Schauer, and Halper 1976).

> Following the procedure of the previously described experiments, we again presented a stimulus object parafoveally, now generally a colored shape. The shape was either a rectangle, a triangle, or a cross; the color was either black, red, or blue. The sizes of the shapes were, on the average, about 1 cm, subtending a visual angle of about 0.75 degree. They were positioned in one of the quadrants formed by the cross in the same location as the small squares of the previous experiments, so that their furthest points were 2.25 degrees from the fixation mark. Because these figures were now colored, a colored mask was used. It was a square grid containing 28 rows and 28 columns of small adjacent squares randomly assigned one of eight colors. Following the subjects' response to the line length task and to the question about seeing anything else on the inattention trial, they were given a recognition test of 6 black shapes (to avoid correct response by using color), namely a square, diamond, and an X, in addition to the three shapes used in the critical trials. Subjects were to give their best guess as to shape, color, and quadrant (figure 3.3).

In addition to the experiment just described, several follow-up experiments were performed because the initial results indicated that shape was not perceived on the inattention trial. We explored this issue by creating conditions that improved the conditions of presentation of the shape:

> In one experiment we varied the mask to see if the mask used was more effective in masking shape than color. In another variation, we converted the cross task to one of color discrimination between the vertical and

horizontal line on the assumption that the line length task is a type of shape judgment and thus might interfere with the perception of the critical shape. Color perception, however, had been excellent, perhaps because the line length task had nothing to do with color. So now we made the attention task one of color discrimination. In yet another experiment, we improved the recognition test by providing correct context, namely, by presenting each shape among the other five in the color and quadrant in which it had appeared on the inattention trial, but all six shapes were the same color. In the last variation we allowed a brief pause following the critical trial, during which time the subjects were to think about the shape they might have perceived. Then the recognition test was given. We thought that the immediate presentation of the recognition test screen in the previous experiment might have overridden a subject's perception by serving as an unwanted, additional mask. In this last variation we also suspended the requirement of reporting on line length on the critical trials, and subjects were *not* required to report on color or location. Thus the recognition test followed immediately upon the pause, which in turn followed upon the offset of the 200 msec. trial.

The pattern of result of the original experiment on shape together with the results of all the variations were the same—shape perception was at a chance level in the inattention trial while color and location were quite accurately perceived. In the control trial, for all these variations, shape, color, and location were correctly perceived. The results for the three critical trials for the detection of shape are shown graphically in figure 3.4.

The results for all the experiments described thus far in this chapter are presented in figure 3.5. The contrast between shape and all the other properties tested is quite evident. For the five variations of experiments on shape perception, 18 of a total of 79 subjects (23%) failed to see anything besides the cross figure. This result is similar to that obtained in the experiments on the detection of a single small square, and of squares in more than one quadrant. The shapes were larger than the small squares and also were colored. It would be plausible to think that large size would decrease IB, as would color, because both of these qualities are likely to attract attention. However, they apparently did not.

Outline Shape
One other experiment that we performed on the question of the perception of shape should be mentioned, although the results are not entirely clear. We decided to investigate whether outline shapes are perceived without attention, in part because they yield a higher spatial frequency than the solid shapes used thus far. One could maintain that since all of our solid shapes have a similar spatial frequency, they are not readily discriminated from one another.

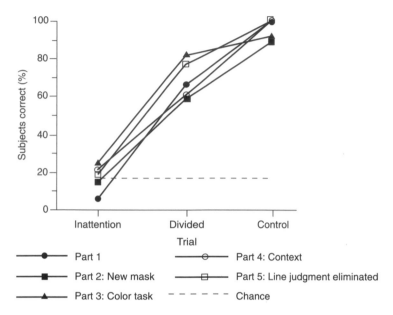

Figure 3.4
Summary of results of shape experiments.

Three outline figures were tested: a triangle, a cross, and a rectangle; they were either black, blue, or red. The three masks used were composed of random shapes of different colors, each characterized by a low spatial frequency profile. Otherwise, the procedure followed that of the previously described experiments in which the figures were presented parafoveally. There was a recognition test consisting of six black outline shapes after the critical trial.

Ten of the 27 subjects reported not seeing anything else on the inattention trial, an IB effect of 37%. This value is somewhat larger than the IB effect obtained in all the solid shape experiments (average IB of 23%). Therefore, it can hardly be argued that an outline shape is more perceptible or attention attracting than a solid shape. However, of the 17 who saw something on the inattention trial, 7 reported and selected the correct shape (41%), which is significantly better than the shape perception of those seeing something in the five combined experiments with solid shapes in which only 10 of 79 subjects were correct [12.5%] (X^2 [df 1] = 7.8, p < .01). A possible explanation is that acuity is better for an outline than a solid shape in the parafoveal location in which the shapes were presented.

On the control trial, all 27 subjects were aware of the object and 26 (96%) correctly reported the shape as well as the color. All 27 reported

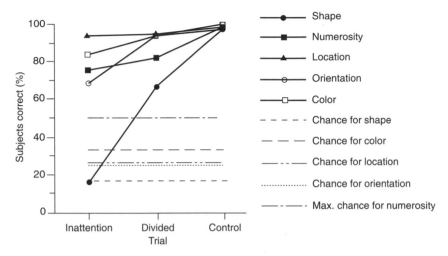

Figure 3.5
Summary of results for properties investigated.

the location correctly. So, if improved acuity explains the improved performance in the inattention trial it would have to be an interaction effect with inattention since acuity is obviously completely adequate in the control trial.

There are some further facts of interest about the results of this experiment. On the inattention trial, of the 17 who saw something 15 reported the correct color and 16 the correct location. Compared to these successes, the fact that only 7 subjects identified the shape correctly is not very impressive, even if it is better than what occurs with solid shapes. Curiously, while none of the 10 subjects who reported seeing nothing besides the cross, that is, the IB cases, correctly guessed the correct shape, 4 guessed the color and 7 the correct location. These values are higher than chance, particularly the one for location, and suggest the possibility of perception below the level of conscious awareness, because forced guessing brings out considerably more correct responses. The phenomenon experience of the subjects was that they were just guessing and had no conscious idea what the correct response was.

The Perception of Motion[3]

Thus far in this chapter we have noted that, apart from IB, the presence of individual connected objects is perceived, as is color, and that when an object is seen, its location is also detected although the precision with which it is detected is not yet clear. Shape, however, is not well discriminated. Another perceptual property we investigated in the early stages of our research was that of motion. It is widely believed that motion of objects attracts attention, particularly when the moving object is in the periphery of the visual field.

In order to determine whether motion is seen under conditions of inattention, the motion had to occur within the 200 msec. interval during which the distraction cross was present and the subject was engaged in judging its longer line. In order to do this we presented the motion stimulus along with the cross on the critical trial. The motion stimulus was either a narrow, black bar (1.4 degrees by 0.2 degree) or a small, black square (0.3 degree on a side) located in a quadrant of the cross where it remained for 50 msec. with the exception noted below. It was displaced discretely three times either vertically, horizontally, or on a 45 degree oblique path, and was present for 50 msec. at each of its three other locations. There was no interstimulus interval (ISI) separating these steps (ISI = 0). The displacement was either horizontal, from the upper right to the upper left quadrant of the cross; vertical, from the upper right to the lower right quadrant; or diagonal, moving from the lower left quadrant through fixation to the upper right quadrant. The sizes of the displacement steps examined were: 0.2, 0.7, 1.7, and 3.4 degrees. The full extent of the displacements were therefore 0.6, 2.1, 5.1, and 6.8 degrees (figure 3.6).

The motion was apparent rather than real, although with the smallest step size the apparent motion approximated real motion because each step was equal to the width of the motion stimulus itself. Thus each step placed the stimulus immediately adjacent to itself. When the step size was 3.4 degrees, the stimulus displaced only twice, remaining at each of its locations for 33 msec. with a 50 msec. ISI.[4] The third trial of each of the 3 testing conditions (inattention, divided attention, and full attention) was the critical trial in which the displacing stimulus was present. All presentations were masked.

A total of 114 subjects were tested. (Twelve subjects were tested with the small square as the motion stimulus that moved in 0.2 degree steps. Twenty subjects were tested with the small square displacing in 0.7 degree steps. Twenty subjects were tested with the narrow vertical bar as the motion stimulus that moved in 0.2 degree steps. Twenty were tested with the bar displacing in 0.7 degree steps and twenty were tested with the bar that displaced in 1.7 degree steps. Twenty-two subjects were run with the bar that moved in 3.4 degree steps.) There were three trials in each of the three conditions: inattention, divided attention, and full attention. The moving stimulus appeared on the third trial in each of these conditions. The inattention condition was first. Immediately following the third, the critical trial, in this condition and following the subjects' reports of line length, they were asked if they had seen anything that had not been present on the preceding trials. Those subjects

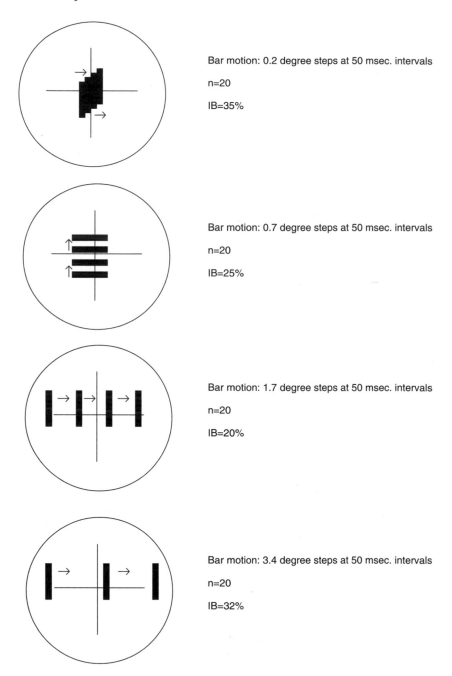

Bar motion: 0.2 degree steps at 50 msec. intervals

n=20

IB=35%

Bar motion: 0.7 degree steps at 50 msec. intervals

n=20

IB=25%

Bar motion: 1.7 degree steps at 50 msec. intervals

n=20

IB=20%

Bar motion: 3.4 degree steps at 50 msec. intervals

n=20

IB=32%

Figure 3.6
Schematic representation of bar motion and IB.

that reported seeing something new were asked to describe it. If they reported having seen a small object, they were asked if it moved. If they reported motion, they were asked whether the motion was vertical, horizontal or oblique. If they reported motion spontaneously, they were also asked its direction.

The results appear in figure 3.7. Because the results differed for the bar and the small square, they are reported separately. Of the 82 subjects tested with the bar, 21 failed to detect the presence of the critical stimulus on the inattention trial. IB was therefore 26%, which is consistent with the reports of IB for stationary stimuli presented in a quadrant of the cross. With the two smallest sized motion steps, the large majority of the subjects who detected the critical stimulus also perceived its motion. With a motion step of 0.2 degree, 91% of the subjects reported the motion; with a motion step of 0.7 degree, 93% of the subjects reported it. This number falls to only 56% when the motion step size was 1.7 degrees and to only 33% with a motion step of 3.4 degrees. In fact, only 40% of the subjects presented with a bar moving in 3.4 degree steps reported seeing motion in the inattention condition.

When the critical (motion) stimulus was a small square rather than a vertical bar, the amount of IB increased to 50%, and 61% of the subjects who reported seeing something new on the critical trial failed to perceive the motion. Both the increase in blindness and the decrease in the perception of motion occurred despite the fact that the spot moved either in 0.2 degree or 0.7 degree steps, displacements that produced the best motion percepts when the critical stimulus was the bar. It should be noted that motion was quite consistently perceived in the full attention conditions indicating that with attention the stimulus conditions supported a motion percept. Performance on the cross task was consistent with all earlier studies.

These results suggest several things. First, the presence of a stroboscopically displacing stimulus does not eliminate IB despite the general view that motion is automatically processed and perceived or that it attracts attention. Second, the difference in the frequency of IB obtained with the small square and the narrow bar suggests that the size of the stimulus may affect its perceptibility under conditions of inattention because the area of the small square was 9 mm^2 and the area of the bar was 24 mm^2, a finding consistent with results reported in chapter 7 that we obtained concerning size for stationary objects. Finally, the finding that the motion of the bar was more frequently perceived when it displaced in either 0.2 or 0.7 degree steps than when it displaced in 1.7 or 3.4 degree steps is consistent with a distinction between short and long range apparent motion (Braddick 1980).[5]

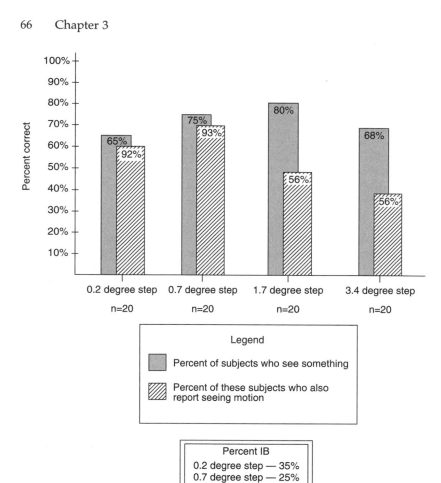

Figure 3.7a
Summary of results of motion experiments with Bar.

Of some interest is the finding that despite the fact that the critical stimulus always fell within the elliptical area we consider the zone of attention defined by the cross, IB nevertheless occurred for a moving object. This, like the finding of IB in the other experiments described in this chapter, suggests that attention must still be attracted to things when not expected or intended, even when they are within the zone of attention.

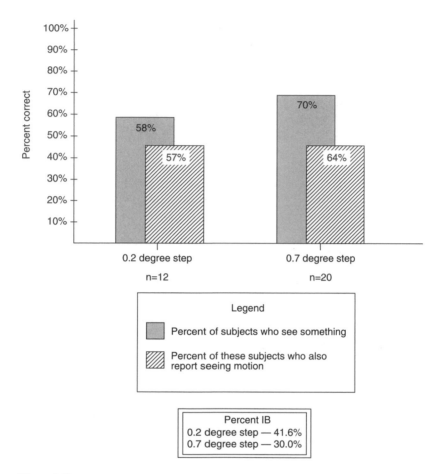

Figure 3.7b
Summary of results of motion experiments with Square.

Equiluminance

Given the interest in equiluminance, we decided to include a test for
the perception of an equiluminant colored circle the diameter of which
was one degree. Equiluminance decreases contrast and thus if contrast
is a stimulus factor that attracts attention, we should predict an increase in IB. Equiluminance was measured by means of a photometer
and was achieved by adjusting the luminance of the critical stimulus
so that it matched the luminance of the background. It appeared in the
same location as the shapes in the prior experiments and was again
approximately 2 degrees from the center of the cross and the fixation

mark. Except for the critical stimulus the procedure followed that of the previous experiments.

Two equiluminant colors, red and green, presented on a medium gray background were used. The red spot yielded an IB effect of 25%, the green spot an IB of 60%. The average of the two was 43%. With full attention in the control trial, virtually all subjects perceived the spots and knew their locations. The average IB of 43% is somewhat higher than the IB obtained in the experiments on shape. However, given the well-known difficulty of perceiving equiluminant stimuli under ordinary conditions with full attention, this result is hardly surprising. As noted above, an equiluminant stimulus object would be less likely to attract attention. We have no explanation to offer concerning the striking difference between the outcome for the two colors.

Experiments with Critical Object at Fixation

We turn now to experiments in which the critical stimulus was presented at fixation, which means, of course, that it stimulated the foveal region of the retina. As noted in the description of the general method, the 200 msec. exposure on the critical trial was followed by a pattern mask in most of our experiments. The mask was black and white when the critical stimulus was black, but colored when the critical stimulus was colored. The intended purpose of the mask was to limit the amount of time that the critical stimulus was available for processing, either because the mask camouflaged that stimulus or otherwise stopped any further processing of it. In some experiments, however, we did not use a mask, either because we were curious to see whether failed perception or IB would still occur, or because a mask would have interfered with the question the experiment was investigating. (These latter experiments will be described in chapter 8.)

We did not begin our research on inattention with foveal presentation of the critical figure because we thought that it would be difficult to entirely disengage attention from the region of fixation. Although it had been known since Helmholtz's time that one can attend to a peripheral location, it was not known whether one can resist attending, at least in part, to an object presented at fixation. Because we wanted a condition of inattention to the critical stimulus, we deliberately avoided presenting it at the fovea.

The Role of the Mask

In one experiment we sought to test the role of the mask in producing IB by holding everything in the procedure constant except for the presence or absence of the mask. Each condition, one with a mask and one without a mask, was given to a separate group of 18 subjects. Subjects in both groups were presented with one of three black shapes, (either a triangle, a rectangle, or a cross) as the critical object on the inattention (fourth) trial. The subjects were assigned to one of the two groups by a prearranged randomization.

However, unlike many of our previous experiments with these shapes, in which they were presented parafoveally in one of the four quadrants created by the cross figure, in this experiment the critical stimulus was always presented centered at the point of fixation. In other words, it stimulated the foveal region.

> The cross was presented parafoveally in one of four locations randomly selected from trial to trial. The center of the cross was the same distance from the fixation point—approximately 2 degrees—as the center of the critical figure was from the fixation point (and center of the cross) in experiments in which the critical stimulus was peripheral. The cross was always centered on an imaginary 45 degree oblique whose origin was the fixation mark. Because it was present for the usual 200 msec., there was insufficient time for subjects to move their eyes from the central fixation mark to the position of the cross. The subject, therefore, had to view the cross in somewhat peripheral vision but, surprisingly, this did not increase the difficulty of the length judgment task. For example, for all subjects of the two groups combined, 78% were correct on the third trial and 61% were correct on the fourth (critical) trial, values that compare reasonably well with performance on the cross task in experiments in which the cross was centered at fixation and the critical shape was located in the parafovea.

The results of this and other experiments we performed with the critical stimulus presented at fixation were completely surprising. Not only did IB occur, but it was substantially *greater* than the IB obtained in experiments in which the critical stimulus was presented in the parafovea. For the group given the mask, 15 of the 18 subjects failed to see anything other than the cross, an IB effect of 89%. For the group who viewed the stimulus arrays without a mask, 9 of 18 subjects did not see the critical shape, an IB effect of 50%. The difference between the groups is significant (P = .01). A further result of some interest is that virtually all subjects who did report seeing something besides the cross were correct about its shape in the recognition test immediately afterward, and almost all of these cases were in the "no mask" group.[6]

The results for both groups on the control trial were as follows. Only 3 of the 36 subjects of the two groups combined failed to see something besides the cross. Of these 33, 30 were correct about the object's shape. Thus it is clear that the failure to perceive the critical stimulus on the inattention trial was the result of inattention and not the difficulty of perceiving a briefly presented small object that was masked (on half the trials). There is no difficulty in perceiving it when attention is directed to it.[7]

Two conclusions seem warranted by these results. First, there is a very high level of IB for foveally presented target objects even without a mask, and second, the mask increases the effect to a level at which hardly any subjects perceive the foveally presented critical shape. These are, intuitively at least, very surprising and dramatic findings. One would think that observers would perceive a solid black shape subtending a visual angle that averaged about 0.75 degree, present for one fifth of a second, and appearing at the very spot where they are fixating, even though they don't expect it, and despite the fact that their focus of attention is directed away from its position. Why, therefore, is the presence of the shape so seldom detected and why is the failure to perceive it even greater than when it is presented in the parafovea as in the earlier experiments?

Our thinking about this question at the time we performed this experiment was as follows. When the shape is presented parafoveally, attention is obviously focused on the cross, the center of which is at fixation. The subjects expect nothing else to be presented, and there is no a priori reason to think that any regions of the display are actively inhibited. In fact, the zone of attention is likely to include the circular area defined by the length of the cross's lines. But when the shape is presented at fixation and, on the first three trials, nothing appears where the fixation point had been, and the cross always appears away from the fixation point in one direction or another, the subject can conclude that he or she should *not* attend to the fixated region. That realization may lead to an active inhibition or suppression and a consequent failure to process input from that region. There is the further fact that when the cross is peripheral and can appear in any of four locations, there is a very large spatial zone to which the subject may be preparing to attend, namely, the locus of points bounding the four parafoveal areas in which the cross may appear. If so, then attention will be spread more widely or diffusely in this condition.[8]

A Test of the Diffuse Attention Hypothesis

An experiment was performed to investigate this latter interpretation concerning the need to spread attention widely. Instead of a fixation point on each trial, a small arrow was used. The subject was instructed to fixate on it. The arrow pointed to the one of the four possible locations of the cross that would be selected by the computer on that trial.

As in all previous experiments, the fixation stimulus, here the location cueing arrow, was present for some interval before the distraction cross was presented, which in this experiment was 1 second. On the critical trial the cuing arrow was replaced by the critical stimulus. Hence the subject could focus his or her attention to a particular parafoveal region and thus narrow the zone of attention to that region. With the further exception that the critical shape was either black, red, or blue, the procedure was the same in this experiment as in those just described. A colored mask was used.[9]

The result was that of 20 subjects, 17 failed to see the shape at the fixated region, an IB of 85%. For the 3 subjects who did see something, the subjects were virtually always correct about both the shape and color. On the control trial, which came last, 19 of the 20 subjects reported seeing something (95%) and 15 of them reported both the shape and color correctly. Because the result on the inattention trial was roughly the same as the result in the previous experiment (in which a mask was also used), this seems to disconfirm the hypothesis that the increased IB obtained in that experiment resulted from the diffuse zone of attention arising from the fact that the subjects did not know in advance where the cross would appear. At this point we were left with the hypothesis concerning suppression or inhibition of attention to the fixated region because in both experiments this could have occurred and could account for the increase in IB. In both experiments subjects knew that they should not attend to the fixated region since the cross would never appear in that location.

Further Experiments Comparing Foveal and Parafoveal Presentation

Several other experiments were done to explore what is perceived when the critical object is presented over the fixation mark. Another reason for these additional experiments was to investigate an alternative explanation for the high degree of IB when the critical stimulus is presented at fixation.

> In the first of this series of experiments, one of three colored shapes was presented at fixation on the inattention trial followed by a multiple-color pattern mask. In fact, three different masks of this kind were used and one of these was selected randomly on any given trial. As in the previously described experiments, following the subject's response to the question "Did you see anything else?" a recognition test was given in which the subject had to choose one of six black figures. Three of the six were the figures used in the inattention trial, namely, a rectangle, triangle, or cross; the other three were a diamond, a square and an X. Even when they reported seeing nothing other than the cross, subjects were forced to choose.

The result of the inattention trial was that 15 of 24 subjects reported seeing something additional, 12 of whom correctly reported the color, and 5 of whom correctly reported the shape. Nine reported seeing nothing else, an IB effect of 38%. Why this IB effect for foveal presentation of the critical stimulus was lower here than in the experiments previously described and those described later is not clear. On the control trial, all 24 subjects perceived the critical object, all of whom correctly reported the color and 22 of whom reported the correct shape.

Tests of the no change Hypothesis

A possible explanation of the high IB that occurred in experiments in which the critical stimulus was presented at fixation rests on the fact that the critical shape appears where the fixation mark had been a moment before. Therefore, subjects may have regarded the shape as the fixation mark, albeit somewhat enlarged and different in shape, at least if these changes were noticed. If so, subjects might not consider it as anything additional to be reported when they are asked "Did you see anything else besides the cross?" [10] We therefore sought to test this possible explanation by varying the procedure in certain respects.

In one experiment we used only black shapes and made the fixation mark a small red outline square visible for 850 msec. instead of 1 second. The red outline square then disappeared for 150 msec. Following this the black critical shape replaced the red square during the 200 msec. inattention trial and the cross appeared in one of the four peripheral locations. By virtue of the change in color and the use of an outline fixation figure and the temporal gap between its disappearance and the appearance of the critical stimulus, the subject was less likely to regard the critical black shape as merely a continuation of the fixation mark. Otherwise the procedure followed that of the previous experiment. The result was that 11 of 18 subjects saw nothing additional, an IB effect of 61%. This result would seem to rule out the suggested explanation of the IB effect.

Further Tests of the Role of Location and Different Masks

We then decided to examine more rigorously the difference between experiments in which the unexpected shape appeared at fixation and those in which it appeared in the periphery. A further purpose was to examine the effect of different masks, because we believed we had found certain differences in outcome as a function of the type of mask employed. One mask was designated *A* and the other *B* (figure 3.8).

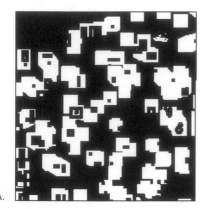 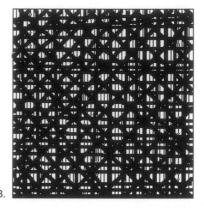

A.   B.

Figure 3.8
Two different masks.

Except for the difference between masks, the procedures were otherwise identical and the experiments were all conducted in the Berkeley laboratory, by the same experimenter. In one condition the critical shape was at fixation and in another it was in the periphery. The design therefore included four cells: critical stimulus at fixation with mask A; critical stimulus at fixation with mask B; critical stimulus in the parafovea with mask A; and critical stimulus in the parafovea with mask B. In all other respects the procedures were exactly like those described above. There were 18 different subjects assigned to each of the four cells. The results are presented in table 3.1.

On the inattention trials combining the results with both masks, there were 22 cases of IB out of 36 subjects (61%) when the critical stimulus was presented at fixation. There were 10 cases of IB out of 36 subjects (28%) for the conditions in which the critical stimulus was located in the parafovea. The difference is highly significant (X^2 (df 1) = 8.1, p < .01). For both masks combined and both locations combined there were 32 cases of IB out of 72 subjects on the inattention trials (44%) whereas there were only 3 such cases on the control trials (4%). This difference is, of course, also highly significant (X^2 (df 1) = 31.7, p < .001). For all four conditions (i.e., the inattention, divided attention, and full attention conditions) there were 16 cases of IB of 72 subjects when mask A was used (or 22%); whereas there were 19 cases of IB of 72 subjects when mask B was used (26%). This difference is not significant. There is a trend for the greater effect on IB of mask B in the inattention conditions only, but the difference is also not significant.

Thus although the two masks did not have significantly different effects, the experiment as a whole does clearly show again that IB is

Table 3.1
Summary of inattentional blindness results with two different masks: critical stimulus at fixation and in parafovea.

	Critical stimulus at fixation		Critical stimulus in parafovea	
	Inattention trial	Control trial	Inattention trial	Control trial
Mask A	50%	11%	28%	0%
Mask B	72%	6%	28%	0%
Combined mean	**61%**	**8.5%**	**28%**	**0%**

greater when the critical stimulus is at fixation than when it is peripheral. In addition, the experiment clearly shows that inattention leads to a considerable failure to see the critical stimulus whether it is presented foveally or parafoveally. These results therefore confirm those of the experiments reported earlier in this chapter.

Flicker

The high IB obtained for objects located at the region of fixation led us to wonder whether a stimulus known to attract attention and presented at fixation might be perceived by most subjects. We therefore repeated the procedure we had been using for foveal location of the critical stimulus object, but caused it to flicker during the 200 msec. period.

> There were three complete on-off cycles during the 200 msec., with the on and off periods equal in duration, namely 33.3 msec. Besides the flicker, these conditions produced two or three onsets of the stimulus during the exposure period. (Abrupt onset was also encountered in the experiments on apparent motion reported above.) One ought not to regard our more typical condition of presentation—in which some critical object appears simultaneous with the cross and disappears when the cross goes off—as an instance of abrupt onset. In other words, in most of our experiments, no object comes on or goes off *during* the 200 msec. period. But in this flicker experiment and the apparent motion experiments, there is an onset and offset during that period. Many investigators have regarded abrupt onset as automatically attention attracting (see, for example, Yantis 1993; Yantis and Jonides 1990; Jonides and Yantis 1988).

The critical stimulus that flickered was either a cross, a triangle, or a rectangle of the kind used in previous experiments. Of 18 subjects,

15 reported that they did not see anything besides the cross (IB = 83%). Of the 3 subjects who reported seeing something, 2 incorrectly identified the shape in the recognition test. On the control trial, 17 of the 18 subjects reported seeing the flickering object and 15 of these selected the correct shape in the recognition test. The subject who claimed to have seen nothing else guessed the shape correctly. In conclusion, apparently even a flickering, stimulus fails to overcome the effect of inattention to the fixated region.

Conspicuity

A issue that we have not yet raised concerns the importance of the nature of the background against which the critical stimulus is displayed. In the experiments described thus far in this chapter, on the critical inattention trial the only stimulus other than the distraction stimulus, that is, the cross, was the critical stimulus itself. Because we know that an object that appears alone in an otherwise empty field is more conspicuous and therefore is more likely to be seen than if it were presented among a group of many other objects, we thought it important to directly explore the role of conspicuousness under conditions of inattention. This issue mattered to us because if perception under conditions of inattention requires the capturing of attention then we should predict that the conspicuousness of the critical stimulus would play a role in its perception. Despite the fact that in most of our experiments described thus far except for the experiments on grouping, texture segregation, and pop out[11], the critical stimulus is an isolated object on a uniform background and therefore ought to be conspicuous, IB occurs very frequently.

To examine the role of conspicuity, we ran a few experiments in which we deliberately decreased it by presenting the critical stimulus on a background that was not homogeneous.[12] However, we were constrained as to the kind of background we could introduce for the following reason. If the background consisted of a random, noisy array of elements, then we could not question the subject directly after the inattention trial as to whether he or she had seen the critical item. That is, there would be no way to specify what object we were asking about. Therefore the background had to have some kind of uniformity against which the critical item could be distinguished.

> In our first experiment on this question, the background consisted of parallel, oblique lines. The critical stimulus—a triangle, cross, or rectangle—appeared in one of the four quadrants in the parafovea in the space between the lines (figure 3.9d). We reasoned that the presence of this kind of background, although regular, still ought to make the shape less

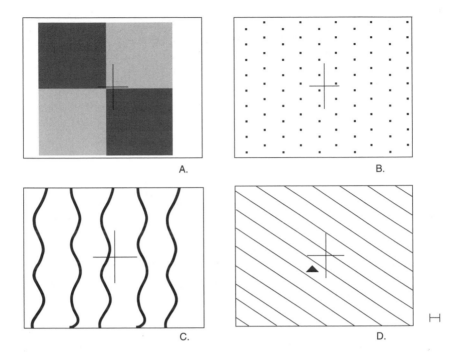

Figure 3.9
Examples of different backgrounds for experiments on conspicuity.

conspicuous. The lines were gray and filled the monitor screen. They were tilted either 30 or 60 degrees from the vertical, either clockwise or counterclockwise. For reasons explained in previous chapters, we decided to begin these experiments by including a background on the first three trials and the fifth and sixth trial as well, that is, on all the noncritical trials. However, the subject was not asked about this background. Three different kinds of background were used, namely, an array of randomly positioned spots (figure 3.9b), a series of wiggly, vertically oriented lines (figure 3.9c), and a four-part partition centered almost on the cross figure in which one pair of the diagonally opposite regions was dark and the other pair light (figure 3.9a). The oblique lines only appeared on the fourth, seventh, and eighth trials that were, respectively, the inattention, divided attention, and control trials. In all other respects the procedure was the same as in most of our experiments.

The performance on the judgment of the cross figure was somewhat poorer than in previous experiments, no doubt because of the interference of the background patterns. The average for the seven trials and 18 subjects was 60%. However, subjects were correct 78% of the time on the fourth, inattention trial perhaps because the oblique lines interfered less with the cross than the backgrounds presented on the non-critical trials. As to the results for the critical stimulus, only 3 subjects were aware of the shape, (and even they failed to guess the correct shape in the recognition test) an IB of 83%. This value is much higher than the degree of IB obtained in the earlier experiments on shape where the average for parafoveally presented figures was approximately 25%. The difference is great enough to justify ignoring a statistical test. On the divided attention trial 15 subjects were able to see the object and 10 of these subjects identified its shape. On the control trial 17 subjects saw the object and 11 of them identified its shape. However, of the 6 subjects who misidentified the shape, 3 selected the rectangle instead of the square. So by a more lenient criterion, 14 of the 17 subjects were correct about shape.

Therefore it seems clear that lessened conspicuity leads to greater IB. There is something of a paradox here, however, because one would expect the massive stimulus of oblique lines to attract attention virtually all the time. There is little doubt that the subjects were aware of these lines. So we interpret the high IB on the inattention trial to mean that although attention was attracted by the background, the shape was not sufficiently conspicuous to attract attention to itself.

A possible criticism of this experiment is that the presence of the background on the first three trials led the subjects to ignore the background, which would then include the critical stimulus as part of the background. Thus one might argue that the high IB is not so much caused by the shape's inconspicuousness as it is by the ignoring of the background array on the inattention trial. Therefore, we decided to repeat the experiment without any background on the noncritical trials. Except for this difference the procedure was identical.

Only 4 subjects perceived the shape on the inattention trial, an IB effect of 78%. Of the 14 IB subjects, only 3 selected the correct shape (2.3 would have been correct if subjects merely guessed). On the control trial every subject was aware of the critical object. Fifteen selected the correct shape but two of the errors consisted of choosing the rectangle when a square had been presented. Therefore it is clear that while the background lines do not interfere with correct perception of the shape *with* attention, they do interfere to the point of leading most subjects not to see any object at all other than the lines *without* attention. This result answers the criticism raised against the first experiment. It is not the ignoring of the background that leads to the high IB because no background was presented on the first three trials. It is clearly the inconspicuousness of the shape when it is presented with the background of oblique lines that leads to the high IB obtained in both experiments.

Conclusion

In this chapter there is striking evidence that IB is not merely an occasional event, as we had thought early on in our research, but a very frequent phenomenon. Moreover, it is now clear that IB occurs under conditions in which we and many other investigators would have thought it unlikely, namely when the critical stimulus is presented at fixation. This seems unlikely not only because visual acuity is optimal in the foveal region, but because of the customary linkage between the region we fixate and the region to which we attend.

A question that remains is why IB does not occur all the time, or at least more of the time, particularly when the critical stimulus is presented parafoveally as it was in the earlier experiments. One possible answer is that the cross figure to which subjects are always attending does not narrow attention merely to its contours. If attention were confined to the contours of the cross, a critical stimulus presented in one of its quadrants would fall in a region of inattention. But suppose instead as we have suggested that the zone of attention includes the locus of points within an imaginary circular region created by the contours of the cross, the diameter of which is the longer line of the cross, then a stimulus falling within a quadrant of the cross would fall within the zone of attention. The question of the area of attention and the consequence of manipulating it are addressed in chapter 4, where we also review evidence concerning other factors that play a role in the capture of attention. Specifically, these experiment explore the role of the location of the critical stimulus relative to the focus of attention, and attempt to assess the validity of our account of the increase of IB obtained when a stimulus is presented at fixation in terms of the postulated inhibition of attention for stimuli in that location.

Chapter 4
The Zone of Attention and the Distraction Task

A Hypothesis

If IB is caused by the absence of attention to an object, it should follow that anything that decreases the chances that an object will capture attention should increase the likelihood of its occurrence. One way to achieve this in the laboratory using our general method might be to locate the critical stimulus outside the area to which attention is directed, because anything within that area would seem either to stand a better chance of capturing attention or of benefiting from the voluntary attention directed to that location. In every experiment described up to this point the object of the distraction task has been the cross. Because the attention of the subjects is directed to the cross, the zone of attention might plausibly be the notional circle or ellipse defined by its arms, as we suggested earlier. Furthermore, in all the experiments described thus far, whether the critical stimulus contained multiple elements or a single element, it always was located within this circular area. This was so whether the cross was centered at fixation and the critical stimulus was located in the parafovea, or the cross was centered in the parafovea and the critical stimulus appeared at fixation (figure 4.1). In both cases the critical stimulus was always the same distance from the center of the cross and always fell within the area defined by its arms. If, as others have previously suggested (for example, Posner 1980), attention is conceived of as a spot or beam of light, then in these experiments, the critical stimulus fell within its focus and therefore was illuminated by it.[1] This hypothesis could explain why IB, on average, was only 25% with the cross at fixation and the critical stimulus in the parafovea, because it was located in an area to which attention was directed and thus there was a high probability that it would benefit from or capture attention. However, it could not explain the sharp increase in IB when the critical stimulus is at fixation, but, as we have already suggested, this is a special case that may be accounted for by an inhibition of attention to the region around fixation that normally would receive attentional priority. Here, despite the

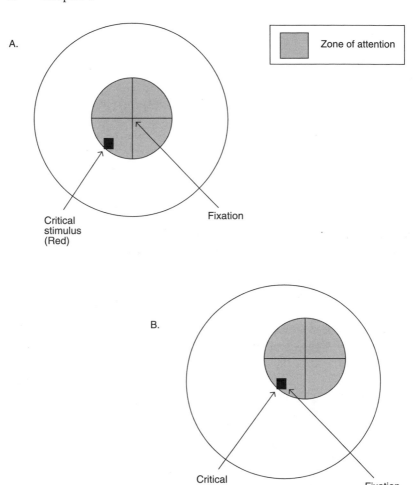

Figure 4.1
Hypothetical zone of attention with:
A. Cross at fixation, critical stimulus in parafovea. Black square was red in the experiment.
B. Cross in the parafovea, critical stimulus at fixation. Black square was red in the experiment.

fact that the critical stimulus falls within the zone of attention defined by the cross, it does not benefit from the attention directed to the cross.

Thus we are proposing two hypotheses concerning the spatial location of the critical inattention stimulus, one of which limits the generality of the other. The first hypothesis states that under conditions of inattention, an unexpected stimulus falling within the zone of attention is more likely to be seen than one outside of the zone. The second hypothesis exempts the region around fixation when the object of attention is located away from fixation, and asserts that stimuli within this region are subject to an active inhibition of attention that reduces the likelihood that they will be seen even though they fall within the zone of attention.

The first experiments to be described explored the first hypothesis that unanticipated stimuli falling within the zone of attention are more likely to capture attention and be seen than those falling outside this region. (Of course, not every unanticipated object falling within this region will be seen, because these objects are not the *objects* of attention and so do not benefit from either the intention or expectation to see them that we found plays a role in IB, [see chapter 9]). If this is correct, it should be possible to manipulate the frequency of IB by varying the position of the critical stimulus relative to the postulated zone of attention and by varying the size of the distraction stimulus and thus varying the area of attentional focus.

Other experiments described in this chapter explored whether it is possible to increase IB by using arrays designed to encourage the inhibition of attention to locations other than fixation and thus mimic the IB found at fixation. The finding of this kind of inhibition would lend support to the *inhibition-of-attention-at-fixation* hypothesis. Finally, experiments are described that explored the question of whether IB can be demonstrated using other attention engaging distraction tasks. This should be possible if IB is caused by the absence of attention.

The Critical Stimulus on the Distraction Cross[2]

The first experiment addressed the question of whether the zone of attention is limited to the contours of the stimulus to which attention is directed, or, as we had reason to believe, was the entire area surrounding that stimulus and defined by its contours. To answer this question the critical stimulus was placed on the cross itself.

> The same crosses used in previously described experiments served as the distraction stimuli. They were centered at fixation, and the critical stimulus, a small black square 0.2 degree on a side, was either at one of

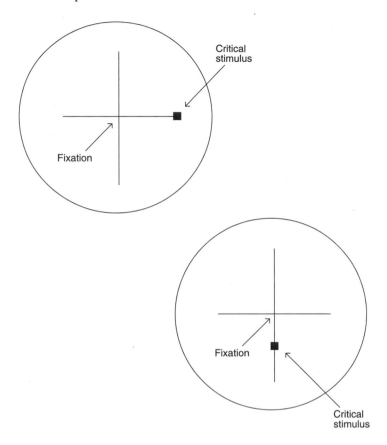

Figure 4.2
Critical stimulus on the distraction cross.

the four ends of the cross arms or at the center of one of the four seg-
ments of the cross (figure 4.2). The distraction task, as always, was to
report the longer arm of the cross. Each presentation was followed by a
mask. Twenty subjects were tested and their results were compared to
those of another group of 20 subjects for whom the critical stimulus was
in one of the four quadrants of the cross (its more typical location) 1.5
degrees from the center of fixation on a 45 degree oblique angle from
fixation.

Eighty percent of the subjects (16 of 20) reported seeing the square
when it was located on the cross (IB = 20%) and the same number, 16
of 20 (IB = 20%), did so when it was in a quadrant of the cross. Moreover, when the critical stimulus was on the cross, it did not matter

where on the cross it was. This was true even though one might have expected the square located at one of the ends of the cross lines to be seen more frequently, because in order to perform the cross task, subjects had to attend to how long the arms were, which was determined by their endpoints. Of the 16 subjects in this condition who saw the critical stimulus, only 3 were mistaken about which segment of the cross the square was on, although 9 subjects were wrong about its absolute location, that is, whether it was at the end or middle of an arm segment.[3] Of the 16 subjects who saw the critical stimulus when it was in a quadrant of the cross, 14 correctly identified the quadrant it was in. Of course, the identification of its quadrant location does not require precise location information. Thus whether the critical stimulus is on the distraction stimulus or falls within its bounds, it has an equally good chance of capturing some of the attention directed to the distraction stimulus and therefore of being perceived. The results support the view that the zone of attention is not simply limited to the contours of the stimulus to which the subject is attending and therefore increase the likelihood that it is the entire area surrounding the attended stimulus.

The Spatial Relation Between Critical and Distraction Stimulus

The next group of experiments to be described manipulated the spatial relationship between the critical stimulus and the distraction object using a reconfigured distraction stimulus, which was a closed figure, and therefore had a clearly defined inside and outside. Instead of a cross the distraction stimuli were rectangles with the same vertical and horizontal dimensions as the arms of the crosses previously used. As with the cross, the subjects were asked to report which dimension of the rectangle was longer, the width or the height, so that the task remained very similar to that of the earlier experiments. Assuming that the zone of attention hypothesis is correct, anything presented within the rectangle is clearly within the focus of attention. Anything outside the rectangle is, just as clearly, outside its focus.[4] Thus, with the rectangle as the stimulus for the distraction task we believed we could more adequately control the position of the critical stimulus relative to the spatial focus of attention and thus better assess its impact on IB. The obvious prediction is that under conditions of inattention, if the critical stimulus is inside the rectangle it will be seen significantly more often than if it is at the same distance from fixation but outside the rectangle. The experiments that follow give clear evidence that this prediction was confirmed.

General Description of the Inside/Outside Experiments[5]

A total of 140 subjects were tested in different versions of what came to be called *the inside/outside experiments.* In all but one of these experiments the rectangle served as the object of the distraction task and, with one exception, it was located either immediately to the right or left of the fixation mark.

> When the rectangle was to the left of fixation, its right vertical edge abutted the left end of the small fixation cross. When it was to the right of fixation, the reverse was true. The maximum distance between the fixation mark and the far vertical side of the rectangle was about 4 degrees. (This distance varied as a function of the dimensions of the rectangle.) The center of the vertical side of the rectangle was level with fixation. The critical stimulus, which was either a small stationary or moving solid black square (0.2 degree), was located on an upward or downward 45 degree virtual oblique line, 1.5 degrees from the center of fixation. It was thus in about the same location, even somewhat closer, relative to fixation than the critical stimulus in many of the experiments described in chapter 3. When the critical stimulus was located on the same side of fixation as the rectangle, it fell inside it. When it was on the opposite side, it was the same distance from fixation but outside the rectangle (figure 4.3).
>
> In the first of these experiments 20 subjects recruited from the New School student population were tested. The position of the rectangle varied randomly from the right side to the left side of fixation from trial to trial and subjects never knew on which side it would appear. As with the cross in earlier experiments, the exact dimensions of the rectangle varied from trial to trial. The critical stimulus was a small stationary black square 0.2 degree on a side, comparable to the small square stimulus used in experiments described in chapter 3. As usual with experiments performed at the New School, there were three conditions, (inattention, divided attention, and full attention), each of which was comprised of three trials, and on the last of which the critical stimulus was present (i.e., on the third, sixth, and ninth trials). Ten subjects were tested with the critical stimulus on the side opposite the rectangle on the critical trial (outside) and 10 subjects were tested with it on the same side as the rectangle (inside) in the inattention condition. All trials were masked. On the critical inattention trial immediately following the report of the longer side of the rectangle subjects were asked whether they had seen anything that had not been present on prior trials, and if so, what it was and where it was located. The subjects who were presented with the critical stimulus inside the rectangle on the inattention trial were presented with it outside the rectangle on the divided attention trial and inside it on the control trial. The reverse was true for the subjects who were presented with the critical stimulus outside the rectangle on the inattention condition. Subjects indicated the location of the criti-

A. Inside the zone of attention

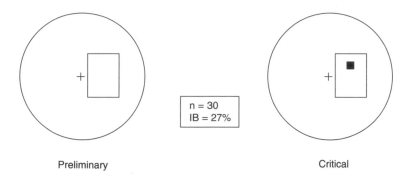

Preliminary   Critical

n = 30
IB = 27%

B. Outside the zone of attention

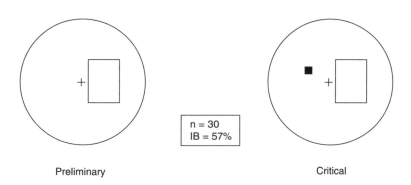

Preliminary   Critical

n = 30
IB = 57%

C. Choice array

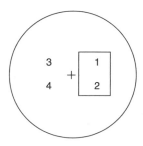

Figure 4.3
Displays with critical stimulus inside and outside hypothetical zone of attention with
IB results.
A. Inside
B. Outside
C. Choice array for location.

cal stimulus by telling the experimenter on which side of fixation it had appeared, and then by indicating its more precise location by picking it out from a set of possible locations presented on a choice sheet given to the subject at this point in the experiment (figure 4.3).

When the critical stimulus was outside the rectangle, 5 of the 10 subjects failed to see it (IB = 50%) on the critical inattention trial, while 3 of the 10 subjects tested with the critical stimulus inside failed to do so (IB = 30%), ($X^2(df\,1)$ = .83 > .30). Although this difference is in the correct direction it is not significant. Nevertheless, it may be noted that of the 7 subjects who reported seeing something when the critical stimulus was inside the rectangle, all identified its location correctly, whereas only 2 of 5 did so when the critical stimulus was outside.

There were no significant differences trial to trial in the accuracy with which subjects reported the longer side of the rectangle. Accuracy was comparable to the accuracy with which subjects performed the cross task in earlier experiments. Results from the divided attention condition make it clear that both detecting the critical stimulus and the longer side of the rectangle are possible when subjects are asked to do so in advance. All but 2 of the 20 subjects reported its presence and location, and all but 2 correctly identified the longer side of the rectangle. Because for half of these subjects the critical stimulus was inside and for half it was outside, it is evident that this factor is irrelevant when attention is divided. All subjects were completely correct in the full attention condition.

The direction of the difference between the results in this experiment are consistent with the prediction of greater blindness when the critical, inattention stimulus falls outside the object to which attention is directed, but the difference is less than anticipated. The number of subjects tested, however, was small. The next experiment sought to increase IB for the critical stimulus presented outside the rectangle by informing the subject prior to each trial about which side of fixation the rectangle would appear. We thought that if subjects knew the side in advance, it would virtually eliminate the likelihood that they might be attending to the side opposite the rectangle when it appeared, which was where on outside trials the critical stimulus appeared. Had this occurred, the critical stimulus could have inadvertently benefited from this attention, thus decreasing the difference between IB inside and outside.

Twenty new subjects were run in this version, which differed from the previous one only by virtue of the information concerning the side of fixation on which the rectangle would appear, which was given to the subjects in advance of each trial in both the inattention and divided attention conditions.[6] Subjects were told immediately before each trial

began that the rectangle would appear either to the left or right of fixation. For 10 subjects the critical stimulus was outside and for 10 it was
inside, and for half the subjects the rectangle was to the right of fixation
on the critical trial and for the other half of the subjects it was to the left.

This modification had the predicted effect of increasing the inside/
outside IB difference on the critical inattention trial. Now only 2 of the
10 subjects (20%) reported seeing the critical stimulus when it was
outside (IB = 80%), whereas 7 of the 10 subjects (70%) saw it when it
was inside (IB = 30%), $(X^2 (df 1) = 5.04$, p. < .02). Six of the 7 observers
who reported seeing something else when the critical stimulus was
inside the rectangle located it correctly, and both subjects who reported seeing something else when the critical stimulus was outside
correctly located it. Every subject reported and correctly located the
critical stimulus in the full attention control condition and 80% did so
in the divided attention condition.

Inside/Outside Without a Mask

Another version of this experiment was performed that examined the
role of the mask. This issue concerned us because its influence was not
always consistent. Sometimes the mask seemed to cause a significant
increase in IB whereas in other experiments it did not. For example, in
the grouping experiments, the mask seemed to have no affect, whereas
in the shape-at-fixation experiments it did. Therefore, a group of 20
new subjects were tested, 10 of whom were presented with the critical
stimulus outside and 10 with it inside the rectangle. Subjects were
again told prior to each trial on which side the rectangle would appear
but no mask was used. Without the mask only 4 subjects failed to see
the critical stimulus when it fell outside the rectangle on the inattention trial (IB = 40%), and only 2 failed to do so when the critical stimulus was inside the rectangle (IB = 20%). Now when the critical
stimulus fell outside there was less IB than there had been when the
mask was used, although this difference is not quite significant. (The
comparison is between 40% IB without a mask and 80% with a mask,
$(X^2 (df 1) = 3.33$ p. > .05.) Nevertheless, there is a suggestion that the
mask makes a difference here. The combined IB results for the 60 subjects participating in one of the three versions of this experiment are
given in figure 4.3.

Outside Inattentional Blindness to Motion

In the next experiment the critical stimulus was changed from a stationary to a moving square because we thought the motion might be

more likely to capture attention, even if it fell outside the area to which attention was directed.

> The critical stimulus again was a 0.2 degree black square. It was located either 2 degrees left or right of fixation and displaced stroboscopically up or down a distance of 1.2 degrees in three 0.4 degree steps with zero ISIs. The square remained present for 50 msec. in each of its four locations[7] (figure 4.4). All trials were masked. A fresh group of 40 subjects was tested, 20 of whom were presented with the critical stimulus outside and 20 with it inside the rectangle. As in the preceding experiment subjects were told immediately prior to each trial on which side of fixation the rectangle would appear. A mask was used.

Sixteen of the 20 subjects (80%) presented with the moving stimulus inside the rectangle on the inattention trial reported seeing it and correctly identified its location and direction of motion (IB = 20%). In contrast, only 6 of the subjects reported seeing the moving critical stimulus when it was presented outside the rectangle (IB = 70%). This difference is significant (X^2 (df 1) = 10.10, p < .01). In other words, when the moving stimulus was outside the rectangle, only 6 subjects even were aware that a stimulus was present, which means that for the other 14 subjects, the question of motion did not even arise. Of the 6 subjects who did report seeing something, 5 of them correctly reported its location and direction of motion.

On the divided attention trial the inside/outside difference had no effect on perception. All subjects correctly identified the longer side of the rectangle, and all but 4 subjects reported the critical stimulus, its location and direction of motion. (The 4 subjects who failed to do so were presented with the critical stimulus outside the rectangle.) In the full attention control condition all subjects reported seeing the critical stimulus regardless of whether it was inside or outside the rectangle. Moreover, all subjects were correct about the critical stimulus' motion, its direction and its location.

These results demonstrate that under conditions of inattention a moving stimulus generally fails to be seen when it is outside the area to which attention is directed, even though the same stimulus at the same distance from fixation is almost invariably perceived if it is inside the spatial envelope to which attention is directed. The reader should bear in mind that these results reflect the fact that the subjects who are presented with the moving stimulus outside the rectangle are not simply failing to see its motion, but are failing even to detect its presence.

We continued to worry about whether knowing on which side of fixation the rectangle would appear might be skewing fixation despite

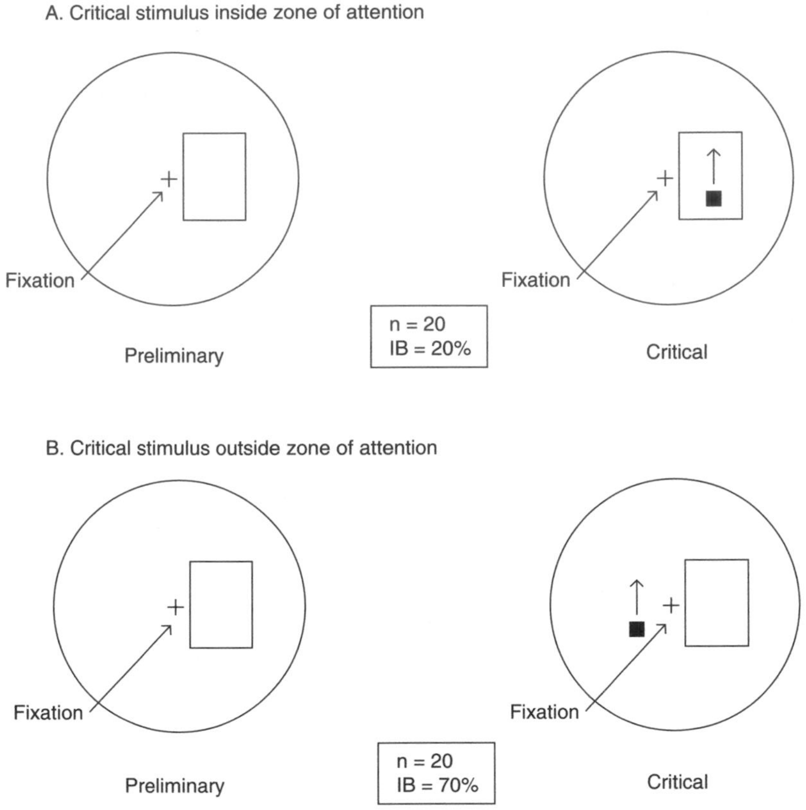

A. Critical stimulus inside zone of attention

Fixation	Fixation
Preliminary	Critical

n = 20
IB = 20%

B. Critical stimulus outside zone of attention

Fixation	Fixation
Preliminary	Critical

n = 20
IB = 70%

Figure 4.4
Schematic display of moving critical stimulus inside and outside zone of attention with
IB results.
A. Inside
B. Outside

our alerting subjects to the importance of carefully maintaining fixation. Had this occurred, it would have displaced the outside stimulus
toward the retinal periphery, so that the decrease in its detection might
have been caused by a loss of acuity. We therefore ran an experiment
with 20 new subjects identical to this one in every respect except that
subjects were not informed in advance about which side of fixation the
rectangle would appear. The results effectively eliminated this concern. All of the 10 subjects tested with the moving stimulus inside
reported it (IB = 0) while only 4 of the 10 subjects presented with it
outside on the critical inattention trial did so (IB = 60%).

Inhibition and the Spatial Focus of Attention

The results thus far indicate that the more effective the conditions are in eliminating attention to a stimulus, the greater the likelihood that it will not be perceived. If this is correct, then if subjects were to tacitly learn to ignore a particular location, (i.e., inhibit attention to it), because on trials prior to the critical one an object irrelevant to their task was located there, and the critical stimulus appears at that location, it should not be seen by most subjects. This postulated inhibition of attention should resemble the inhibition of attention presumed to account for the increase in IB for targets presented at fixation under inattention conditions. Furthermore, if the location the subjects tacitly learn to ignore is located outside the spatial focus of attention, it should be even less likely to be seen.[8] In the next experiment we explored the combined influence of the spatial focus of attention with the postulated inhibition of attention on IB.

> In order to induce the proposed inhibition of attention to the critical stimulus, two identical, stationary, small black squares were presented on every trial. One was 2 degrees to the right and the other 2 degrees to the left of fixation (figure 4.5). On every trial one was inside and the other outside the rectangle. Every trial was masked. For 5 subjects the rectangle always appeared to the right of fixation in the three inattention trials and for 5 it always appeared to the left on these trials. Subjects knew in advance on which side the rectangle would appear and were cautioned against moving their eyes toward it and away from the fixation mark. On the third trial, the critical trial, the outside black square moved up or down. (The motion was like that in the experiments just described.) Thus, for all 10 subjects tested, the critical stimulus was always the small black square opposite, that is, outside the rectangle.

Only 1 subject reported seeing anything different on the critical inattention trial. Thus IB was 90% and almost complete.[9] Moreover, only 1 of the subjects correctly guessed which square moved and that subject incorrectly reported its direction of motion. Ninety percent of the subjects failed to see the moving stimulus on the inattention trial, although all but 1 subject did so on the divided attention trial, and all did so in the full attention control condition. Subjects' reports of the longer side of the rectangle were 100% accurate on both the critical inattention and divided attention trials.[10] This result established that the resources of attention that were available were sufficient for the perception of the critical stimulus and of the longer side of the rectangle.

The final experiment in this series examined the relation between attention and IB in a different way. This experiment was an attempt to assess whether subjects would be more likely to perceive the motion

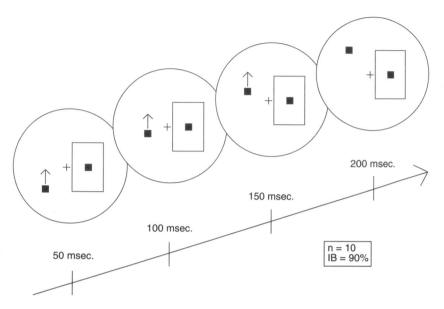

Figure 4.5
Inhibition of attention display with moving stimulus outside zone of attention with IB results.

of the outside critical stimulus if it were located where they had come to expect the rectangle to appear and thus in a location to which attention might be directed. In other words, the question was whether after having built up an expectation about where the rectangle would appear, would unexpectedly switching it to the opposite side of fixation and presenting the critical stimulus in its place increase the probability that the critical stimulus would be seen? Evidence that this was the case would not only add support to the hypothesis about the importance of attention for perception, but also provide evidence of the role of expectancy.

In this experiment, like the previous one, two small black squares were always present—one to the right and one to the left of fixation—in order to encourage the development of inhibition. On every trial prior to the critical one, the rectangle appeared on the same side of fixation. We increased the number of trials prior to the critical inattention trial from two to eight in order to increase expectancy about where the rectangle would appear. On the ninth and critical trial the rectangle unexpectedly switched to the opposite side of fixation, and the black (upwardly or downwardly moving) square appeared on the side where the rectangle had been on the prior eight trials. The critical stimulus was always outside but located where the rectangle was expected to be. For half the subjects the rectangle appeared to the right of fixation for eight trials and switched to the left on the ninth trial. The reverse was true for the remaining subjects. A mask was used. Twenty subjects were tested.

The results were in the predicted direction. Now instead of only 10% of the subjects (1 of 10) perceiving the critical stimulus when it was outside, 50% detected it, (10 of the 20 subjects), and of these 10 subjects 8 reported seeing motion and located it on the correct side. This difference is significant (X^2 (df 1) = 4.59, p < .05). There was no significant decrease in the number of correct reports of the longer side of the rectangle on the critical trial, despite its unexpected change of position. Seventeen of the 20 subjects were correct about the longer side.

These results suggest that there was some division of attention occasioned by the unexpected switching of the location of the rectangle and its replacement by the unexpected critical stimulus which, as predicted, increased the frequency with which the critical stimulus was perceived.

Substitution of the Cross for the Rectangle

In order to ascertain whether the inside/outside differences we obtained when the distraction stimulus was a closed figure could be generalized to cases in which the distraction stimulus was an open figure, we ran another experiment in which the cross task replaced the rectangle task.

> The set of crosses that had been used in other experiments served as the distraction stimuli in this experiment. The crosses were located in the position held by the rectangle in the inside/outside experiments, that is, immediately to the right or left of fixation. The critical stimulus that appeared on the third, sixth, and ninth trials was a small square that moved on a 45 degree oblique trajectory through 2.1 degrees in three 0.7 degree stroboscopic jumps (ISI = 0). When the motion was on the same side of fixation as the cross, its origin was the center of the cross. (We considered this condition to be analogous to the inside condition with the rectangle.) When it was on the side opposite the cross, its origin was the identical position on the opposite side of fixation. (We considered this condition to be analogous to the outside condition with the rectangle.) All trials were masked. Forty subjects were tested, 20 with the critical stimulus in the inside position on the critical trial and 20 with it outside. All subjects knew in advance on which side of fixation the cross would appear.

In the inattention condition 14 of the 20 subjects (70%) of the subjects reported seeing something different on the critical trial when the critical stimulus was inside the cross. All of these subjects reported motion.

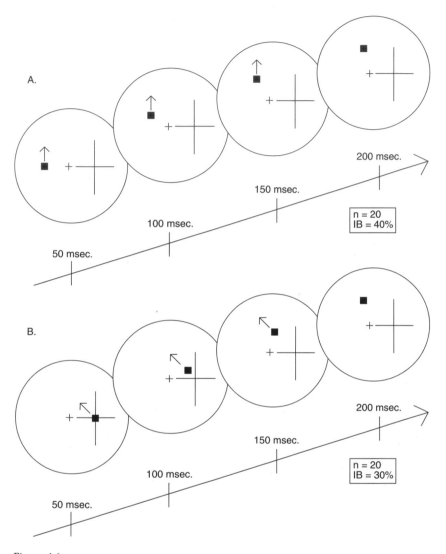

Figure 4.6
Inside/outside displays with moving stimulus and cross as distraction stimulus with
IB results.
A. Outside
B. Inside

Thus IB was only 30%. In contrast, only 6 of the 20 subjects reported seeing something different on the critical trial when the stimulus was outside the cross (IB = 70%). All 6 of these subjects, however, reported seeing motion (X^2 (df 1) = 6.4, p. < .02). These results are evidence that the two tasks—the cross and the rectangle—are comparable, and that the postulated zones of attention are also comparable.

Spatial Focus and a "Preattentive" Distraction Task

The next experiment in this series asked whether the inside/outside difference in the detection of the critical stimulus, which we attribute to the location of the zone of attention, would occur if the perception required by the distraction task was one that some other investigators have assumed is preattentive and accomplished by parallel rather than sequential processing (see, for example, Beck 1967; Julesz 1980). We speculated that if the distraction task were only to entail preattentive processing then, by virtue of the fact that focused attentional processes are not engaged, the critical stimulus might stand a better chance of capturing attention and thus of being seen under conditions of inattention. This ought to be even more likely if the perception of the critical stimulus itself is considered to be based on preattentive processing. In other words, the question addressed by the next experiment is whether the spatial focus of attention controls the perception of the critical stimulus under conditions of inattention, even when both the distraction task and the inattention stimulus are thought by some other investigators to be perceived without attention on the basis of parallel processing.

We chose texture segregation based on a vertical-horizontal orientation difference as the distraction task and a moving spot as the inattention stimulus. Both this kind of texture segregation and motion have been found to pop out in the standard search paradigms and thus are considered to result from parallel processing (Treisman 1982; Julesz 1980; Braun and Sagi 1990; Braun and Sagi 1991).

> The texture segregation patterns were identical to those used in the grouping experiments (see figure 2.2, chapter 2). Both homogenous and segregated patterns were used. The homogenous patterns consisted of either all vertical or all horizontal small line elements. In the heterogenous patterns, one quadrant of elements was rotated 90 degrees, so that, for example, three quadrants of the pattern had vertical elements and one had horizontal elements. The overall pattern was 3.1 × 2.9 cm and subtended a visual angle of approximately 4 degrees vertically and horizontally. The critical stimulus was a small black square which moved vertically up or down, or horizontally toward fixation, a distance of 1.2 degrees in three 0.4 degree stroboscopic steps (ISI = 0). The entire tex-

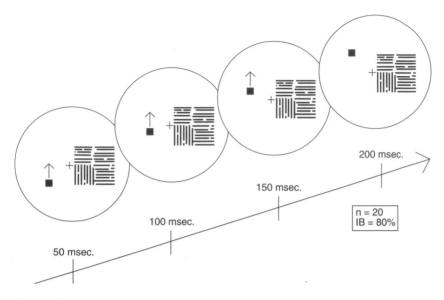

Figure 4.7
Texture segregation as distraction task; critical stimulus moving outside attention zone with IB results.

ture pattern was presented immediately to the right or left of fixation (figure 4.8). On the critical trial (the third, sixth, and ninth trials), the moving spot appeared 2 degrees from fixation on the side opposite the texture pattern. In other words, the critical stimulus was always outside the spatial focus of attention (see figure 4.7). The subject's assigned task was to report whether the pattern was homogenous or heterogenous, and if heterogenous, to locate the odd quadrant by pointing to one of the four quadrants of an outline square divided into quadrants, which was shown to the subjects after they reported whether or not they had detected it. All trials were followed by a mask. Following the critical inattention trial, subjects were asked about the critical stimulus. Twenty subjects were tested. Ten subjects knew prior to each trial on which side of fixation the texture pattern would appear; the other 10 did not know. On the critical inattention trial the texture pattern always had an odd quadrant.

Only 5 of the 20 subjects tested detected the presence of the critical stimulus in the inattention condition (IB = 75%). Two of the 10 subjects who knew the location of the texture array in advance reported seeing the critical stimulus on the inattention trial, and 3 of the 10 subjects who did not know the side in advance did so. This difference is not significant. Eighty-five percent of the subjects correctly reported an odd quadrant on the critical trial in this condition, although only 58%

of these subjects correctly located it. In contrast, all the subjects saw the critical stimulus on the critical trial in the divided and full attention control conditions, and almost all were correct about the texture pattern in the divided attention condition.

These results fail to reveal any decrease in IB, and thus show no facilitation in perceiving the critical stimulus outside the focus of attention when the perception of both it and the distraction task are based on what has been thought to be parallel processing. Thus, not only is it clear from the obtained results that these conditions do not facilitate attentional capture by the critical stimulus which presumably is necessary for its perception, but, like the results reported in chapter 2, they weigh against the assumption that the perception of texture segregation and motion are preattentive. Furthermore, if we assume, as others presumably do, that preattentive perception is always based on the parallel processing of input, then these results also argue against the view that the perception of texture segregation and motion required by these arrays is dependent on parallel processing.[11]

Texture Segregation and Dot Motion Reexamined

The results of this last experiment led to a further examination of the perception of motion under conditions of inattention when the distraction task entailed texture perception. This next experiment, however, differed from the one just described in several ways. Most importantly the texture pattern was now centered at fixation, and the moving target stimulus was superimposed on the texture array. It was therefore inside the focus of attention.

There were three different conditions of testing on the critical trial that were of particular importance in the inattention condition. They were designed to provide additional information about the relation between attention and the perception of the critical stimulus when the subjects were engaged in searching for texture segregation.

> For 15 subjects the texture pattern contained an odd quadrant and the motion of the critical stimulus occurred within that quadrant. For another 15 subjects on the critical trial, the texture pattern contained an odd quadrant, but the motion of the critical stimulus was confined to one of the other quadrants. Finally, for 15 different subjects the texture array was homogenous on the critical trial, that is, there was no odd quadrant, and the motion of the critical stimulus was in one of its four undifferentiated quadrants. The critical motion of the small square was either horizontal to the left or right, or vertical up or down. The square was 1.3 degrees from the center of fixation at its closest and moved a distance of 2.1 degrees in three 0.7 degree stroboscopic steps (figure 4.8).

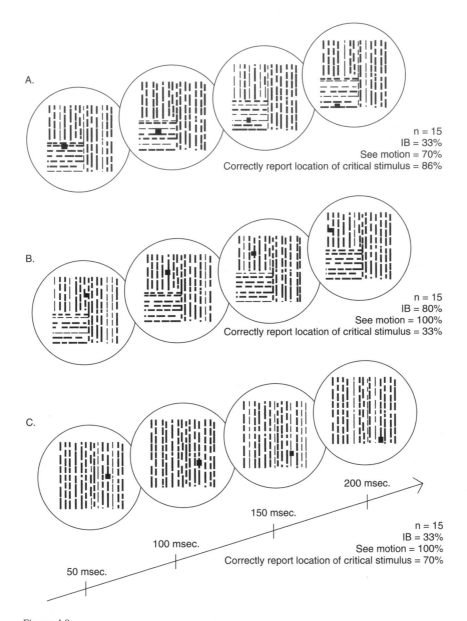

A.

n = 15
IB = 33%
See motion = 70%
Correctly report location of critical stimulus = 86%

B.

n = 15
IB = 80%
See motion = 100%
Correctly report location of critical stimulus = 33%

C.

200 msec.

150 msec.

100 msec.

n = 15
IB = 33%
See motion = 100%
Correctly report location of critical stimulus = 70%

50 msec.

Figure 4.8
Texture segregation as distraction task with IB results.
A. Critical stimulus motion inside odd quadrant.
B. Critical stimulus motion outside odd quadrant.
C. Homogeneous texture: critical stimulus moves in a quadrant.

Table 4.1

Location of critical stimulus (CS)	Number of subjects	Percent of inattentional blindness	Percent of subjects who see motion	Percent of subjects who correctly report location of CS
Odd quadrant	15	33%	70%	86%
Not in odd quadrant	15	80%	100%	33%
No odd quadrant	15	33%	100%	70%

The results are consistent with those from the prior experiment and confirm the strong causal link between the spatial focus of attention and perceiving the inattention stimulus even when both the distraction stimulus and the critical stimulus are thought by some others to require only parallel processing. The results are presented in table 4.1.

When the critical stimulus was located in the odd quadrant in the inattention condition or when there was no odd quadrant, IB was much less frequent (33%) than when the critical stimulus was located outside the odd quadrant and an odd quadrant was present on the inattention trial (IB = 80%), (X^2 (df 1) = 4.57, p. < 05). These results suggest that when the subject is searching for texture segregation and it is present, the odd quadrant attracts attention, so that if the critical stimulus is within it, it is likely to be perceived. However, if it is outside it, it is less likely. If, however, there is no odd quadrant, attention appears to be distributed over the entire texture array, so that wherever the critical stimulus is , as long as it is within the array, it stands a good chance of receiving some attention and therefore of being perceived. The fact that the critical stimulus is moving does not seem to increase the likelihood that it will be perceived.

There were no differences in the number of subjects seeing and correctly identifying the location of the odd quadrant—when there was one—between the condition in which the moving square was inside and the one in which it was outside the odd quadrant. Furthermore, the location of the critical stimulus relative to the odd quadrant had no effect in the divided or full attention conditions. Almost all the subjects reported the target motion in these conditions.

These results are consistent with the other results thus far reported in this chapter that attest to the strong causal link between the spatial focus of attention and the perception of the inattention stimulus. Moreover, like the results from the preceding experiment they provide no evidence that the critical stimulus is more likely to be seen under inattention conditions when it and the distraction task entail percepts that

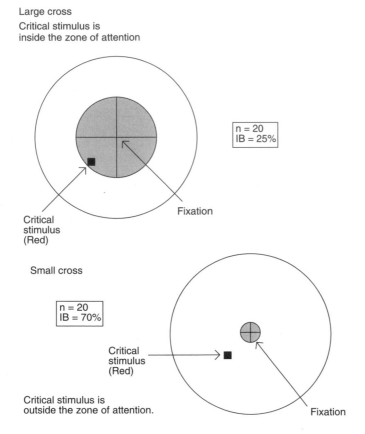

Large cross
Critical stimulus is
inside the zone of attention

n = 20
IB = 25%

Fixation

Critical
stimulus
(Red)

Small cross

n = 20
IB = 70%

Critical
stimulus
(Red)

Critical stimulus is
outside the zone of attention.

Fixation

Figure 4.9
Hypothetical zone of attention: small and large cross at fixation with IB results. Black
square was red in the experiment.

in the past have been thought to be preattentive, but that clearly in
these instances are not.

Small Versus Large Crosses[12]

The next experiment addressed the question of the relation between
the spatial focus of attention and the perception of the inattention stimulus in yet another way—by comparing the amount of IB found with
a small and an identical large distraction stimulus (figure 4.9). The
reduction in the size of the cross was designed to sharply shrink the
zone of attention and to assess how this affected the perception of
the critical stimulus under conditions of inattention.

We compared the frequency of IB for a 0.6 degree solid red square, centered 2.3 degrees from fixation along a 45 degree oblique trajectory, when the longer arm of the cross was either 0.6 degree (small) or, as in all the earlier experiments, approximately 4.0 degrees (large) (see figure 4.9). The subject's task once again was to report the longer arm of the cross that was centered at fixation. Because the critical stimulus was the same distance from fixation and from the center of the cross in both the small cross and large cross conditions, any difference in the frequency of IB between these two conditions must be due to the relation of the critical stimulus to the zone of attention. We predicted a significant increase in IB in the small cross condition.

Twenty subjects were tested with the large crosses and 20 with the small crosses. The large crosses were chosen from the set of those used in all our other experiments in which the distraction task was to report the longer arm of a cross. Fifteen subjects were tested in the small cross condition. The largest of the small crosses subtended a visual angle of 0.6 degree vertically or horizontally. The difficulty of determining the longer arm of the smaller crosses was matched to that of the larger crosses so that any difference between the results of these two conditions could not be attributed to the different levels of difficulty of the distraction task. The experiments conformed to our standard testing pattern, except that in both conditions there were five trials prior to the critical trial in the inattention and divided attention conditions. All trials were masked with a colored pattern.

In both the inattention and divided attention conditions subjects performed as well on the line length task with the small crosses as they did with the standard large crosses. With the large crosses, only 5 of the 20 subjects failed to see the critical stimulus on the inattention trial (IB = 25%), which is consistent with the prior results. In contrast, 14 of the 20 subjects tested with small crosses failed to see the critical stimulus (IB = 70%), [X^2, (df 1) = 5.24 p > .05]. Thus by only changing the size of the crosses that are the focus of the subject's attention in the inattention condition, the amount of IB is tripled, and this is true despite the fact that the critical stimulus is identical and located in the identical position relative to fixation and the center of the cross.

Small and Large Crosses in Parafovea

The results of additional experiments are not only consistent with all the results reported in this chapter, but also provide some additional clarification. These are results from experiments in which the placement of the critical inattention stimulus and the distraction stimulus were varied in order to manipulate the zone of attention and its relation to the critical stimulus. The critical stimulus was a solid red circle

0.6 degree in diameter, and the distraction stimuli were the small set of crosses used in the prior experiment. The next figure shows the various critical arrays that were used (figure 4.10), and for the sake of comparisons also includes a representation of the standard display in which one of the larger distraction crosses appears centered at fixation and the critical stimulus appears in one of its quadrants (figure 4.10a).

> In one version of this experiment the crosses were centered at fixation and the red critical stimulus appeared in one of the four standard positions around fixation (figure 4.10b). In another the red critical stimulus appeared at fixation with the small crosses in one of the four standard parafoveal locations (figure 4.10c). In another variation the small crosses appeared in one of the four parafoveal locations and the critical stimulus appeared in another of these locations (figure 4.10d). In this version the distance separating the distraction stimulus from the critical stimulus was almost twice as large—4.0 degrees—as that normally separating these stimuli. The last variation was one in which the crosses appeared in one of the standard parafoveal locations above fixation while the critical stimulus only appeared below fixation in one of the two other possible parafoveal positions (figure 4.10e). Colored masks were used and 20 subjects were tested in each of these variations.

The inattention results are also summarized in figure 4.10, along with the results from a prior standard experiment in which the critical stimulus falls within the zone of attention (figure 4.10a) to make comparisons easier. What we find is a sharp increase in IB relative to the standard experiment when the critical stimulus is outside the zone of attention (figures 4.10b and 4.10e). (For example, when the position of the crosses is limited to one particular area of the parafovea, namely to the two positions above fixation, as it is in figure 4.10e, and the critical stimulus appears below fixation, it is outside the attentional zone and therefore suffers considerable blindness.) There is also the now familiar increase in IB when the critical stimulus is at fixation and the small crosses are parafoveal (figure 4.10b), which we have attributed to the inhibition of attention for objects at fixation when attention is focused on a stimulus located elsewhere. However, when both the critical stimulus and the crosses appear in the parafovea and are now further apart than is usual (figure 4.10d), there is no increase in IB, because here the critical stimulus falls within the zone of attention, which is quite large. In fact, it includes the entire parafoveal area in which the crosses may appear. In contrast, when the crosses are centered at fixation (figure 4.10a), their position is completely predictable and attention can be focused at that location, narrowly if the crosses are small and more broadly if they are large. It therefore makes sense that simply reducing the size of the crosses when they appear in the

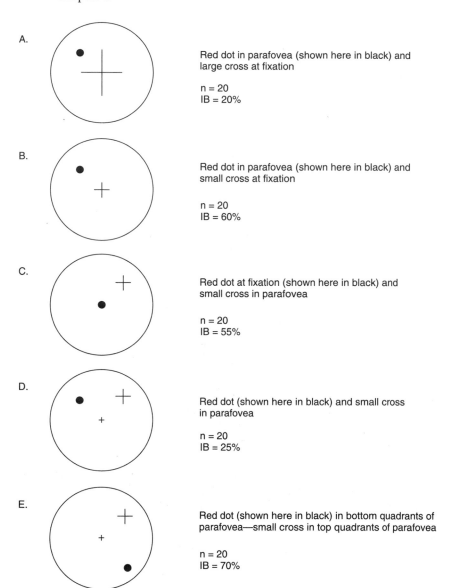

A.
Red dot in parafovea (shown here in black) and large cross at fixation

n = 20
IB = 20%

B.
Red dot in parafovea (shown here in black) and small cross at fixation

n = 20
IB = 60%

C.
Red dot at fixation (shown here in black) and small cross in parafovea

n = 20
IB = 55%

D.
Red dot (shown here in black) and small cross in parafovea

n = 20
IB = 25%

E.
Red dot (shown here in black) in bottom quadrants of parafovea—small cross in top quadrants of parafovea

n = 20
IB = 70%

Figure 4.10
Displays varying the placement of the cross (large and small) and critical stimulus (red disc) with IB results.

parafovea does not have the same effect of reducing the zone of attention as it does when the crosses are at fixation. All these results once again underscore the intimate, causal relation between attention and inattentional blindness.

An Attempt to Diffuse the Zone of Attention

The question of the relationship between the zone of attention and IB was explored in the Berkeley laboratory using a different procedure, which attempted to transform the zone of attention from one with clear boundaries to one in which the boundaries were more diffuse.[13]

> The distraction task in these experiments was to discriminate the shade of gray of the background that was one of three different homogeneous grays. The critical stimulus was one of three familiar geometric shapes, (a cross, a rectangle, or triangle) used in the shape experiments described in chapter 3. These solid shapes were either red, black, or blue. They were presented in one of the four typical parafoveal locations, 2.0 degrees from fixation. Fixation position was always marked. The subjects reported their perception of the shade of gray of the background on every trial except the control trial by assigning a number to it. If they thought it was the lightest gray, they were told to assign the number 1, intermediate gray they were to assign the number 2, and the darkest gray they were to assign the number 3. The subjects were familiarized with the three shades of gray prior to the first actual experimental trial. As in other experiments performed in Berkeley, the critical stimulus was presented on the fourth, seventh, and eighth trials. The fourth trial was the critical inattention trial. The seventh trial was the implicit divided attention trial and the eighth trial was the full attention, control trial. Whether or not subjects perceived the critical stimulus, they were asked to select it from among an array of five shapes. They also were asked what color the stimulus was.

In the first experiment the entire screen was one of the three shades of gray. Twenty-three subjects were tested. Performance on the new distraction task was worse than general performance on the cross task. On trial one, only 43% of the subjects correctly identified the shade of gray, and on the fourth trial only 52% of the subjects did so. A large number of subjects also failed to detect the critical stimulus on the inattention trial. Seventeen of them suffered IB (74%). Of these 17 subjects, 6 correctly reported the color and only 2 selected the correct shape. Of the 5 subjects who reported seeing something new on the critical inattention trial, 3 correctly reported both the color and the shape. One reported the color only and 1 failed to correctly identify either shape or color. Almost all the subjects reported the shape and its color correctly on the control trial.

> In the second version of this experiment the gray background surrounded a white circular area 2.4 degrees in diameter, which contained the fixation mark at its center. The critical stimulus was presented outside this area, but inside the gray area of the screen that was the object of attention. Thus the critical stimulus nominally fell within the zone of attention but, of course, subjects might have performed the distraction task by always attending to one side of fixation that might not have been the side of fixation on which the critical stimulus appeared. Again subjects were asked to assign the number 1, 2, or 3 to the background grey. A new group of 28 subjects were tested.

By the fourth trial subjects were performing quite well on the distraction task. Seventy-five percent of them assigned the correct number to the background gray. On the other hand very few (only 3) subjects detected the critical stimulus on the inattention trial (IB = 89%). Of these only 7 correctly guessed the color, and only 2 correctly guessed the shape. In contrast, 27 of the 28 subjects saw and correctly identified the shapes and their colors on the control trial.

The last experiment in this series asked whether the reduction in the usual contrast between the critical stimulus and the background produced by changing the background from the usual white to a shade of gray might have accounted for the high IB just as a reduction in conspicuousness was shown to increase IB in chapter 3. Therefore, the cross task now replaced the shade of gray discrimination as the distraction task, but the cross now appeared against a background that was one of the three shades of gray. The experiment was otherwise identical to the first experiment in this series. A group of 19 new subjects were tested.

The results support the conclusion that some of the IB obtained in the first two experiments was caused by the decrease in contrast between the critical stimulus and background, because in this experiment we obtained an IB effect of 53%—10 of the 19 subjects failed to detect the critical stimulus. This is twice as large an IB effect as that obtained for the same stimuli presented under the same conditions except for a white background (see chapter 3).

The meaning of these combined results is not entirely clear because the procedure was such that even though the critical stimulus was nominally within the area to which subjects had to attend in order to perform their assigned task, they could attend to any section of it, and so they might well have been attending to the right side of the background pattern when the critical stimulus appeared on the left.

Thus, although it fell within the background area that was the object of the distraction task, it might well have been well outside the zone of attention. This then would account for the high IB. If so, this would mean that this procedure, which was meant to explore the effect of diffuse attention on IB, was simply another, perhaps less precise, version of the inside/outside procedure used to explore the relation between IB and the zone of attention.

A More Cognitive Distraction Task

The next experiment examined two different questions, one of which again concerned the effect of shrinking the zone of attention. The other question concerned the nature of the distraction task itself. Thus far the distraction tasks had been visual and spatial and, if attentional resources are modality specific, these tasks call upon the same resources as those required for the perception of the critical inattention stimulus (Kahneman 1973). This experiment therefore examined whether IB was limited to cases in which attention was preoccupied with a visuospatial task. The distraction task used in this next experiment was both cognitive and visuospatial. However, it was only visuospatial to the degree that its performance required that the subjects look at the area in which the information necessary to do the cognitive task was presented.

> The new task required the subject to subtract 7 from a three-digit number that appeared for 200 msec. on the screen in a small rectangular box subtending a visual angle of 0.7 degree horizontally and 0.6 degree vertically. This box was centered around the fixation point. Because the numbers that appeared in the small box were the object of the subjects' attention, we assumed that the zone of attention was probably no larger than the box containing the numbers and thus was about the same size as the zone of attention when the small crosses served as the distraction stimuli. The subjects were required to report whether the next three-digit number that appeared in the box (also for 200 msec.) was equal to, more, or less than the number produced by their subtraction. There was a 400 msec. interval between the disappearance of the first number and the appearance of the second number that was designed to provide the subject with time to perform the calculation. During this interval the window in which the numbers appeared remained on the screen as did the fixation point at its center. Subjects were urged to carefully maintain their fixation until the mask appeared, which occurred immediately after the second number disappeared from the screen. On the critical inattention trial a 0.2 degree solid red square (the same stimulus in the same location as the critical stimulus used in the preceding experiment with large and small crosses) was presented at the same time as the

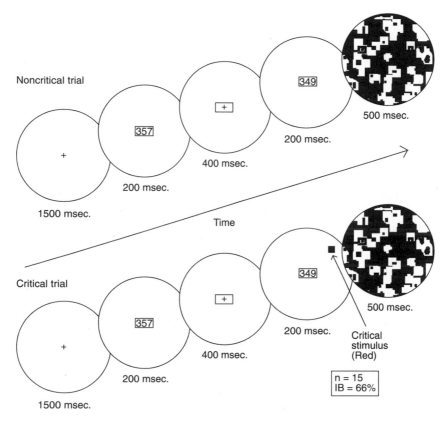

Figure 4.11
Schematic illustrations of noncritical and critical displays with subtraction task and IB results. Black square was red in the experiment.

second number. It was located in one of the four typical parafoveal locations. In this case it was 2.3 degrees from fixation and remained on the screen for 200 msec. (figure 4.11). Each condition (the inattention, divided attention, and full attention control conditions) consisted of three trials on the third of which the critical stimulus was present. Fifteen subjects participated in this study.

Performance on this new distraction task was comparable to performance on the earlier spatial distraction tasks. On the first trial, 47% of the subjects answered correctly, and on the third trial, the critical one, 93% did so. Nine of the 15 subjects, (IB = 66%), failed to detect the critical stimulus on the inattention trial. If we compare the frequency of IB in this experiment with its frequency in the small cross condition of the preceding experiment that used the identical critical stimulus, we find no difference. In the divided attention condition only 1 subject failed to see the critical stimulus and only 2 subjects gave the incorrect answer in the subtraction task. In the full attention control condition, every subject reported seeing the small red square. Thus, the IB effect does not appear to be limited to occasions in which attention is occupied by a purely visual task.

We ran another experiment using the subtraction distraction task. In this experiment the subtraction task was combined with a display that we had established was likely to generate the inhibition of attention to the position of the critical stimulus. The purpose of this experiment was again to extend our understanding of the generality of the IB phenomenon. We wished to find out whether the subtraction task that confined attention to a small area on the screen and to an internal mental process would, when combined with a display which encouraged inhibition to the critical stimulus, lead to an increase in IB.

> In order to answer this question the display was modified so that on every trial, four small black squares—the same size as the critical stimulus—were presented around the number display window. Each occupied one of the four possible positions in which the red critical stimulus would appear. On the critical trial, one of the black squares became a red one. Since the black squares were consistently present and irrelevant to the subject's task, we thought they would generate inhibition of attention to those stimuli and thus significantly increase the likelihood that the red square would not be seen (figure 4.12).

Only one of the fifteen subjects reported seeing the critical stimulus on the inattention trial (IB = 94%). These results therefore duplicate those from other experiments in which we combined narrowness of focus with an attempt to generate an inhibition of attention and found almost total IB.

The combined results of both these experiments support several conclusions. First, the assumption that the zone of attention in this experiment is defined by the small box in which the numbers appeared is plausible because the amount of IB was identical to that found with the small crosses. Second, IB does not appear limited to presentations entailing purely visuospatial distraction tasks because it occurred in this experiment with a more cognitive task. If the subtraction task can be likened to any absorbing conceptual task, then IB may be likened to the experience of *not* seeing, an experience familiar to most of us that occurs when we are deeply engaged in thought.

The question of whether IB would occur with a strictly cognitive task that had no visual component remains. However, it is procedurally difficult to answer because fixation must be controlled in order to

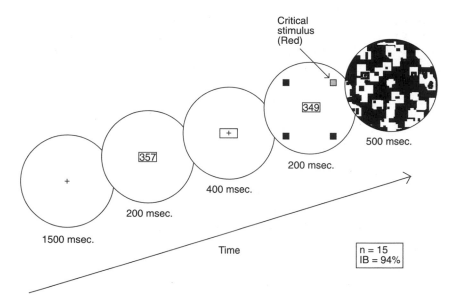

Figure 4.12
Inhibition of attention display with subtraction task and IB results. Textured square was red in the experiment.

maintain the desired relation between fixation and the critical stimulus, and therefore, at the very least, the subject must be asked to fixate some visual mark. As the reader will discover in chapter 8, IB occurs even when the subject's only assigned task is to maintain fixation. Finally, the results lend additional support to the speculation that subjects can tacitly learn to ignore a specific region, and if they do, IB is more likely to occur for any stimulus presented there.

Attentional Load and IB

Several experiments were done that attempted to explore the relationship between the difficulty of the distraction task and the amount of IB. Unfortunately the results of these few experiments were equivocal and this line of research was dropped. However, because the issue of the relation between attentional load and IB is of some interest, we thought it might be useful to briefly describe this research.

In these experiments we attempted to increase the difficulty of the distraction task by giving the subjects two tasks rather than one, one or the other of which was called for after the distraction stimulus was replaced by the mask.

In one experiment the rectangles from the inside/outside experiments were used, but we added a small gap in one of their sides. In another experiment the larger crosses were used, and a small gap was introduced in one of the arms. In both cases the distraction stimulus was centered at fixation and the critical stimulus appeared in the parafovea. The subjects were instructed that on any trial they would be asked to report either the longer axis of the rectangle (or cross) or the location of the gap. In both experiments the critical stimulus was a solid black disc, 0.3 degree in diameter.

The results obtained from these experiments were compared with those obtained when the subjects had only a single distraction task, namely, reporting the longer arm of the cross or the longer side of the rectangle. We obtained no differences between the one and two task conditions. In both cases IB was close to the 25% normally obtained when the critical stimulus is in the parafovea and the distraction stimulus is centered at fixation. While the finding of no difference does not permit a strong conclusion, these results do *not* support the hypothesis that attentional load play a role in IB, although it may be that if the tasks have been more difficult, some effect might have been obtained.[14]

An Oculomotor Distraction Task[15]

The experiments thus far described in this chapter have demonstrated that IB is strongly affected by the spatial focus of attention and that it does not appear to be contingent on a particular mode of attention. It occurs as strongly when attention is engaged by a cognitive task with a spatial component as it does when it is engaged by a strictly visuo-spatial task.[16] The next experiment demonstrates that even the engagement of attention by an oculomotor distraction task causes frequent IB. There were several reasons for doing this experiment. First, we wished to determine whether a visuomotor task that involves no cognitive component would produce blindness.[17] Second, because the task was simply to fixate two consecutively presented targets that required only that the subjects execute a saccade from one to the other, it was possible to query the subject about the critical stimulus immediately after the critical trial without having to wait until the subjects reported either their line judgment or the outcome of their subtraction. Were blindness to occur, it would be much more difficult to attribute it to a failure to remember the critical stimulus, because there would now be only an extremely brief delay between its disappearance and the subject's being asked about it. Finally, this experiment allowed for a significant increase in the presentation time of the critical stimulus. In every experiment thus far described, the critical stimulus was present for no more than 200 msec. Had it been present for longer, it would have been possible for the subjects to move their eyes to it, because the average latency for a saccadic eye movement is 250 msec. We wished to avoid this possibility. In the present experiment the critical stimulus was visible for 700 msec., (i.e., three and one-half times longer than had previously been the case). Because the subjects' only task was to move their eyes from one saccadic target to the next, it seemed unlikely that they would attempt to move their eyes to the critical stimulus that was quite distinct from the saccadic targets. At any rate, had they done so, it probably would have acted to reduce IB so that any evidence of IB would be more compelling.

> The experiment began with the appearance of a small black fixation cross at the center of the display screen that was present until the first saccadic target appeared. After 1500 msec. the first saccadic target, a small red spot, appeared in one of the four possible locations, 2 degrees from fixation. These were approximately the same locations as those used for presenting a critical stimulus within a quadrant of the cross. It remained visible for 350 msec. and was followed by a second saccadic target, a small blue spot that appeared at one of the other three possible locations with the restriction that it was either vertically up or down or horizontally right or left from the first saccadic target (see figure 4.13). It too remained on the screen for 350 msec. and was followed by a pattern mask that remained on for 500 msec. and covered the entire area in which stimuli were presented. On the third trial in each of the three standard conditions (inattention, divided attention, and full attention), the critical stimulus—a solid black circle 0.6 degree in diameter—appeared at fixation with the onset of the first saccadic target and remained visible until the mask appeared. Consequently it was visible for 700 msec. and during that time it was only 2 degrees from each of the saccadic targets. The subjects' task on all trials in the inattention condition was to move their eyes as precisely and quickly as they could to the first target, which they were told would be a red dot, and then to move them as quickly as possible to the second target, which they were told would be a blue dot. They were told that we were interested in the accuracy of their changes in fixation. On the critical inattention trial, immediately after the mask appeared, subjects were asked if they had seen anything that had not been on the screen on the earlier trials. If they answered yes they were asked what they saw and where it was located. Even if they failed to report seeing a difference, they were told that something had been present and they were asked to try to select it from an array of five shapes, one of which was the target circle. In the divided attention condition, subjects were asked to perform the saccadic task and to report anything else they saw on the screen, while in the full attention, control

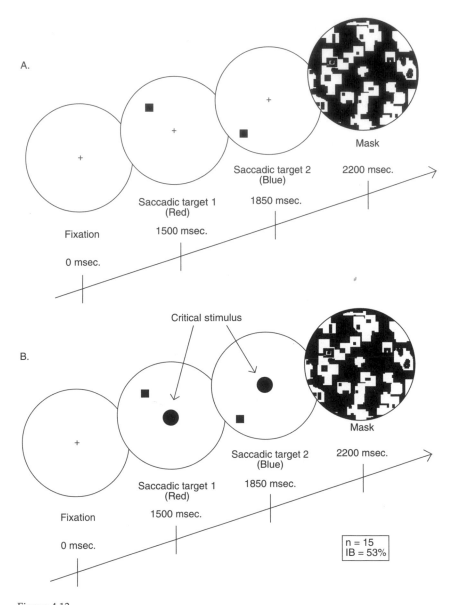

Figure 4.13
Critical and noncritical displays for saccadic eye movement experiment with IB results.
Black square was red in the experiment.

condition, subjects fixated the fixation mark and simply reported what they saw. Eye movements were not recorded because their accuracy was not at issue. Fifteen subjects were tested.

Only seven of the 15 subjects detected the critical stimulus in the inattention condition, (IB = 53%). None of the 8 (inattentionally) blind subjects selected the correct shape from the recognition test array. Not surprisingly, all the subjects correctly identified the critical stimulus in the full attention condition, and 11 subjects did so in the divided attention condition.[18] The fact that 73% of the subjects in the divided attention condition perceived and identified the critical stimulus is clear evidence that, with some attention to the critical object, it can be perceived under the conditions of this experiment.[19]

These results are powerful evidence of IB under conditions in which attention is engaged only by an oculomotor task and the critical stimulus is present for almost three-quarters of a second. An interesting aspect of these results is that they may represent IB that is less closely tied to the focus of attention. In this experiment the subject had to be attending rather broadly in an effort to detect the appearance of the saccadic targets because the subjects did not know in advance where they would appear. Because the critical stimulus appeared at the position of the original fixation, it is possible that this location was included within the area attended to, at least while the subject was waiting for the second saccadic target. Of course, this might account for why 46% of the subjects detected the critical stimulus.

Conclusion

The general conclusion that all the experiments in this chapter support is that observers tend to be blind to a suprathreshold object that appears either at or close to fixation when they are not searching for it, when they are occupied with any task that engages their attention, and when the critical object is located outside the boundaries of the area to which attention is directed. Thus, if the critical stimulus is outside the zone of attention, it will cause significantly more IB than if it is at the same distance from fixation but inside the attentional zone. Perhaps most compelling of all the data reported in this chapter is that which demonstrates that IB occurs even if the subject's only task is to execute two saccades and the critical stimulus is present for 700 msec.

The experiments described in chapter 5 reveal interesting and extremely important exceptions to these conclusions. These experiments are concerned with the question of whether there are stimuli that almost invariably are seen under conditions of inattention, and which therefore must be capable of capturing attention even under conditions that make this unlikely. In all the experiments described thus far, the critical stimuli have been more or less semantically neutral, for example, a geometric shape or some feature such as color, location, or motion. In the next chapter we describe experiments in which the critical stimulus is more meaningful, either for a particular subject or for all subjects.

Chapter 5

Meaningfulness: Names[1]

A Question

All the evidence presented in the last chapter can be interpreted as support for the hypothesis that there is no perception without attention. By decreasing the probability that attention would be paid to some object, we significantly reduced the probability that its presence would be perceived and, in fact, demonstrated in a few experiments that this probability could be reduced almost to zero. In fact, in no experiment we have described has any stimulus presented under conditions of inattention been reliably perceived when efforts were made to shield it from attention by placing it: (1) outside the focus of attention (2) at fixation where a process that inhibits attention seems to operate, or (3) in a location that subjects have come to ignore. In other words, the evidence thus far presented supports the conclusion that in the absence of attention observers are functionally blind to a highly visible stimulus that is imaged at or within a few degrees of fixation.

The question remains, however, as to whether there are not some objects that would capture attention even though they are not anticipated, they appear when attention is engaged with some other task, and they are located outside the focus of attention. One possible candidate whose credentials have been well established in the selective attention literature is one's own name.

In the standard selective attention experiments that typically engage audition rather than vision, subjects are asked to shadow a message delivered to one ear while a different message is delivered simultaneously to the other ear. The general findings are that subjects hear very little of the unattended message, but about a third of them do report hearing their own names if it occurs in the unattended message (Moray 1959). This phenomenon has an ordinary life analogue which has been called the "cocktail party effect" (Cherry 1953), and refers to the experience of hearing one's own name across a crowded and noisy room while one is engaged in some other conversation. Although the significance of this phenomenon has been debated in the selective attention literature, its occurrence has not been. Somewhat surprisingly, there seems to have been no effort to determine whether there is a comparable effect in vision. Does one's written name, which is undoubtedly seen less frequently than one's name is heard, have the same power as one's spoken name to capture attention—or to be more theoretically neutral—to be perceived under conditions of inattention? Anecdotal evidence suggests that it might, since one's own name does seem to leap off a page of text even in the absence of any expectation of finding it there.

Given this background, constructing an experiment in which one's written name serves as the critical inattention stimulus seemed worth doing even though there were compelling reasons to think that the effect might not occur in vision. If so-called low-level features of visual stimulation, like color, motion, texture segregation, or flicker go undetected, and simple geometric shapes are not discriminated from one another, why would something as complex as a word be perceived? After all, a word or a name consists of many different features and shapes grouped together in particular ways. Nevertheless, even though we were pessimistic about its outcome, we proceeded to design and run an experiment in which the subject's own name was the critical stimulus presented under conditions of inattention.

Seeing Your Name

This experiment followed the pattern of our other experiments. One of the four standard crosses centered in one of the four possible parafoveal locations around fixation served as the focus of the distraction task, which again was to report its longer axis. On the third and critical trial in the inattention condition the subject's own first name unexpectedly appeared centered at fixation along with the cross. (We restricted subjects to those with first names of between three and five letters in order to control the size of the inattention stimulus. The smallest name subtended a visual angle of 0.733 degree while the largest subtended an angle of 1.4 degrees.) Immediately after the subjects reported the longer axis of the cross, they were asked whether they had seen anything else and if so, what. In the divided attention condition that came next, the critical stimulus, which also appeared on the third trial, was the word *House*[2] (visual angle, 1.23 degrees), which is among the most frequent five-letter concrete nouns in the English language (Kucera and Francis 1967). On the third trial of the final condition, the full attention control, the critical stimulus was the word *Time* (visual angle, 0.933 degree), which is also among the most frequently used four-letter concrete nouns. All trials were masked. In order to avoid alerting subjects to the possibility that their name would play a role in the experiment, subjects, primar-

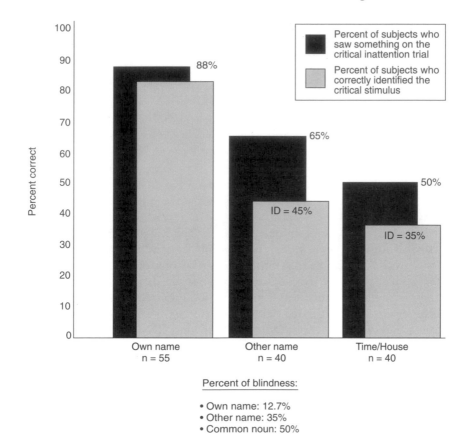

Figure 5.1
Summary of results of experiments with own name, other name, and familiar noun as
critical stimulus with IB results.

ily students at the New School, were recruited some time before they
were tested. When they were recruited, they were asked to give us their
names and telephone numbers. Before they arrived in the laboratory to
be tested, their first names were entered into the display program. Forty
subjects were tested, although for some of them the conditions of testing
varied slightly from those just described. However, because these variations (for example, whether the mask consisted of a matrix of lines or of
black and white novel shapes, or whether the center of the cross was 1.5
or 2.0 degrees from fixation) did not affect the results, all the results are
reported together and are summarized in figure 5.1.

Only seven of all the subjects tested failed to perceive their own
names in the inattention condition (IB = 12.7%), which is astonishing

given our findings that any stimulus thus far tested when presented at fixation has a low probability of being seen. Without even being asked, most subjects reported seeing their own names. Moreover there was no decrease in performance on the cross judgment task associated with the detection and identification of the name. In the divided attention condition subjects reported both the longer cross line and the critical stimulus with a high degree of accuracy and all the subjects reported correctly in the full attention, control condition. Given the fact that there was so little IB, that is, that most subjects reported seeing and identified their own names, it perhaps is not necessary to point out that there were no differences between either the detecting or identifying of three- and five-letter names despite the size difference between them.

In order to make certain that there was not something special about a lexical stimulus presented at fixation under conditions of inattention, we tested two new groups of subjects. For one group of 20 subjects the critical stimulus in the inattention condition was someone else's name. We chose either the five-letter name *David* (visual angle, 1.13 degrees) or the four-letter name *Alex* (visual angle, 0.87 degree) because they were the most common four- and five-letter names in our subject pool. We tested a separate groups of 20 subjects using the four-letter word *Time* and another group of 20 subjects using the five-letter word *House* as the critical stimulus in the inattention condition. The remaining conditions of testing were unchanged.

When the critical stimulus was someone else's name, 35%, or 14 of the 40 subjects, were blind to it and of the 26 subjects who reported seeing something different on the this trial, fewer than half of them (45%) correctly identified it. When the critical stimulus was a common word (time or house), 50%, that is, 22 of 40 subjects, failed to see it and only 35% of the subjects who reported seeing something, correctly identified it. Again there was no tendency for subjects presented with a five-letter critical stimulus to report it more often than subjects presented with a four-letter one, and there were no significant differences in the accuracy with which the longer line of the crosses was reported.

These results establish the generality of the own name effect, which seems to be significantly more pronounced in vision than in audition. The difference between the frequency with which subjects detect their own names and either an extremely common English noun or someone else's name under conditions of inattention is highly significant (X^2 (1df) = 18.35 < .001). If attention is a precondition of perception, then one's own name appears to be a stimulus that almost invariably captures it.

This finding raises many questions, the most critical of which has been widely discussed and fought over in the selective attention literature and remains unresolved. The question at issue is whether these results are consistent with the hypothesis that the attentional selection implicated in perceiving one's own name occurs early in the processing hierarchy on the basis of gross stimulus features of the input (Broadbent 1958; Treisman 1969) or occurs much later, after deep and perhaps even full semantic processing has been completed (Deutsch and Deutsch 1963). If selection is early and occurs on the basis of sensory features of the input, then how is it possible that one's own name, which would seem to require semantic processing, is perceived on the unattended channel? Those who believe in some version of what has come to be called the theory of "early selection" have argued that the reason names are perceived on the unattended channel is that very little information is necessary for their perception, because they have a very low perceptual threshold and sufficient information gets through even the coarse, early filter on the unattended channel to permit recognition (Treisman 1969). In other words, according to a theory of early selection, an input attenuator operates early on the unattended channel, but preserves sufficient information to permit stimuli with very low recognition threshold to be perceived. One's own name is such a stimulus.[3] According to this theory the reason other stimuli are not perceived on the unattended channel is that they require far more information for their perception and this information is lost as the relevant input passes through the attenuating filter. Another fact that emerged from the selective listening research that is consistent with the early selection hypothesis is the finding that subjects are generally able to detect the gender of the voice speaking over the unattended channel (Moray 1959). According to the theory of early selection, this is possible because the coarse information required for this gross discrimination survives the filter.[4]

In contrast, those who favor a late selection theory (Deutsch and Deutsch 1963) explain the perception of one's own name when it is spoken over the unattended channel in a dichotic listening-shadowing experiment by the assumption that the attentional gate or filter operates late in the processing chain after meaning has been assessed. According to this theory it is the meaning of the stimulus that is responsible for the capture of attention, and for its consequent perception. In other words, all input is assumed to be processed to a semantic level at which point both selection and capture may occur.

Reduced Exposure Time

In an effort to determine what it is about one's own name that leads it to be perceived under conditions of inattention when so little else seems to be, we obtained data that support a late selection theory of visual attention. The experiments designed to explore this question attempted to determine whether global aspects of a name could account for its perception, because it is these properties of a stimulus that might be the basis for its early selection. Before turning to the most decisive of these experiments, however, we briefly describe a variation of the name experiment that underscores the strength of the finding.

In this experiment the presentation times for the displays were reduced by 50% from 200 msec. to 100 msec. Instead of presenting the crosses that continued to serve as the objects of the distraction task for 200 msec. we presented them for only 100 msec. On the critical trial in which the name was presented along with the cross, presentation time was also only 100 msec. No mask was used. Of the 15 subjects who participated in this study, 11 reported seeing something different on the critical inattention trial (IB = 26%) and 8 of these subjects correctly identified their names. Thus, although somewhat fewer subjects see their own names when the exposure time is reduced by 50%, many do, which is a striking finding.[5] Subjects continued to perform the cross task at about the same level of accuracy in the inattention condition. However, in the divided attention condition significantly fewer subjects correctly reported the longer line of the cross although only 2 of 15 subjects failed to report seeing something other than the cross on the critical divided attention trial. Eleven of these subjects correctly identified the critical stimulus on this trial.

We compared the results obtained with these subjects with those from another group of 15 subjects who were presented with the familiar word *Time* on the critical inattention and full attention control trials and with the word *House* on the critical divided attention trial. (These were stimuli that had been used earlier when they were presented for the normal duration of 200 msec.) All stimulus presentations were only 100 msec.

Only 3 subjects reported seeing anything other than the cross on the critical inattention trial (IB = 80%), and none of the subjects who reported seeing something else correctly identified it as *Time*. Subjects did not do well on the critical divided attention trial either, since 53% of them were blind to the critical stimulus on this trial. In fact, even on the full attention control trial when *Time* again was the critical stimulus, 4 subjects did not even detect its presence and only 6 of the 11 subjects who did correctly identified it. A comparison between the effects of halving the presentation time on the detection and identification of one's own name with its effect on the detection of a highly familiar word (X^2, $df1 = 8.64$, p. $< .01$) attests again to the uniqueness of one's own name and its ability to capture attention.

Modifications of Own Name Produces IB

A series of experiments were done to determine whether we could find support for the view that the perception of one's own name under conditions of inattention is based on its gross or global features which, if true, would be consistent with an early selection theory of attention. Conversely, evidence that this is not the case would argue for a theory of late selection. The most telling of these experiments was one in which a single, seemingly modest modification was made to the subject's name, which had a far from modest effect. If the subject's name did not begin with a vowel, the first vowel was replaced by another vowel, for example, *Ken* became *Kon, Jack* became *Jeck,* and *Megan* became *Magan.* For the two subjects whose names began with a vowel, *Adam* and *Adina,* the second vowel in their names was replaced, so that their names became *Adem* and *Adena.* All other conditions of testing were identical to the main name experiment. The reasoning behind this experiment was that if the perception of one's own name under conditions of inattention is based on the processing of low-level or coarse stimulus information, then a simple vowel switch within the name should have very little effect. This might not be true if either the first or last letter of the name were altered, because these letters might be thought to occupy privileged positions that are more critical in identifying one's own name. A new group of 20 New School students was tested.

The result was that now 12 of the 20 subjects were blind (IB = 60%) whereas in the exactly comparable experiment with 20 subjects for whom testing conditions were identical except that the names were not modified, only one of the 20 subjects failed to see their names, (IB = 0.5%). This difference, of course, is highly significant (X^2 ($1df$) = 13.8 p < .001). Thus changing a single letter embedded within one's name that neither begins nor ends it strongly affects its visibility. Again, it is not simply that subjects fail to identify the critical stimulus. *They do not see that it is there at all.* Of the 8 subjects who reported seeing something on the critical inattention trial, 5 reported seeing their name. No subject correctly reported seeing the modified version of his or her name.[6] It is telling that 35% of the subjects continued to be blind to the critical stimulus even in the divided attention condition, and of the 13 subjects who saw something besides the cross in this condition, only 3 correctly identified the modified name. The others reported seeing their actual names. Most subjects who reported seeing something in either the inattention or divided attention conditions and were able to describe it in some way made what is familiarly known as the "proofreader's error." This was true even in the full attention control condition where, although all subjects reported seeing something, only 45%

reported what was actually there, while the remaining subjects reported seeing their names.

A reasonable inference from the early selection account of the perception of one's name is that subjects ought to make a proofreader's error and misperceive the modified version of their own names as their actual name based on its global features. However, because only 5 did so on the inattention trial, this too does not support an early selection theory. The proofreader's error not withstanding, the fact that 60% of the subjects in the inattention condition were blind to a modestly altered version of their own names, whereas almost all subjects see and recognize their unmodified names under identical viewing conditions, would appear to argue strongly against any early selection theory of attention.

In order to better understand the meaning of the results from the modified name experiment, we compared its results with those from an experiment in which the critical stimuli were similarly modified versions of the words *Time* and *House*, which had served as the critical stimuli in earlier experiments. We wondered whether modifying these stimuli in the same way that we had modified subjects' own names would produce similar results, namely, increase the amount of IB. So we presented a new group of 10 subjects with *Teme* as the critical stimulus and a group of 10 other subjects with *Hause* as the critical stimulus on the inattention trial.

Four of the 10 subjects tested with the modified version of *Time* and 5 of the 10 subjects tested with the modified version of house were blind on the inattention trial, (IB = 45%). If we now compare this result with the frequency of IB when the unmodified *Time* or *House* served as the critical stimulus, we find no difference. Almost the same number of subjects were blind to the unmodified versions of the critical stimuli (IB = 55%). Thus, altering these common words has *no* effect on their detectability, whereas modifying a subject's own name has a significant inhibitory effect.

This outcome also seems easier to interpret in terms of a late selection theory that could explain the increase in IB for a modified version of one's own name by arguing that the modification changes the stimulus from one that is highly meaningful and capable of capturing attention to one with little meaning that is much less likely to capture attention. In the case of the modified words, which, even without modification, are not reliably perceived under conditions of inattention, modification has very little effect, because these stimuli are simply not ones that are likely to capture attention under any conditions. An early selection theory, however, seems to have no ready explanation of these results, unless the assumption is made that changing one internal letter in a subject's name significantly transforms its global features while a similar modification of a common word does not. This seems highly unlikely.

To restate the argument: if it is some sensory aspect of one's name as a visual stimulus that captures attention at an early processing stage, the vowel switch should have little or no effect. The fact that it has a significant effect seems to be strong support for a late selection theory. According to our version of this theory, attention is captured at a late stage of visual processing, probably at the stage in which meaning is assessed, because the hypothesis that it is its meaning that captures attention seems plausible. So to use an actual example, if your name is *Susan* and you are presented with *Sosan* under conditions of inattention, you will not perceive it because even though *Susan* is salient for you and will capture your attention, *Sosan* is not salient and consequently will fail to do so. For this to be true the entire word must be seen and its meaning encoded.[7]

Several other unsuccessful attempts were made to determine what aspects of one's own name might be important in its perception under conditions of inattention, but because they added no new insights, we mention them only briefly. In one of these experiments involving 10 subjects, the critical stimulus was again a modified version of the subject's name. Either one or two letters in the middle of a subject's name were replaced by dashes, for example *Jose* became *J__e* or *Sarah* became *S_r_h*. (The size of the critical stimulus was between 0.928 and 1.46 degrees.) All the other conditions of testing remained unchanged. The rationale for this experiment was similar to that which motivated the modification by vowel switch. We thought that if global aspects of the name were responsible for its perception, then it might follow that the subjects would perceive their names when the first and last letters of it were present in their appropriate positions and the absent letters were marked by space holders so that the overall size of the name was maintained. The results failed to confirm this conjecture. Fifty percent of the subjects were completely blind in the inattention trial. Of the 5 subjects who reported seeing something else, only 1 was correct and no subject reported seeing his or her own name even in the divided and full attention conditions.[8]

A Lexical Distraction Task

Because the name effect was obtained using a spatial distraction task, it seemed reasonable to ask whether the difference between the kinds of processes underlying the distraction task and those responsible for perceiving and reading a word might, at least in part, explain the

robustness of the effect. This seemed unlikely given the results reported in chapter 4, where we review experiments in which IB was
almost total despite the fact that the processes responsible for the distraction task and for the perception of the critical stimulus were designed to be largely independent of each other. (For example, a
subtraction distraction task coupled with a critical stimulus that did
not engage cognitive processes such as detecting a colored spot did
not reduce IB.) Nevertheless, the name effect was of sufficient theoretical significance to merit the exploration of this possibility. This was
accomplished by providing the subjects with a lexical distraction
task.[9]

> The subject's assigned task in the inattention and divided attention con-
> ditions was to report whether a stimulus presented in one of the four
> standard parafoveal locations, 2.3 degrees from fixation, was a word or
> not. Ten different stimuli were used, five of which were words (*Time,
> Shoe, Bath, Hour, Iron*) and five of which were not (*Mulk, Exom, Exut, Werk,
> Poge*). Twenty subjects participated in this experiment. For 10 of them
> the critical stimulus was their own first name. (Subjects again were re-
> stricted to those with names of between three and five letters.) For the
> remaining 10 subjects the critical stimulus was again the word *Time*.

Performance on the distraction task resembled performance on the
cross task. On average subjects were correct 70% of the time. Of more
importance is that fact that the lexical distraction task did not reduce
the name effect. Only 2 of the 10 subjects tested with their own name
failed to see it and identify it on the critical inattention trial (IB = 20%).
This seems clear evidence against the hypothesis that the nature of the
distraction task can account for the perception of one's own name under conditions of inattention.

Additional support for believing that the nature of the distraction
task does not account for the IB effects is gained from the results from
the inattention condition in which *Time* was the critical stimulus. Sixty
percent of the 10 subjects who were presented with *Time* were blind to
it, and only one of the four subjects who reported seeing something
different correctly identified *Time*. With the small number of subjects
in each group, the difference is not statistically significant, but the
trend exactly parallels the results of our other experiments in which
one's name is the critical stimulus and the cross judgment served as
the distraction task.

Own Name and Narrowed Zone of Attention

If, as we have suggested, one's own name captures attention by virtue
of its meaning to the subject, then it might be reasonable to assume

that it would do so even if the name were presented outside the zone to which attention was directed. If input to the retina is processed deeply and selection occurs only after processing is complete, then it should not matter whether a stimulus falls inside or outside the zone of attention. In the experiments described in this chapter so far, the name was always presented at fixation and fixation fell within the zone of attention, although we believe that attention ordinarily is inhibited from this location. The exception to this occurred in the immediately preceding experiment in which a lexical distraction task was used that might be thought to narrow the attentional zone to the area immediately surrounding the lexical stimulus. If this is correct, then the results of that experiment provide some evidence that one's own name captures attention even when it is located outside the zone of attention at a location that normally is subject to the inhibition of attention. Of course, whenever one's name is seen when it is presented at fixation, it must overcome this inhibition. However, an experiment described in Chapter 4 provides reason for doubting whether reducing the size of the attentional zone when the critical inattention stimulus is located at fixation will influence the frequency of IB. In that experiment reducing the size of the attentional zone by using the smaller rather than the larger crosses located in one of the four standard parafoveal locations and placing the critical stimulus—a red circle—at fixation had no affect on the frequency of IB. This outcome is understandable in light of the fact that when the distraction stimulus can occur in any one of four parafoveal locations, the focus of attention is likely to be broad and include this entire area thus negating any effect of reducing the actual size of the distraction stimulus. This then is a reason to suspect that reducing the attentional zone when one's name at fixation is the critical stimulus also may have no affect on the amount of IB.

The next experiment reconfirmed the finding that one's own name defeats the inhibition of attention at fixation and captures attention.

> In order to investigate this issue, we narrowed the zone of attention by replacing the standard larger crosses with the smaller crosses described in chapter 4, which subtended no more than 0.6 degree along their longer dimension. The crosses were centered in one of the four standard parafoveal locations and were 2 degrees from fixation along an oblique trajectory. Because the critical stimulus was presented at fixation, it now fell outside of the zone of attention defined by the longer arm of the small crosses, and, because it was at fixation, it also was subject to the inhibition of attention that occurs at that location. The experiment, as usual, involved the inattention, divided attention, and full attention conditions. Twenty subjects were tested with their own names as the critical stimulus and twenty subjects were tested with someone else's name as the critical stimulus. The other names were selected from among the

group of names of the subjects tested with their own names, creating a partial yoked control. The names chosen were *Terry, Joe, Megan, Sandy, Chris, Lisa, Patty, Ralph, Eran,* and *Laura*. The longest name subtended a visual angle of 1.1 degree and the shortest 0.68 degree. A mask was used.

Of the 20 subjects tested with their own name, 13 (65%) saw something, and of these subjects 8 (72%) correctly identified it. IB was 35%. In contrast, 70% of the subjects tested with someone else's name were inattentionally blind and of the 6 subjects who reported seeing something else on the critical inattention trial, only 3 correctly identified it. This difference between the frequency of IB in these two conditions is significant (X^2 ($df1$) = 4.91, p < .05), and more subjects identify their own name than someone else's. However, if we compare the frequency of IB for one's own name obtained here with that obtained in the comparable experiment in which 20 subjects were also tested but with the larger cross so that the name fell within the zone of attention, we also find a significant difference, 35% compared to 5% (X^2, $1df$ = 5.62 < p. < .02). More subjects detected and identified their own name when it fell within the zone of attention than when it fell outside it. It is not clear, however, why, in this case, narrowing the zone of attention increased the frequency of IB, whereas it did not do so earlier. The possibility exists that reducing the size of the distraction stimulus actually continues to reduce the size of the attentional zone even when the critical stimulus is at fixation and the distraction stimulus is in the parafovea. If so, we should predict the obtained increase in IB because now the critical stimulus lies outside the attentional zone but this, of course, leaves the discrepancy with the earlier result unexplained.

Another attempt was made to explore the depth of the capacity of one's own name to capture attention. Here, instead of narrowing the attentional zone and locating the name outside it, we attempted to increase the inhibition of attention at the location in which the name was presented. This was done by presenting letter-like stimuli at fixation where the name was to appear on the trials preceding the critical one. The general method was the same as that used in other experiments in which the subject's own name was presented at fixation under conditions of inattention with this single modification. The rationale for this experiment was similar to that which motivated the experiments described in chapter 4. In those experiments we were able to produce a significant increase in IB for a stimulus presented within the zone of attention by preceding it by an irrelevant stimulus that occupied that location on trials prior to the critical one. The stimuli meant to enhance inhibition were created by decomposing the line elements of letters and recombining them into letter-like forms (figure 5.2).

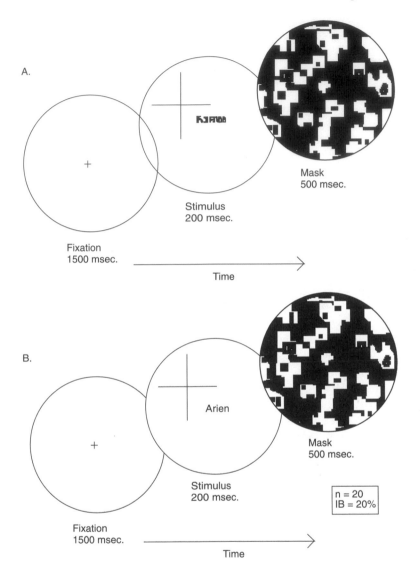

Figure 5.2
Inhibition of attention to critical stimulus using letter-like stimulus with IB results.
A. Noncritical trial.
B. Critical trial.

The letter-like stimuli were presented on every trial except the critical ones, (i.e., the third, sixth, and ninth trials) and subtended approximately the same visual angle as the critical name stimulus. Twenty subjects were presented with their own name as the critical stimulus in the inattention and full attention control conditions and with the name *Jane* on the critical trial of the divided attention condition. Twenty additional subjects served as yoked controls and were presented with one of the names of the 20 subjects tested with their own name as the critical stimulus in the inattention and full attention conditions and with *Jane* as the critical stimulus in the divided attention condition.

The results reveal *no* increase in IB. One's name was still perceived significantly more often than someone else's name, despite our attempt to increase inhibition. Sixteen of the 20 subjects tested with their own names reported seeing something else on the critical inattention trial (IB = 20%) and 13 of these subjects correctly identified it. In contrast, only 9 of the 20 subjects tested with someone else's name detected it (IB = 55%) and only 3 of these subjects correctly identified what they saw. This difference in the frequency of IB is again significant (X^2 (1 df) = 5.23, p < .05) as is the difference in the frequency of correct identification. All subjects were 100% correct on the full attention control trial in both conditions and all subjects saw and most correctly identified *Jane* in both conditions on the critical divided attention trial.

The failure to find any significant increase in IB despite the presence of the irrelevant letter-like stimuli on trials prior to the critical one (which were meant to increase inhibition) may be due to the fact that inhibition was already very high and therefore difficult to increase, or because one's own name is able to overcome the increase in inhibition. If we compare the amount of IB for one's own name in this experiment with that obtained when nothing was presented at fixation on the trials prior to the critical trial, we find no significant difference (5% versus 20%), which is also the case if we compare the frequency of IB for someone else's name in these two situations (35% versus 55%), although the direction of both differences is consistent with an increase in IB caused by an increase in inhibition. Thus, both of the experiments that were designed to address the question of whether one's name captures attention when the difficulty of capture is increased revealed a small, nonsignificant increase in IB, but one's name continued to be seen significantly more often without attention than was someone else's.

One's Own Name Pops Out and the Capture of Attention

Having established that one's own name, unlike any other stimulus explored thus far, is predictably seen under conditions of inattention, we wondered whether one's own name might also pop out in a standard array containing multiple objects. This question seemed important for several reasons. First, because if one's own name pops out, it would add to the accumulating evidence that it is not only simple features in isolation that pop out (for example, color or motion), which was originally thought to be the case when pop out was first investigated (Treisman and Gormican 1988). Later studies revealed that feature conjunctions also pop out (see Nakayama and Silverman 1986; Wolfe, Cave, and Franzel 1989), upsetting the original account of pop out, which asserted that a conjunction of features required focused attention and serial search (Treisman and Gelade 1980). Moreover, later work also demonstrated pop out even for high-level features such as surface representation (Nakayama and Silverman 1986; He and Nakayama 1992), depth from shading (Kleffner and Ramachandran 1992) and three-dimensional structure (Enns and Rensink 1990).

Perhaps most relevant to the question of whether one's own name will pop out is the finding that familiarity plays a role during search (Reicher, Snyder, and Richards 1976) and specifically during pop out (Wang, Cavanagh, and Green 1994).[10] These investigators found that when search was for a familiar target, a Z or a N, among familiar distractors, for example a Z among N's, search for the target was faster than when these same stimuli were rotated by 90 degrees, an orientation in which they no longer appeared familiar. They also report that whereas search for an unfamiliar target, for example, a Z rotated 90 degrees, among familiar distractors, for example, an upright Z, was extremely rapid and appeared to be parallel, the reverse was not the case. Searching for a familiar target among unfamiliar distractors appeared to be serial and slow. This asymmetry effect was first described by Treisman (Treisman and Souther 1985; Treisman and Gormican 1988) who explained it by proposing that a canonical stimulus, for example, a vertical line, elicits less neuronal activity than a noncanonical stimulus, for example a tilted line, so that if the noncanonical stimulus is the target, the difference between the signal it generates and the signal generated by the canonical background stimuli is highly noticeable, whereas the reverse is not true. If the canonical stimulus is the target, the activity it elicits is not enough to readily differentiate it from the greater activity generated by the noncanonical background elements. However, while this explanation seems plausible when the stimuli are vertical and tilted lines, it seems less so when the stimuli are more complex and involve conjunctions of features, as is the case of the letters used in the Wang, Cavanagh, and Green (1994) experiment referred to above. Further evidence of the role of top down processes in parallel search is found in the report that "set" plays a role in search, so that searching for the letter O among digits is faster than searching for the digit *0* among other digits (Jonides & Gleitman 1972; Egeth, Jonides, and Wall 1972).

The fact that it has now become impossible to think of parallel search as a phenomenon restricted to simple, or primitive, features was one of the reasons why it seemed reasonable to ask whether one's own name, which is a highly familiar stimulus but one that conjoins many different features, will pop out. Evidence that it does, and therefore that is processed in parallel would drive the explanation for pop out beyond that of the parallel processing of simple features, and even beyond the level at which it takes account of the role of familiarity. If one's own name pops out, this would significantly enlarge the range of stimuli that are subject to parallel processing, to include both simple features like color or motion as well as the complex assembly of many different features that are organized into a stimulus both familiar and idiosyncratically meaningful.

Another reason for exploring the question of whether one's own name pops out was to try to clarify the relationship between parallel search and perception without attention. At the outset of our research we thought that stimuli that had been found to pop out and therefore were considered to be processed without attention might be perceived under conditions of inattention. However, in the research reported thus far we have found no relationship between pop out and perception without attention, because stimuli that pop out during search (for example, color, shape, motion, and texture segregation) are not detected under conditions of inattention. If one's own name pops out, this would be an exception and might not only further clarify the processes underlying parallel search but also might provide some understanding of the relation between pop out and perception without attention.

Given the general explanations of pop out, there is no obvious reason to expect to find that one's own name will pop out. On the other hand, the fairly common experience of having one's own name leap off a page of text when you have no reason to expect that it is there seemed an unexplored instance of pop out in every day life. That experience coupled with finding that one's own name captures attention under conditions of inattention provided some grounds for optimism.

The experiments designed to explore the question of whether one's name will pop out used the standard methodology, and, like all such search experiments, subjects were instructed to look for a target and to report its presence or absence as quickly as possible. The dependent variable in these experiments is typically the subject's response time and this was case in these experiments as well.

> Like all other standard pop out experiments the number of elements in
> the array on any trial was varied. There were an equal number of trials

Target present:

House   House   House   House

House   House   House

        House   Irvin

House   House   House

Target absent:

House   House   House   House

House   House   House

        House   House

House   House   House

Figure 5.3
Twelve item pop-out display: Irvin as target.

in which only 1, 6, or 12 elements were present. On half the trials, the target was present and for half it was absent. In one of the 2 conditions of the first experiment, the target was the subject's own name and in the other the target was the name of some other subject participating in the experiment, thus creating a yoked control. The order of the trials was random. The nontarget items, referred to as *distractors* were also words with the same number of letters as the subject's name. Only subjects whose first or last name contained between three and five letters were tested. When the target name had three letters, the distractor item was *Cat* (visual angle 0.53 degree), when it had four letters, it was *Time* (0.75 degree), and when it had five letters it was *House* (1.81 degrees). All three words occur with almost equal frequency in English (Kucera and Francis 1967). The visual angle subtended by the distractor item was always within 0.1 degree of that of the target name, and distractor items were always identical to each other. Both the distractor items and target were arranged in a 4 × 4 matrix. Their positions within this matrix were random. The words were printed in Chicago 12-point type face. The first letter of both the distractors and the target was capitalized (see figure 5.3). All subjects completed 50 trials in each of the following six display conditions, both when the target was their own name, and when the target was someone else's name: (1) one item present that was the target, (2) one item present that was not the target, (3) six items present including the target, (4) six items present with no target, (5) twelve items present including the target and (6) twelve items present with no target.

Trials from each of these conditions were randomly presented. Thus there was a total of 300 trials in one complete run in which the subject's name was the target and 300 in one complete run in which someone else's name was the target. Subjects were required to search through two entire runs in each condition, that is, twice with their own name (i.e., 600 trials) and twice with someone else's name as target (i.e., 600 trials) for a total of 1200 trials per subject.

Before the actual experiment began the experimenter explained the procedure and subjects then completed 60 practice trials. Response times from these trials were not included in the data analysis. Half the subjects reported the presence of the target by hitting the B key on the computer keyboard and its absence by hitting the M. For the remaining subjects the meaning of the keys was reversed. The significance of the keys was maintained throughout the entire experiment for each subject, and subjects used their left index finger to hit the B key and the right one for the M key. After each trial the subjects received feedback about their performance. A plus sign (+) appeared on the screen if they had responded correctly and a minus sign (−) appeared if they had made an error. Subjects controlled the pace of the trials and had 1000 msec. to respond on every trial. If they did not respond during this interval, the trial was terminated and subsequently was repeated. Each 300-trial run was broken up into three equal parts, each containing 100 trials. Subjects were given a 20 minute break between parts. No subject was permitted to complete more than 300 trials in a given day. Half of the subjects were tested with their own name as the first target followed by testing with someone else's name as target, and half were tested in the reverse order. Ten subjects participated in the experiment, 2 with their last name as target and 8 with their first name.[11]

The results are reported in figure 5.4 and provide clear evidence that one's own name pops out. In the context of the literature on preattentive processing this seems quite remarkable. When the subjects were searching for their own names and it was present, search was not only extremely rapid—5.7 msec. per item—but the number of distractors had virtually no impact on response time. These are the two major hallmarks of parallel processing and pop out. Treisman and Souther have noted that:

> When a target in a visual search task is detected with little change in latency as the number of Distractor items is varied, we infer that its critical property (or properties) is processed spatially in parallel. Because detection occurs without focused attention, we assume that it is mediated by a relatively early stage of visual processing. The consistent pattern which defines pop-out, as we use it in this article, is a flat or almost flat function (less than 5 or 6 msec per item) relating detection latency to the number of

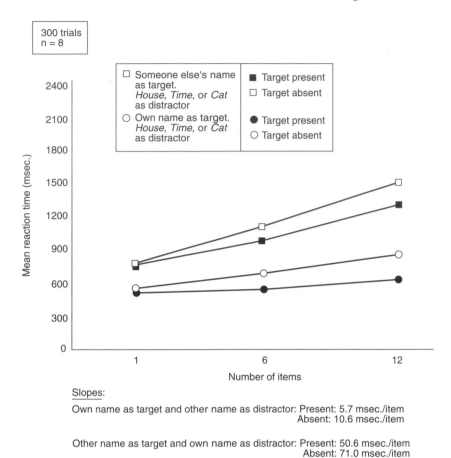

Figure 5.4
Summary of results: searching for own name or other name among common English words.

Distractor items on trials when the target it present. (Treisman and Souther 1985, 287)

By this description one's own name appears to be searched for in parallel and to pop out and this conclusion is strengthened by the results obtained when one's own name was absent from the array. Response time was doubled (10.6 msec./item) and increased slightly as a function of the number of items in the display. This also conforms to the description of the search for a pop out target when it is absent from the display. As Treisman and Souther continue:

When the target is absent from the display, the function may also be flat if subjects are confident that the target would pop out if present, but may increase (usually not linearly) if subjects check to make certain that they are not missing the target. (Ibid.)

In contrast, as they also note, searching for someone else's name is clearly a serial and slow process. "The main diagnostic for a serial search is a linear increase in search latency as distractors are added to the display" (ibid). When the target is present search time per item was 50.6 msec. and when absent, it was 71.0 msec. per item. The time to search for someone else's name in an array of six items is approximately 30% faster than the time required to search an array of twelve items.

These findings therefore provide clear support for the hypothesis that one's own name, although composed of a conjunction of many different features, behaves as a single unit and is subject to parallel processing. This kind of effect has also been remarked upon by Treisman and Souther. "We might infer that extended and consistent perceptual learning leads to the formation of new feature detectors responding to the targets as unitized wholes rather than as a conjunction of features" (ibid., 287). However, the argument that one's name becomes unitized over time and activates a specially created detector is difficult to reconcile with the fact that subjects are significantly more likely to be blind to a marginally modified version of their names than to the unmodified version under conditions of inattention.

Having found clear evidence that one's own name pops out when searched for among a common and comparably sized word, we wished to determine whether the asymmetry effect found by Wang, Cavanagh, and Green (1994) and earlier by Treisman (Treisman and Souther 1985; Treisman and Gormican 1988) also would occur for one's own name. On the assumption that one's own name bears the same relationship to another's name or common word that a vertical line bears to a tilted line, then someone else's name or the common word should pop out among an array of own name distractors, while the reverse—one's own name as target among an array in which someone else's name or a common word is the distractor—should not. Evidence of an asymmetry effect would suggest an underlying similarity between the processes involved in name pop out and in the other examples of pop out described in the literature.[12]

In this experiment the target stimulus was either the subject's own name or the name of some other subject tested in this experiment. The name of every subject served as the target stimulus both for that subject and for one other subject. When the target stimulus was the subject's own name, the distractor stimulus was the name of another subject that had the same number of letters. When the subject's own name served as the distractor stimuli, the target stimulus was someone else's name. So each subjects was tested with two stimuli, both of which served alternatively as the target and the distractor. One of these was the subject's own name and the other was some other subject's name.

> There were 300 trials in each of the two conditions, preceded by 60 practice trials, the results of which were not included in the data analysis. In all other ways this experiment was the same as the preceding one. Half the subjects were tested with their own name as the first target and the remaining subjects were tested in the reverse order. Ten new subjects were tested in this experiment.

The results summarized in figure 5.5 failed to reveal an asymmetry effect like that found by Treisman and Souther, 1985 and subsequently by Wang, Cavanagh, and Green (1994). Searching for one's own name as target among someone else's continues to be done in parallel with a search time of 6.50 msec./item when the target name is present and 10.60 msec./item when the name is absent. In contrast, when the search is for someone else's name among distractors that are the subject's own name, search is much slower and serial. If the target was present in the array search time per item was 80.72 msec., whereas if it was absent, search time was 142.45 msec./item. With one's own name as target the effect of increasing the number of distractors was small but large when someone else's name was the target.

The failure to find the predicted kind of asymmetry effect thus suggests that there may be a difference between the processes responsible for searching for one's name and those responsible for the pop out of a single feature or some simple conjunction of features, which, if true would be consistent with the view that the processes responsible for perception without attention, in fact, are different from those underlying the standard divided attention tasks like those used in experiments exploring pop out. This possibility is also supported by the finding that features which pop out in search experiments fail to be perceived under conditions of inattention.

In a further attempt to understand the relation between seeing one's name under conditions of inattention and searching for one's own name among distractors, we looked at the speed with which a subject could search for his or her own name when its first internal vowel was changed. This modification, as previously noted, produced a large increase in IB. Ten new subjects were tested in each of three conditions, the order of which was counterbalanced among them. In one condition the subject searched for his or her own name among distractors that were the subject's altered name. In another condition the subject

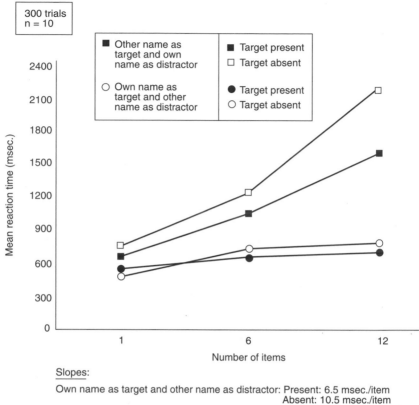

Figure 5.5
Summary of results: searching for own name among other names, or other's name among own names.

searched for his or her altered name among unaltered own name distractors. Finally, there was a condition in which subjects searched for their altered names among distractors which were someone else's altered name matched for length (figure 5.6). The procedure was otherwise identical to that used in the preceding search experiments.

The results are summarized in Figure 5.6, and reveal that all three searches were slow and serial, which may not be surprising when the distractors and target differ by only one letter, but is more revealing when the distractors are someone else's modified name. This result seems consistent with the speculation that the processes underlying

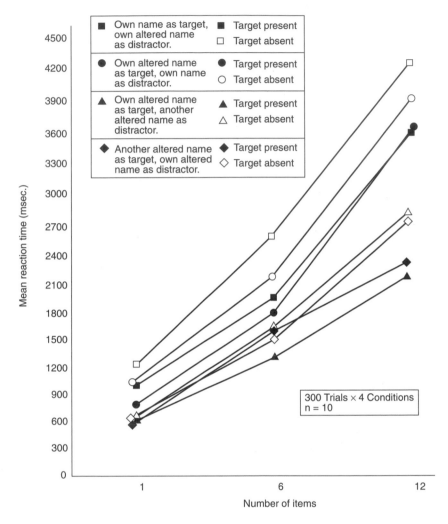

Figure 5.6
Summary of results: searching for own name with vowel change.

search for one's name may be the same as those underlying its perception under condition of inattention. One's own unaltered name pops
out when searched for and is seen without attention. One's altered
name, however, is much less frequently seen without attention and
does not pop out when searched for. Were the letters of one's name
to form an emergent global unit rather than be subject to a letter-by-
letter (if not feature-by-feature) analysis, these results should not have
been obtained.

Conclusion

Whatever is the correct interpretation of these results, the fact that one's own name pops out and is thus far the only stimulus to be predictably perceived under conditions of inattention provide collective proof of the perceptual importance of one's name and of its capacity to capture attention. The implication of this finding coupled with the finding that a modest modification in the spelling of one's name causes IB and destroys pop out argue for a theory of selective attention that places the selection at some late stage, which may be the stage in which meaning is assessed. We account for the fact that other features that are found to pop out in a search paradigm are not seen under conditions of inattention by the assumption that these stimuli fail to capture attention because they have no intrinsic importance for the perceiver.

We now propose that not only does attention enter at a late stage of processing, but for that processed input to reach consciousness, it must be attended to. If attention is voluntary, as it is when we are searching for something, its importance is guaranteed by the fact that it is what we are looking for. However, when it is not an object of search, its capacity to capture attention becomes paramount because it must capture attention to be consciously perceived. From the results with one's own name it seems reasonable to propose that only stimuli that are important to the observer and perhaps extremely familiar will capture attention and therefore be seen. On the basis of this reasoning there are no grounds for necessarily expecting that something that pops out when searched for will capture attention and be perceived under conditions of inattention, because stimulus discontinuities may underlie parallel search (Nothdurft 1992), but are not likely to be relevant to perception of stimuli without attention.

Before we can be certain that one's own name is perceived under conditions of inattention because it has high signal value and therefore has the capacity to capture attention, we must examine the role of familiarity. Does one's own name capture attention because it is familiar and *not* because it is important? The fact that familiar words like *Time* and *House* are seen much less frequently under conditions of inattention argues against this possibility, but because of the importance of this question it is reexamined in the next chapter.

If one's own name is perceived under conditions of inattention because it has high signal value, are there other stimuli that share this capacity? We of course already know that simple features like color, motion, shape, or flicker do not, but perhaps other, more complex stimuli that have clear significance for human observers might. The next chapter reports research that examines some likely candidates.

Chapter 6

Inattention: Faces and Other "Meaningful" Stimuli[1]

The finding that one's own name is seen under our experimental conditions of inattention while various basic features of objects and, in fact, entire objects, are not, raises the possibility that it may be *meaningfulness* that is critical in capturing attention. However, while it makes perfect intuitive sense that we consciously see what is important to us, and that what is important to us is more likely to capture our attention, if this proposal is to be taken seriously, it requires additional support. Of course, with attention, particularly with distributed attention, we have the impression that we perceive most of what is present in the immediate scene, even if only in some global fashion. However, this does not appear to be so because recently reported research indicates that observers are very poor in perceiving significant changes in a scene even when they are searching for them (Rensink, O'Regan, and Clark 1997).

So far the claim that what captures attention is what is meaningful and has signal value to the perceiver rests solely on the finding that one's own name is predictably seen under our conditions of inattention. The experiments described in this chapter sought to determine whether there are other stimuli perceived under conditions of inattention that, on the face of it, would seem to be members of what might be agreed were a class of "meaningful" stimuli. The choices of which stimuli to examine were based on guesses about what might constitute an important stimulus, that is, a stimulus with significant signal value for an observer.

Even if we find, as we did, that there are other meaningful stimuli that are perceived under conditions of inattention, there is another question that must be resolved before the hypothesis relating the meaning of a stimulus to its capacity to attract attention can be confidently proposed. This question concerns the role of familiarity. To what extent are these stimuli that we have designated as highly meaningful perceived without attention because they are extremely familiar? This is an important question because if the effect of meaningfulness were reducible to familiarity, then one might be able to account for it in terms of an earlier processing stage. For example, if highly familiar stimuli have lower perceptual thresholds than less familiar ones (as early selection theorists have proposed) it might be that the processing of global or formal features would be sufficient for their recognition. This then would explain why they are more likely to be perceived under conditions of inattention. However, as we have pointed out earlier, the fact that we found a steep increase in IB when we modestly modified the spelling of the subject's own name weighs against this possibility. Nevertheless, this issue was sufficiently important to demand additional examination, and this chapter describes a set of experiments expressly designed to address the role of familiarity. These experiments were done despite the repeated finding that highly familiar shapes like circles and squares and familiar words like *Time* and *House* tend not to be seen under conditions of inattention.

Faces

Considerable evidence indicates that faces are special stimuli and may be in a class of their own (Bruce 1988; Roll 1984; Purcell and Stewart 1986; Perrett et al. 1985). They certainly are of the greatest importance for the social interactions that constitute much of our daily lives. Thus they seemed an obvious choice of a stimulus to examine as a candidate for attracting attention. We chose to use a schematic, cartoon-like face rather than an actual drawing or photograph because it seemed important to keep the purely stimulus features of the object as simple as possible and not too different from those thus far investigated. In particular it seemed important to keep the size of the stimulus within the range of those thus far investigated. We wished to eliminate the possibility that if faces were perceived, their perception could be attributed to aspects other than their meaning. We chose a cartoon-face icon (figure 6.1) that had the same circumference as the circle that had served in various prior experiments as the critical stimulus, even though it is an extremely impoverished representation of a face. Had it not been perceived under conditions of inattention, we would have tried a more realistic representation, but, in fact, it was seen.

> The first set of *face* experiments followed the procedures of the name experiments. The critical stimulus was presented at fixation and the distraction stimuli were the standard crosses, which were presented in one of the four parafoveal locations, 2.3 degrees from fixation. All presentations were masked. In the first of these experiments the critical stimulus was either a smiling face, a sad face, a scrambled face, or the outline of the face without any inner detail (figure 6.1). The only difference between the happy and sad faces was in the orientation of the mouth,

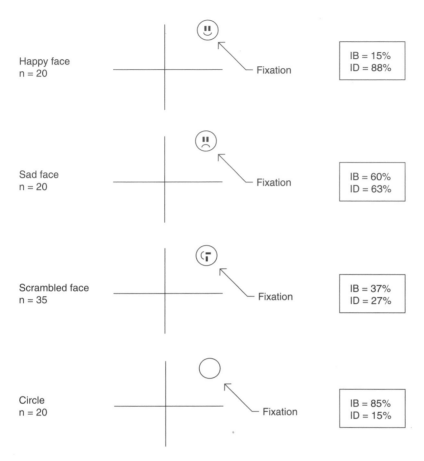

Figure 6.1
Schematic illustrations of face displays and IB results.

which was upturned or downturned. The scrambled face was created by simply placing the features—the representations of nose, eyes and mouth—in different locations within the face contour, and, finally the figure that was just the outline circle with no inner detail. The diameter of each of these figures subtended a visual angle of 0.6 degree. The contours of the figure, like the lines of the cross, were black on a white background. As usual, subjects were tested first in the inattention condition, followed by the divided and full attention conditions, each of which had three trials. The critical stimulus was present on the third trial in each condition. The questioning of the subjects on the critical trials also followed the normal procedures. Subjects who reported seeing something new but did not spontaneously identify it on the critical trial and subjects who failed to see anything were asked to select what had been presented from an array of five figures, one of which was

Figure 6.2
Recognition arrays used in face experiments.

the critical figure (figure 6.2). Subjects who reported seeing nothing but the cross on the critical trial were told that something else in fact had been presented, and they were to try to guess what it was by picking it out from the five-figure array.

A total of 95 subjects recruited from the New School student population were tested. Twenty subjects were tested with the "happy face," 20 with the "sad face," 20 with the outline circle, and 35 with the "scrambled face."

The results are summarized in figure 6.1. Note that when the happy face was the critical stimulus only 3 subjects were blind to it on the inattention trial (IB = 15%) and 88% of the subjects who did not suffer IB correctly identified it.[2] In contrast, when the sad face was the critical stimulus, IB was 60% and 63% of the subjects who did not suffer IB correctly identified it. The difference is significant (X^2, $1df$ = 8.64, p < .01). When the critical stimulus was a scrambled face, IB was only 37%, but only 27% of the seeing subjects correctly identified it. Although the difference between the frequency of IB for the scrambled and happy faces is not quite significant (X^2 $1df$ = 3.03 p > .05), this may be due to the small number of subjects tested in the happy face condition. (There is no significant difference between the frequency of IB for the sad face and scrambled face (X^2, $1df$ = 2.68). When the critical stimulus was an outline circle, IB was extremely high (85%) and was

Figure 6.3
Neutral face.

significantly different from both the happy and scrambled faces. (The difference between the frequency of IB for the scrambled face and the circle is highly significant [X^2, $1df$ = 11.76 p < .001].) This suggests that degree of articulation of the stimulus may be a relevant factor in the capture of attention.

The fact that the happy face was seen much more frequently than either of the other comparable stimuli adds support to the hypothesis that meaningful stimuli with signal value capture attention and are likely to be seen under conditions of inattention, although the issue of the role of its familiarity remains unresolved. We have no explanation for the finding that the sad face is seen less frequently than the happy face, although two possible explanations suggest themselves. Either happy-face icons are more familiar than sad ones, and familiarity plays a role in the capture of attention, or sad faces are somehow aversive and therefore repel attention.

On the chance that the reason why the sad face produced significantly more blindness than the happy one was related to the affect communicated by the curve of the mouth, the only difference between the two stimuli, we repeated the experiment using a "neutral" face as the critical stimulus. If, under conditions of inattention, the neutral face were not to be seen any more frequently than the sad face, it would rule out an explanation in terms of communicated affect. The neutral stimulus was created by simply converting the contour representing the mouth from a curve to a straight line. (figure 6.3). Fifteen new subjects were tested. Nine subjects failed to see the neutral face (IB = 60%), and only one of the inattentionally blind subjects chose the neutral face from the recognition array. In contrast, 4 of the 6 subjects who reported seeing the critical stimulus correctly identified it. Because there was no difference between the frequency of IB for the neutral face and sad face, it seems safe to conclude that the negative affect communicated by the curve representing the mouth was not the source of the IB.

An Inverted Face

Before turning to the research expressly concerned with the possible role of familiarity in both the happy face and own name effects, we review the results of several other experiments in which a face served

Figure 6.4
Upside down face.

as the critical stimulus. In one of these experiments the happy face was turned upside down. Because we know that inverting a shape with a canonical orientation decreases its recognizability and we know that faces in particular are more difficult to recognize when they are inverted (Rock 1974), we examined whether an upside down face would be seen significantly less often than the same stimulus in its upright orientation. Finding that it was, would add significant support to the *meaningfulness-signal value* hypothesis, because otherwise the upside down version should fare as well as the normally oriented one given that they are structurally identical. The upside down face experiment was identical to those described above except that the inverted happy face was the critical stimulus (figure 6.4). All of the 10 new subjects who failed to spontaneously detect and identify the critical stimulus were asked to select it from a choice array consisting of five figures. Only 3 subjects reported seeing something different on the critical inattention trial (IB = 70%), and all 3 of these subjects correctly identified what they saw. In contrast, none of the inattentionally blind subjects did so. Four of them chose the sad face, 2 the diamond, and 1 the circle from the choice array. Eight of the subjects correctly identified the upside-down face on the divided attention trial and all 10 subjects did so on the full attention trial.[3]

It seems that simply inverting the happy face leads to a large and significant increase in blindness. Again, the reader should bear in mind that subjects are not merely failing to identify the critical stimulus, they are failing to *detect its presence*. The fact that the upside down face produces as much IB as the sad face (70% compared to 60%) might be a consequence of the change in the shape of the mouth when the happy face is rotated by 180 degrees. This change in orientation produces a downward, "sad," curving mouth, and since recognition of an upside-down face requires mental correction of all the features (Rock 1974), if for some reason it did not occur for the mouth, it would be registered as a sad mouth and thus might explain the frequency of IB, which is like that for the sad face.

Modified Faces

Because the happy face, like one's own name, appears to attract attention and consequently to be perceived under conditions of inattention,

Table 6.1
Summary of results: modified faces.

Face stimuli used		Percent IB	Percent ID
☺	Happy face without eyes	20%	38%
☹	Sad face without eyes	70%	0%
◡	Happy face without an outline	53%	71%
◠	Sad face without an outline	50%	80%
◡	Smile without eyes or an outline	80%	50%

we sought to discover what features of the face were responsible. In a group of experiments that paralleled those described in the last chapter (in which subjects were tested with modified versions of their own names) we tested subjects with modified schematic faces as the critical stimuli. The various modifications are pictured in Table 6.1.

In one version either the happy face or the sad face was presented without eyes. Ten subjects were tested with each of these as the critical stimulus. In another version both the happy and sad faces were presented without the surrounding contour. All subjects were asked to select the critical stimulus from the choice array, whether or not that had reported seeing something on the critical trial. Thirty-five subjects were tested. Fifteen subjects were tested with the happy face version and 10 with the sad face version. In the last of these manipulations 10 subjects were tested with only the happy mouth as the critical stimulus.

The results are also presented in table 6.1. The absence of only the eyes had no effect. When only the eyes were missing, the results did not differ from those with the complete faces. The happy face version tended to be seen, whereas the sad version tended not to be. When the critical stimulus was either a happy or sad face without the outer contour, the difference in the perceptibility of the happy and sad faces disappeared. When the critical stimulus was only the happy-face smile, inattentional blindness was almost complete (80%).

On the attention condition all subjects tested with either the happy or the sad face without eyes saw and identified the stimuli correctly, and all subjects tested with either the happy or sad face without its outer contour also saw and correctly identified it. Finally, in this condition when the critical stimulus was only the smile, 7 of the 10 subjects saw and correctly identified it.

These combined results confirm the perceptibility of the happy face icon without, however, completely clarifying what aspects of this stimulus are critical. The results do suggest that as long as the smiling mouth and outer contour are present, the stimulus is likely to be detected under conditions of inattention. Thus, this minimal representation of a face, but only a happy one, seems to be capable of capturing attention under these conditions.

A Few More Face Experiments

Before finally turning to the important question of the role of familiarity in the capture of attention, there are several other experiments in which the face icon served as the critical stimulus that merit a brief description. One experiment repeats a procedure used when exploring the own name effect. In this experiment, all stimulus presentations were reduced by 50%, so instead of presenting the crosses and critical stimulus for 200 msec., they were presented for only 100 msec. This reduction in presentation time had little effect on the perception of one's name, and it also turned out to have little effect on the perception of the happy face as well.

> Two groups of 15 subjects were tested. One group was presented with the happy face on the critical inattention trial and the other was presented with the sad face. If subjects did not spontaneously describe what they saw, or reported that they saw nothing besides the cross on the critical inattention trial, they were shown an array of pictures that included a circle, a diamond, a sad face, a happy face, and a scrambled face. On the divided attention trial the critical stimuli were reversed so that the group that had seen the happy face on the inattention trial was presented with the sad face on the divided attention trial, and the reverse was true for the other group of subjects. On the full attention control trials subjects were presented with the stimulus they had been shown in the inattention trial. The distraction task entailed reporting the longer line of the cross. The standard crosses were used and were presented in any one of the usual four parafoveal locations. The critical stimulus was at fixation. All trials were masked, which is the main difference in procedure between this and the experiment with names.

Only 4 of the 15 subjects in the happy face condition failed to detect its presence on the critical inattention trial (IB = 27%), and 10 of the 11 subjects who detected the critical stimulus correctly identified it. The 1 subject that did not selected a circle from the choice array. (Only 1 of the 4 subjects who failed to detect the critical stimulus selected the happy face from among the choice array, so there seemed to be no bias to choose the happy face icon.) All but one subject saw and identified the sad face in the divided attention condition, and all of them identified the happy face in the control condition. In contrast, twice as many subjects (8) failed to detect the presence of the sad face when it was the critical inattention stimulus (IB = 53%), and only 3 of the 7 subjects who reported seeing something else on the critical inattention trial correctly identified the sad face. Only 1 subject who failed to detect the critical stimulus selected the sad face from the choice array. All of these subjects correctly reported the sad face on the control trial. Given the few subjects tested, the difference between the frequency of IB in the two cases is not statistically significant even though there is almost twice as much IB for the sad as for the happy face. Nevertheless, these results, combined with those from the other experiments on faces, lend support to the view that a happy face icon is more likely to be seen under conditions of inattention.

One other face experiment deserves mention. We compared IB for the happy face icon with that for a solid black circle of the same size, using the saccadic eye movement task described in chapter 4. Either the face or the circle was presented at the initial fixation location for 700 msec., during which time the subject executed saccades to the sequenced eye movement targets. With the black circle IB was 56%. In contrast, it was only 27% for the happy face icon. So this also provides evidence of the capacity of the face icon to attract attention.

It might occur to the reader to ask whether the happy face pops out from an array of distractors, just like one's name (which is the other stimulus thus far described that is seen reliably under conditions of inattention). We designed an array to explore this question in which the happy face was the target and sad or scrambled faces were the distractors, but when we ourselves looked at these displays, it was immediately obvious that the happy face did not pop out. In fact, it took a serious effort to find it. At about this same time, an article appeared that confirmed our observations (Nothdurft 1993), and made a formal experiment of our own unnecessary. Nothdurft reports that neither a schematic happy nor sad face pops out among other faces. This makes the finding that one's name pops out more puzzling.

Familiarity and Inattentional Blindness

Names and faces are not only important stimuli, they are also extremely familiar ones. The question therefore arises as to whether extreme familiarity—independent of meaning, salience, or signal value—contributes to, or is responsible for the fact that these two stimuli are seen under conditions of inattention. As previously mentioned, there are prima facie reasons for doubting this, because many of the stimuli we tested that failed to be seen under conditions of inattention—simple geometric shapes, words like *Time* or *House* and a brightly colored or a moving square—must be at least as familiar as the happy face icon or even one's own name, which may be heard frequently, but is not that frequently seen. Nevertheless, we thought it appropriate to directly investigate the role of familiarity. To do this we chose the word *The* as the critical stimulus. We did so for two reasons. First, it is the most frequently occurring word in the English language, and second, it has no meaning independent of the noun it modifies. Thus, if familiarity alone captures attention, *The* should be seen under conditions of inattention. We chose to compare the frequency with which *The* is detected under conditions of inattention with that of another lexigraphically similar word that not only occurs less frequently but, unlike *The*, carries independent meaning. The word we chose was *Tie*, which differs from *The* in appearance only by virtue of the contour which turns the *i* into an *h*.

> The procedure used to assess the perceptibility of these words was identical to that used for names and faces. The larger crosses served as the objects of the distraction task and were located in one of the four parafoveal positions, 2 degrees from fixation. *Tie* and *The* were presented at fixation on the third trial in each of the three standard testing conditions. Twenty-five subjects were tested with *The* as the critical stimulus in the inattention conditions, and 25 were tested with *Tie*. *The* subtended a visual angle of 0.53 degree and *Tie* subtended a visual angle of 0.565 degree. All trials were masked.

Sixteen of the 25 subjects (IB = 37%) presented with *The* under conditions of inattention reported seeing something on the critical trial, although only 6 of these 16 subjects (37%) correctly identified it. (Most of the other subjects were unable to describe what it was that they had seen.)[4] All the subjects saw and identified *The* on the full attention control trial, and many did so on the divided attention trial. Fifteen of the 25 subjects failed to detect *Tie* (IB = 60%), and only 4 of the 10 subjects who detected it correctly identified it. All 25 subjects did so with full attention. If we compare these results with those obtained with *The* we find the direction of difference consistent with the importance of familiarity, but the difference is not statistically significant (X^2, $df1 = 2.88$ p. $> .05$).

Unfortunately, these data are not as clear as they might be because they suggest, although not strongly, that familiarity may be a factor in determining what is seen under conditions of inattention. However, even if the difference between the frequency of IB for *The* were significantly less than that obtained for *Tie*, we still would have reason to believe that familiarity could not be the sole factor responsible for the name and happy face effect, because there is a highly significant difference between the frequency of IB obtained when one's own name is the critical stimulus under comparable conditions where IB is 5%, and when *The* is the critical stimulus (IB = 36%), (X^2, $df1 = 15.8$, p $< .001$).

Similarly, there is also a significant difference between the IB for the happy face icon (15%) and *The* when viewed under comparable conditions (X^2 *df*1 = 5.7 p < .02).[5]

In order to pursue a possible difference in the perception of *The* and *Tie*, we repeated the experiment just described using the smaller set of crosses as distraction stimuli. In every other respect the experiments were identical. We thought that if, in fact, there was a real difference between the perceptibility of these two words under conditions of inattention, it might become clearer, if they were presented not only at fixation (where we believe attention is inhibited) but on one view *outside* the zone of attention as well.

> Forty additional subjects were tested in this version of the experiment. Twenty were presented with *The* as the critical inattention stimulus and 20 were presented with *Tie*. The results are almost identical to those obtained with the larger set of crosses and again the obtained difference in IB was not significant, although, like the earlier results, it too is in the predicted direction. Thirteen of the 20 subjects shown *The* detected it (IB = 35%), and 9 shown *Tie* did so (IB = 55%), (X^2 *df*1 = 1.62 p > .20). Thus these results also fail to support the hypothesis that a familiar stimulus is more likely to be seen under conditions of inattention than an unfamiliar one.

Another Test of the Role of Familiarity

Despite all the evidence suggesting that familiarity does not account for either the name or face effect, we thought the issue of sufficient importance to perform one more experiment in which we again compared the frequency of IB for a highly frequent word with little meaning with that for a meaningful word that is encountered far less often. The words chosen were *And* and *Ant*. *And* is listed as the fourth most frequently appearing word in the English language (Kucera and Francis 1967).

> Except for the change in the critical stimuli, this experiment was identical to the one described above in which *The* or *Tie* served as the critical stimulus. The visual angle subtended by *And* was 0.64 degree and by *Ant* 0.6 degree. Twenty subjects were presented with *And* on the critical inattention and full attention control trials, and with *Ant* on the divided attention trial. Twenty additional subjects were tested with *Ant* as the critical stimulus on the inattention and control trials and with *And* as the critical stimulus on the divided attention trial.

The results again revealed *no* significant difference in the detection of two words that differ only in one letter but that differ significantly in their frequency of occurrence. As with *The* and *Tie*, the difference obtained was in the direction predicted by a role for familiarity in the capture of attention, but it was also not significant. Fifteen of the subjects presented with *And* on the inattention trial detected its presence, (IB = 25%), and 11 of the subjects presented with *Ant* did so (IB = 45%), (X^2 *df*1 = 1.77). There was also no difference between the number of subjects who correctly identified *And*, of which there were 8, and those who identified *Ant*, of which there were 7. All the subjects saw and correctly identified *And* on the control trial and 19 of them did so when *Ant* was presented. There were also no differences on the divided attention trial.

Because once again we failed to find any evidence that familiarity alone facilitates perception under conditions of inattention, we conclude with some confidence that familiarity does not account for the perception of one's own name, a happy face, or the few other stimuli discussed below, which we found are quite reliably seen under conditions of inattention.[6]

One More Test of the Role of Familiarity

Other evidence that suggests that familiarity alone does not provide the basis for the capture of attention was obtained in an experiment in which a solid, 0.6 degree black circle was the critical stimulus in the inattention condition. In this experiment the inattention condition was preceded by ten trials, the purpose of which was to familiarize the observer with the stimulus that subsequently was to become the critical stimulus in the inattention condition. For these ten trials the subjects were asked to report whether two figures, presented sequentially at fixation for 200 msec. each, were the same or different. The circle figure, which later was the critical stimulus, was always a member of each of these stimulus pairs. Thus immediately prior to the inattention testing condition, the subject had attended to the critical stimulus on ten separate occasions. If simply being familiar with a stimulus were sufficient to capture attention, then it would seem to follow that, under conditions of inattention, the observers should report the presence of this critical stimulus significantly more often than a group of subjects who had not benefited from this prefamiliarization experience.

> The ten shape discrimination trials were immediately followed by the standard experiment for determining what is perceived under conditions of inattention. Twenty subjects were tested. For 20 of them the critical stimulus was presented on the third inattention trial. For the other 10 subjects the critical stimulus was presented on the first inattention trial in order to determine whether presenting it immediately after the prefamiliarization trials would increase the likelihood that this experi-

ence would facilitate its perception under condition of inattention. In all cases the critical stimulus was presented at fixation and the cross was located in one of its typical parafoveal position 2.3 degrees from fixation. A mask was used.

Fifty percent of the subjects were blind to the circle when it was presented on the third trial in the inattention condition and 60% were blind to it when it was presented on the first of these trials. Thus, not only did the time of its occurrence relative to the prefamiliarization experience not matter, the familiarization experience itself made no difference, since an equal amount of IB was obtained from a group of subjects tested without it. (Ten subjects were tested with no prefamiliarization experience, 5 of whom failed to see anything but the cross on the critical inattention trial IB = 50%). The weight of the evidence clearly is against the speculation that familiarity or the recency of encountering a stimulus plays an important role in the perception of an object to which attention is not intentionally directed.

Other Meaningful Stimuli

If meaning or signal value, rather than familiarity, accounts for the fact that one's own name or a happy face icon is seen under conditions of inattention, then perhaps there are other stimuli which, because they also have significant signal value, may be seen as well. A series of experiments explored this question and provided some evidence that this is so. Because there is no valid index to which one can refer to determine the meaningfulness or signal value of a stimulus, the candidates we chose to investigate were those we guessed might rank high on such an index were it available. Because they were guesses, they could easily have been bad guesses, but we suspect the reader will agree that they at least were not unreasonable ones.

Our general procedure was to decide on some stimulus that seemed as if it might rank high in signal value, and in each case to compare its perceptibility under conditions of inattention with the perceptibility of another stimulus that shared all or most of its features combined differently. The set of stimuli chosen were: *Rape*, which was compared to its anagram *Pear*; *Stop*, which was compared to its anagram *Post*; *Help*, which was compared to *Held*; and a swastika which was compared to one of two novel shapes composed of the same line elements reconfigured. We also looked at a group of what we deemed meaningful shapes for two reasons. First, we did this simply as part of the effort to see if there were other meaningful stimuli that captured attention, and second, to determine whether, as the data suggested, words were more likely to do so. This group of stimuli included a red heart, which was compared with a red circle; a looming black circle, which was compared with a stationary circle, the standard "do not" symbol (a 0.6 degree diameter circle with an oblique line through it), which was compared with an equal size circle with either a vertical or horizontal line. Finally we looked at a dollar sign but did not compare it with any other stimulus. (See table 6.2 for illustrations of most of these stimuli.)

> Each of these stimuli were tested under the conditions used to test faces and names. The critical stimulus was always located at fixation. The larger crosses were the object of the distraction task and were presented in one of the four standard parafoveal locations between 1.5 and 2 degrees from fixation. Masks followed each presentation. In all of the experiments exploring the role of signal value, subjects were shown an array of stimuli following their response to the question of whether they had seen anything other than the cross on the critical trial and, regardless of whether or not they had, they were asked to select what had been shown from this array.

The results obtained in the inattention condition for all these stimuli are presented in table 6.2. If we compare the amount of inattentional blindness for *Rape* and *Pear*, we find that *Rape* is seen significantly more often than *Pear* (X^2, $df1 = 4.285$, $< .05$) despite the fact that *Pear* occurs more frequently than *Rape* in the English language.[7,8] There were no differences between these two words in the full attention control trials in which virtually all subjects saw and identified the critical stimuli. This outcome is consistent with the view that signal value and meaning rather than some low-level property of a stimulus are the attributes that capture attention.

The results also reveal a significant difference in the perceptibility of *Stop* and *Post*. Only 2 of the 15 subjects presented with *Stop* on the inattention trial failed to see it, whereas 10 of the 15 subjects presented with *Post* failed to do so (X^2, $1df = 8.89$ p $< .01$). Moreover, 9 of the 13 subjects who detected the presence of something new on the inattention trial correctly identified *Stop* when presented with it, while 3 of the 5 subjects who detected the stimulus when presented with *Post* on the inattention trial did so.

The other word pair that was examined was *Help* and *Held*, but although a few more subjects (10 of 15) reported seeing something when *Help* was the critical inattention stimulus than when *Held* was, the difference was not significant.

We compared the perceptibility of a swastika and of a novel figure that was constructed by rearranging its parts into either an open or closed figure. Fifteen subjects were tested with the swastika as the critical inattention stimulus, 15 subjects were tested with the closed version of the novel stimulus, and 15 other subjects were tested with

Table 6.2
Summary of results: other "meaningful" stimuli.

Critical stimuli	Percent IB	Percent ID
Rape	33%	90%
Pear	46%	75%
Stop	13%	69%
Post	33%	100%
Help	33%	70%
Held	46%	63%
♥	66%	80%
(In the experiment this was red.)		
●	66%	60%
(In the experiment this was red.)		
$	80%	0%
⊕ Looming circle	50%	0%
⊘	37%	57%
⊖	57%	40%
⌐┘	26%	63%
╜	56%	47%

the open version of this stimulus. All subjects even if they reported having not seen the critical stimulus were asked to identify it by selecting it from an array of five stimuli, one of which was the critical stimulus. The results indicated that the swastika was more likely to be seen under conditions of inattention than either the closed or open novel figure. Of the 15 subjects presented with the swastika on the inattention trial, only 4 (26%) exhibited inattentional blindness, whereas 9 of the 15 subjects (IB = 60%) shown the closed version of the novel figure and 8 of the 15 subjects (IB = 53%) shown the open version detected its presence. If we combine the results from the novel figure conditions and compare them with the results when the swastika was the critical inattention stimulus, we find an *almost* significant difference in the predicted direction (X^2, DF 1 = 3.62 p. > .05).[9] As it turned out, up to this point, the swastika was the only shape, that is, nonlexical, stimulus that subjects proved likely to see under inattention conditions, other than the happy face.

None of the other comparisons produced any significant differences between the stimuli deemed more or less meaningful. Even when the detectability of the widely recognized symbol for "do not" was compared with the detectability of the same circle with a vertical rather than diagonal slash through it, the difference was not significant (X^2 $1df$ = 2.81).

Similarly, a looming black circle was not detected more frequently than a static black circle, the size of which was equal to the end state of the looming stimulus (0.6 degree). In both cases IB was 50%. A red heart was not detected more often than a red circle comparable in size (0.6 degree). In both cases inattentional blindness was 67%. Thus, with the exception of the swastika, none of these stimuli selected for their possible signal value captured attention more often than the stimuli that served as their less salient counterparts. The fact that the looming stimulus failed to do so is somewhat surprising given the fact that very young infants respond with distress to a looming stimulus. However, because we had to keep the angular size of the looming stimulus quite small, the quality of the looming may not have been adequate, although subjects in the full attention control condition did report it.[10]

In our continuing effort to find shapes other than the happy face that might capture attention we decided to compare a stick figure of a man, a Christmas tree, and a schematic representation of a house to see if any of these figures had the capacity to capture attention. To our surprise we found that the stick figure was seen far more frequently under conditions of inattention than either of the other two figures.

> In these experiments[11] the critical stimulus figures were located at fixation and the standard crosses were presented in one of the four typical sites in the parafovea. For most of the experiments no masks were used, but otherwise the experiment followed the normal procedure for experiments in the New School laboratory. Each of the figures subtended an angle of approximately 0.6 degree vertically and horizontally. They were black outlines on an white background (see figure 6.5). Regardless of whether or not subjects reported seeing anything on the critical inattention trial, they were asked to select what had been presented from an array of five figures, three of which were the stick figure man, the house, and the tree. The other two figures were the outlines of a circle and a triangle. Twenty subjects were tested with the man as the critical figure in the inattention condition, 20 with the Christmas tree and 12 with the house.

The results, which also are summarized in figure 6.5, make it clear that the fate of the stick figure of the man differs significantly from that of the other two figures. Only 4 of the 20 subjects failed to perceive the man under conditions of inattention (IB = 20%). The other two figures were seen significantly less often and behaved like all the other stimuli which were not seen under conditions of inattention (x^2 1 $df =$ 7.74 < .01). To make sure that the meaning of the stick figure rather than its shape was responsible for the capture of attention, we tested all three figures in an upside-down orientation. In every other respect the experiment was identical to the previous one. Ten subjects were

Figure	Number of Subjects	IB
	n = 20	20%
	n = 20	55%
	n = 12	67%

Figure 6.5
Stick figure of a man, a Christmas tree, and a house, with IB results.

tested with each of the inverted figures. The results confirm the hypothesis that it is the meaning rather than the shape of the stick figure that is responsible for it being seen under conditions of inattention, because in this experiment only three of the ten subjects tested with that figure reported seeing anything but the cross on the critical inattention trial (IB = 70%). Inverting the tree and the house had no effect. IB for the inverted house was 70%, while that for the inverted tree was 80%. Because these two figures do not capture attention when they are in their canonical orientations, it is not surprising that inverting them fails to significantly increase the frequency of IB. Finally, we ran an additional group of 10 subjects with the upright stick figure as the critical inattention stimulus but added a mask to be certain that the results were not somehow specific to a no-mask condition, and found that adding the mask had no effect.

An interesting question that these new results raise is why, of the many figures we tested, the stick figure of the man and the happy face are, with the exception of the swastika, the only shapes resistant to IB. The hypothesis that immediately suggests itself is that their capacity to attract attention may rest on the fact that they are both schematic representations of a person and may, for this reason, be highly salient to human observers. The one shred of evidence that might support such an hypothesis is that both these representations are often among a child's first attempts to draw faces and people. Moreover, the stick figure representations are found in very early prehistoric cave drawings suggesting that there is something extremely basic about these representations that might make them particularly arresting.

Conclusion

The results of the experiments described in this chapter add support to the proposal that meaningfulness plays an important role in the capture of attention and that familiarity by itself does not, although the possibility remains open that it plays a supporting role.

Before turning to the important question of the fate of stimuli not perceived without attention, explored in chapter 8, in chapter 7 we examine the capacity of stimulus size to capture attention under conditions of inattention. Data already reported provides some suggestion that it may be more likely that a larger stimulus will be perceived without attention than a smaller one. The question of size has theoretical importance, because if confirming evidence of a size effect is found, it would suggest that attention may be engaged at a level much below that at which meaning is processed.

Chapter 7

Stimulus Size, Scenes, and the Capture of Attention

Stimulus Size

A question that is of some interest in its own right, and which is relevant to the question of the level of processing at which attention may become engaged is the question of the role of pure stimulus factors in this process. We have established thus far that there are complex and meaningful stimuli that are perceived under conditions of inattention, and equally complex stimuli—like neutral or sad faces and other people's names as well as simpler and less meaningful stimuli like simple geometric shapes or motion—that are not. These data seem to point to a high-level account of the engagement of attention. But suppose that there are also formal, lower level stimulus characteristics that contribute to perception without attention. Evidence that this is the case would point in the other direction, namely to an account of the relation between attention and perception that brought attention in at a lower level of processing. This then would mean that any account of the relation between perception and attention would have to be flexible enough to allow the engagement of attention at more than one level of processing.

On the face of it, there seems to be little question that purely formal stimulus characteristics can contribute to the capture of attention because our everyday experience teaches us that we do hear unexpected loud sounds and do see unexpected bright flashes and large objects. So, even though we know that a mother usually will hear the almost inaudible cries of her infant while she herself is asleep, and by definition is not attending (which is consistent with the hypothesis that meaningful stimuli are more likely to be perceived without attention than meaningless ones), we also know that we are likely to be awakened by very loud noises that, of course, are potentially very meaningful. So the question that needs to be addressed is whether what might be considered pure stimulus factors contribute to perception under conditions of attention. We already know that certain stimulus properties, which reasonably might have been thought to elicit perception under these conditions do not do so. Neither motion, flicker, nor color are perceived if a stimulus with one of these properties is presented either at fixation or outside the zone of attention. But what about size?

In an experiment briefly referred to in chapter 6 that failed to yield evidence that a looming stimulus was likely to be seen under conditions of inattention, we did find that although a stationary 0.6 degree disc at fixation rarely was seen under conditions of inattention, the same stimulus enlarged to 1.1 degrees of visual angle frequently was seen. The blindness for a black circle 0.6 degree in diameter displayed at fixation was found to be 50%, whereas for a 1.1 degree circle, it was only 25%. In order to be more certain that the size of a stimulus affects its perception under conditions of inattention, we ran a separate experiment in which we simply compared the frequency of IB for a stimulus that subtended a visual angle of 0.6 degrees (its area was 0.49 cm² viewed from 76 cm) with one that subtended an angle of 1.1 degree, (its area was 1.2 cm² also viewed from 76 cm).

> In both cases the critical stimulus was a solid black circle that was presented at fixation in each of the three standard testing conditions. The larger set of crosses was used as the object of the distraction task. The crosses were presented in one of the four typical parafoveal locations, and all trials were masked. Twenty subjects were tested with the larger circle and 40 with the smaller.

On the critical inattention trial, 5 of the 20 subjects tested with the larger circle failed to see it (IB = 25%) and 21 of the 40 subjects tested with the smaller circle failed to do so (IB = 53%). This difference is significant (X^2 $df1 = 7.43$ p. $< .01$), and is consistent with the conclusion that size matters.

The Retinal or Postconstancy Aspect of Size?

Given a difference in the frequency of IB based on the size of the stimulus, the question then arises as to which aspect of size is responsible for this difference. Is it the retinal size of the stimulus or its postconstancy processed aspect that matters? The retinal size of an object refers to the size of the image projected by the object on to the retina. Its size is measured in degrees of visual angle. The postconstancy aspect of size refers to its size following the integration of other sensory information, for example, distance information, which is the basis for the perception of size constancy and its size is measured in linear terms.[1] The question about whether it is the retinal or postconstancy aspect of size that matters is important because it is relevant to the question concerning the level of processing at which attention is engaged. If it is the postconstancy aspect of stimulus size that is the basis for the attraction of attention, it would mean that attention is drawn to the stimulus after the constancy operation is completed. However, if it is the retinal aspect of stimulus size that is important, this would be consistent with attentional capture at an earlier stage of processing. Thus, the answer to this question bears directly on the claim that attention is captured at a late stage in processing.

Before we ran an experiment designed to directly address the retinal/postconstancy aspect of size issue, we wanted to determine whether our viewing conditions supported size constancy perceptions. If not, then the question of whether the postconstancy aspect of size might account for the difference in IB between a larger and smaller stimulus is irrelevant. To answer this prior question we ran a version of a standard size constancy experiment using a display that was identical to the one used in our inattention experiments. However, in this experiment the subject's only task was to match the size of the standard stimulus to a variable set of stimuli shown to the subject immediately after the standard stimulus was shown.

> The standard stimuli were presented at fixation for 200 msec. and a mask was used, thus duplicating the conditions used in exploring perception without attention. There were 33 different sized standards, all of which were black solid circles that ranged in size from 0.71 cm to 2.67 cm. Twenty subjects viewed the stimuli from both our standard viewing distance of 76 cm and from a distance of 139.3 cm. When viewed from the greater viewing distance, the angular size of the stimulus was 54% of the angular size of the same stimulus viewed from the closer distance. The set of 33 stimuli were shown twice, once from each viewing distance in random order. Following the presentation of each stimulus, the subjects were shown a graduated array of 33 black solid circles (figure 7.1), and asked to select the one that appeared to be the same size as the one they had just seen. This array was printed on a sheet of white paper given to the subject after each trial and was not viewed from the same distance as the standard stimuli.

The results support the conclusion that with attention to a stimulus viewed under our standard testing conditions, the perception of its size is based on postconstancy processing rather than on retinal size, because subjects chose stimuli from the choice array that in almost every instance matched the linear and not the angular size of the standard stimulus.

Having established that size constancy occurs under our viewing conditions, we set about trying to determine whether it was the postconstancy or retinal aspect of size that determined whether a stimulus was likely to be seen under conditions of inattention. The experiment

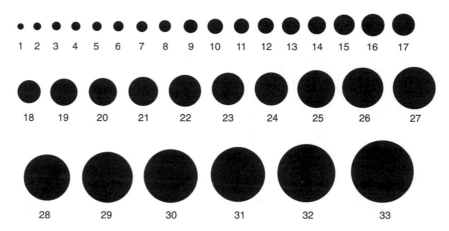

Figure 7.1
Size constancy experiment choice array.

designed for this purpose compared the frequency of IB for comparable stimuli at the two viewing distances used in the preceding experiment, that is, a near viewing distance of 76 cm, and a far viewing
distance of 139.5 cm.

> There were three different sized critical stimuli. One was 0.79 cm in di-
> ameter, one was 1.46 cm in diameter, and one was 2.76 cm in diameter.
> At the near viewing distance the smallest circle (0.79 cm in diameter)
> subtended a visual angle of 0.6 degree. At the far distance it subtended
> an angle of 0.33 degree. The circle that was 1.46 cm in diameter when
> viewed from the far distance subtended a visual angle of 0.6 degree, and
> from the near viewing distance it subtended a visual angle of 1.1 de-
> grees. The largest circle (2.76 cm in diameter) viewed from the far dis-
> tance subtended a visual angle of 1.1 degrees while from the near
> distance it subtended an angle of 2.01 degrees (table 7.1). In every case
> the subject was required to match the perceived size of the target circle
> to one of the 33 circles pictured in the choice array. A total of 80 subjects
> were tested in this experiment.

If the postconstancy aspect of size is the relevant factor, we should
predict no difference between the results for the subjects presented
with the same sized circles, regardless of the viewing distance, despite
the fact that at the near viewing distance the visual angle is almost
twice as large as the angle subtended at the greater viewing distance.
Alternatively, if retinal size is the relevant factor, the increase in viewing distance should lead to a decrease in the frequency with which the
critical stimulus is perceived, and stimuli subtending the same visual
angle should be seen equally often regardless of viewing distance. Ev-

Table 7.1
Summary of size constancy results.

Condition	Size of critical stimulus	Number of subjects	Percentage 1B	Percentage who chose correct circle
Near distance	2.01 degrees 2.76 cm	15	0%	67%
	1.1 degrees 1.46 cm	20	10%	44%
	0.6 degrees 0.79 cm	20	50%	70%
Far distance	1.1 degrees 2.76 cm	15	20%	33%
	0.6 degrees 1.46 cm	15	54%	43%
	0.32 degrees 0.79 cm	15	80%	33%

*Centimeters indicate actual size of critical stimulus.
*Degrees refer to visual angle of image on the retina (proximal).

ery subject was presented with the same stimulus in the divided and full attention conditions.

The results are summarized in table 7.1 and provide confirmation of the earlier finding that, viewed from the same distance, a larger stimulus is more likely to be seen under conditions of inattention than a smaller one. However, they do not provide unequivocal evidence for the role of either the retinal or the postconstancy aspect of size. Support for the role of retinal size is most clearly seen in the comparison between the frequency of IB for the circle with a diameter of 1.46 cm, viewed from near and far. There were significantly more cases of IB at the far distance (53%) than at the near (10%), (X^2, $df1 = 7.89$ p $< .01$), which is what you would expect if retinal size were critical, because retinal size decreases with distance.[2] Also consistent with the importance of retinal size is the fact that there were no significant differences between the frequency of IB for stimuli subtending the same visual angle. In contrast, however, the fact that we failed to find a significant difference in IB for the largest stimulus tested, 2.68 cm viewed from near (2.01 degree diameter), as well as far (1.1 degree diameter), does not support the hypothesis that retinal size alone is the critical factor unless we assume that all stimuli 1.1 degree or larger are equally likely to capture attention. Nor does the fact that we failed to find a significant difference in IB for the smallest stimulus tested (0.80 cm) viewed from near and far (X^2, 1 $df = 3.34$ p. $> .05$), although the difference that was obtained (IB = 50% near, and IB = 80% far) is in the expected direction were retinal size to be critical.

Because the data are somewhat ambiguous, no strong conclusion can be drawn. Nevertheless, we would like to propose that what we have found is some less than unequivocal evidence that there is a *retinal size* threshold effect. Thus, objects that subtend an angular size of about 1.1 degrees or more are likely to capture attention and be seen under conditions of inattention, while those subtending smaller visual angles are less likely to be seen. This is consistent with the finding that for stimuli subtending a visual angle of 1.1 degrees or more, IB ranged from 0% to 20%, whereas for stimuli subtending a visual angle of 0.6 degree or less, it ranged from 80% to 53% (X^2 $df1$ = 13.7 = 13.74 p < .001).

On the assumption that retinal rather than the postconstancy aspect of the size of a stimulus is the relevant factor in the capture of attention, then the account we have offered of when attention enters into the processing must be revised to allow for the possibility that attention is captured at an earlier stage of processing as well. If, as we claimed, it is the meaning or signal value of a stimulus that is the critical determinant of the capture of attention, then it follows that it must be the retinal rather than the perceived size of a stimulus that signals its importance. However, the difficulty with this conjecture is obvious. It is based on completely circular reasoning. It asserts that only what is important captures attention. Consequently, if retinal size captures attention, it is ipso facto important. There does not appear to be any easy way out of this bind other than to propose that the level at which attention is engaged in the processing of visual input depends on the nature of the input. However, this solution also has its problems because it requires that something be proposed about how or on what basis the appropriate level of attentional engagement is determined, and our only answer to this puzzle, at least at this juncture, again implicates meaning.

If retinal rather than perceived size captures attention, then in light of the hypothesis that it is stimulus meaning that is central to the capture of attention, it is necessary to conclude that retinal size carries signal value. This may be a reasonable assumption because an image that subtends a large visual angle (that is, one that occludes a significant retinal area) is often an image of an object that is dangerously close. Furthermore, when a looming stimulus is created, that is, a stimulus that grows in size without the accompanying information indicating that it is coming closer (in fact, even when whatever distance information there is indicates that there is no change in distance at all) both infants and experienced observers respond as if the object was approaching, and very young infants generally will exhibit characteristic distress behaviors. It is only the increase in retinal size that causes the perception of a looming object. This, of course, in no way establishes that our analysis is correct, but at least may lend it greater plausibility.[3,4]

Natural Scenes

Having established that stimulus meaning as well as stimulus size play a role in the capture of attention, we wished to explore to what extent a complete meaningful scene occupying most of the visual field would be perceived under conditions of inattention. As we reflected upon the results of our research, it occurred to us that there may be a contradiction between what contemporary theorists have to say about preattentive vision, that is, about what can be perceived in a brief exposure of multiple elements or objects in a laboratory setting, and what we actually *do* perceive in daily life under conditions that might be considered comparable. Investigators such as Julesz (1984), Beck (1982), and Treisman (1982) have maintained that what we perceive in the laboratory, when an array of elements is presented very briefly, are the basic stimulus features and, that by virtue of parallel processing, we are capable of simultaneously detecting the features of all the elements. There may well be disagreement about what these primitive features are, but there is no disagreement about the limitation that inattention or preattention imposes on processing. Without attention only the "primitive" features in the array are detected and are detected simultaneously.

We have already noted that it is incorrect to think of these search experiments as investigating perception without attention, for the simple reason that the tasks used to study these processes require attention to the display on the part of the subject. Therefore, a better characterization of the level of perception in such cases would seem to be distributed attention. We do not think that this is a trivial point in which we merely substitute one term for another. All the experiments described in this book demonstrate that when one takes the proper measures to eliminate voluntary attention or, better expressed, the intention to attend to what is about to be displayed, there is a drastic reduction in what is perceived, at least on a conscious level. In fact, unless certain kinds of objects are presented in our critical trial, the rule seems to be that nothing is perceived consciously.

However, one major exception are stimuli that, by virtue of some property, seem to capture attention. These exceptions seem to be limited to stimuli that capture attention by virtue of their meaning and stimuli that do so by virtue of their size. Beyond a certain visual angle (or phenomenal size), objects presented unexpectedly in our experimental paradigm are almost always seen. We have interpreted this to mean that the large size attracts attention. Another aspect of the stimulus, clearly related to size, is the presence of elements in the display over a wide area. Although each element may be small, if there are enough elements spread over the display screen, they too will attract attention. Thus the texture segregation or grouping patterns described in chapter 2 were invariably seen on the inattention trial, even though the texture segregation or grouping was not perceived. Because we have not exhaustively searched for other stimulus properties that might have the capability of attracting attention, we are in no position to assert that there are no others. Thus we cannot be sure that size is the only physical stimulus property which is able to attract attention, but we do know that it is one.

When, in our experimental paradigm, attention is attracted to a display of multiple objects filling the screen, one might think that the state of mind of the subject is somewhat equivalent to the one created by the typical experiments on search (for a single unique element or a region consisting of elements that differ from the distractors). That is to say, in both cases we face a condition of distributed attention; we face it in our paradigm because attention is attracted to the entire array, and in the search paradigm because the subject is required to attend to the array by the nature of the task and the instructions. However, one difference is that in our paradigm, even if attention is attracted, there is still no intention to search for anything in particular.

What *can* be perceived with attention distributed over an entire array given a very brief, masked presentation? We have already considered the kind of answer that most contemporary investigators would give, namely that what is perceived without focused attention are the primitive features of all the items in the array that are subject to parallel processing. What is not perceived are all the more complex or higher level aspects of the array. Thus, the combination or conjunction of the features of the stimuli, the perception of shapes when they consist of several parts, the properties of the items that depend on constancy operations, and finally, the identity or meaning of the items if they are familiar are not perceived. However, in the last few years there have been many reports that describe results demonstrating that some of the more complex aspects of items in an array are indeed perceived, so that the thinking of investigators who study attention is now in a state of transition (see, for example, Nakayama and Joseph 1997; Wolfe, Cave, and Franzel 1989).

We now describe research that indicates that what can be seen in brief presentations of pictures of ordinary scenes, presumably based on attracted attention, is very close to being a veridical, if not detailed representation of what is presented—including colored shapes, recognized objects, and appropriate size and shape—based on constancy operations. In this respect, our findings are more in accord with what we see in daily life under comparable conditions of distributed but not focused attention. This latter claim is based on observations we ourselves have made in certain situations in everyday life. For example, in driving, when one views the scene ahead without focusing on anything in particular, one has the impression of seeing the entire scene including all its constituents: the other vehicles, the distant mountains, trees, houses, and so forth. Of course, as we said at the beginning of this book, there are cases in which, in a very similar situation such as driving while conversing with a passenger or thinking in a very concentrated way about something, one has the impression later of having been "blind" to the scene. However, these kinds of experiences are surely less frequent than the one described above.

The Perception of a Photograph of a Scene

We decided to investigate just how good the perception of a picture of a scene would be if the picture was exposed under the conditions of our experimental paradigm. We looked for photographs that contained distinct, familiar objects and in which there was a homogeneous region in the center large enough for the cross figure to be superimposed on it, so that there would not be contours in the picture overlapping or camouflaging the cross when the picture was shown along with the cross on the inattention trial. We settled on two pictures, one to be used on the inattention trial and the other to be used on the control trial. For half the subjects, one picture, which we will call the breakfast scene (figure 7.2), was shown in the inattention trial, and the other picture, which we will call the dog scene (figure 7.3), was shown in the control trial. For the other half of the subjects, the pictures were interchanged.

> The breakfast scene showed about five people sitting around a table eating breakfast. One young man was standing and bending his torso presumably to be sure to be in the picture. The dog scene showed three young people and a dog in an outside setting.
>
> The procedure was essentially the same one used in all our experiments. The cross alone appeared for one of the first three trials and the cross plus one of the two pictures appeared on the fourth inattention trial. However, backgrounds were shown along with the cross on two of the first three trials, consisting of a checkerboard display, the center of which was slightly offset from the center of the cross. The quadrants

Figure 7.2
Photograph of breakfast scene.

of this pattern were of differing colors and the cross was white so that it would be visible. The fifth (control) trial consisted only of the cross and the other picture. As in all of our experiments, the line judgment task was suspended on the control trial. A mask consisting of colored regions followed every trial. Because it would have been very difficult to construct a recognition test with plausible alternatives for these pictures, we relied instead on the subject's verbal description of the scene. However, we questioned them at length after both the fourth and fifth trials, continually asking "Did you see anything more than you just described?" or "anything else?"

Performance on the line judgment task was comparable to most of our other experiments with no decrement to speak of on the two critical trials, despite the complexity of the large picture of the scene that surrounded the cross on those two trials.

Figure 7.3
Photograph of scene with dog.

As we expected, no subject experienced IB. There was however, some difference between the quality of the subjects' perceptions of the two pictures. The breakfast scene appeared to be more difficult. As the reader can see in figure 7.2 there is more detail and there are more objects in the breakfast scene so there is more to report. Hence we have to take this into account in assessing the adequacy of perception on the two trials, should subjects not do as well on the control trial. We first consider results for the two pictures separately. Of the 10 subjects shown the breakfast scene on the inattention trial, 1 was not fluent in English and gave no usable response. Most of the remaining 9 subjects reported seeing people sitting around a table. Others reported seeing several people at a gathering or party. So one might say that subjects picked up the essence or gist of the picture. Beyond these statements there were considerable individual differences in the amount of further detail reported. Some subjects seemed to see the entire picture quite accurately. For example one subject said "family, people around a table, one person standing over them, about three to four people." Another subject reported seeing "some people at a table, someone bending over, she was holding a birthday cake above the table, people facing toward her." This particular report contains some invented reconstruction, that is, either mentioning things not present or mixing features from two people or objects (illusory conjunctions?). The protocols suggest attempts at creative interpretation based on what was seen with certainty and elaborating upon that. A few subjects were wide of the mark, for example, one subject reported seeing "a man, an elderly one, with a red background with blankets."

When this picture was shown in the control trial to 10 different subjects, there is no question that subjects perceived the scene quite accurately and with more details. A typical response was "a picture of people sitting around a table, one person had head tilted, three other people, one of a man who had a beard." Only 1 subject was rather wide of the mark on the control trial and reported that the picture was of a "mother and child, cooking for two kids with some porridge on the table."

Turning now to the dog scene, when it was presented on the inattention trial virtually every subject perceived the essentials of the scene, namely, a few people standing around outside on a sidewalk near a grassy field with one young woman petting a dog. Moreover, much correct detail was also usually noticed, for example, the color of the dog, the clothing the people wore, that some people had shoulder length hair, and so on. As for the 10 other subjects who were shown this scene on the control trial, inspection of their protocols suggest that they performed well but it is not obvious that they did any better than the subjects who saw this scene in the inattention trial. This might be considered the result of a ceiling effect, that is, performance was already excellent in the inattention trial.

This experiment was rerun with an additional 16 subjects. The only difference in procedure was that subjects now were required to rate the adequacy of their perception of the scene, that is, their subjective impressions of how well they were able to see what was in the scene. However, the rating proved to be unreliable since subjects who reported the scene quite accurately were just as likely to give themselves a low as a high rating. The subjects description of what they saw were very similar to those in the first experiment and thus serve as confirmation.

Inverted Photographs

We wondered whether the meaningfulness of the scenes and their coherence and familiarity played a role in the adequate descriptions subjects were able to give of them. In an attempt to explore this question and reduce the recognizability of the objects and presumably to reduce the benefit of context, we ran an additional experiment with the pictures shown upside down. Of the 17 subjects participating in this experiment, 8 were shown the breakfast scene first (inattention) and the dog scene second (control). The other 7 subjects were shown the pictures in the reverse order.

Overall, recognition was poorer here for both pictures, as is to be expected. However, this was more the case for the breakfast scene than the dog scene. This was probably because the dog scene was simple enough for subjects to make out what was represented despite the fact that the picture was upside down. However, even for this scene, perception was not as good as when, in the previous experiment, the picture was right side up. For example, the presence of the dog was detected only rarely in this experiment. But despite the somewhat poorer performance in this experiment, the more surprising aspect of it was the fact that by and large subjects were still able to detect a good deal of what was in each picture.

In the control trial, despite the inversion of the pictures, subjects did extremely well. The descriptions of the scenes given were as good as those given in the control trial of the preceding experiment. Of course, only gross descriptions were required by the task. A picture of a person is still readily recognizable as a person even when presented upside down. Had a finer description been required, we have no doubt that the inversion of the pictures would have resulted in poorer performance.

What conclusions can be drawn from these results? It is clear that, under our very stringent conditions of inattention, subjects are perceiving far more than merely isolated features. They are perceiving, more or less accurately, an integrated scene containing meaningful three-dimensional objects of varying phenomenal sizes, shapes, colors, and locations. We believe that it is the size of the scene that attracts attention and that once this occurs, attention may be distributed over the entire array, or perhaps those parts of the array that carry most meaning are given priority processing and thus are more likely to be consciously perceived. The attraction of attention by these large and meaningful stimuli seem sufficient, at least in these cases, to allow the perception and recognition of the array despite the absence of any expectation or the intention to search for anything in particular. The fact that subjects detect the presence of the multiple elements making up the texture segregation or grouping arrays but fail to perceive the relationship between the elements is consistent with the supposition that it is the meaningfulness of the objects in the realistic pictures that is responsible for the fact that the presence of these pictures are not only detected but that their contents are rather fully perceived. If true, this would support the proposal that meaningfulness plays a dominant role in determining what is consciously perceived.

Figure 7.4
Example of display with unrelated familiar items.

Pictures of Unrelated Familiar Objects

As we have already reported, some of the descriptions of the pictures shown on the inattention trial contained inventive reconstructions. It was as if the subjects were trying to create a coherent and meaningful picture out of the pieces or parts of the array they had perceived. We therefore wondered to what extent the probability of the relationships between the various objects in the pictured scenes was contributing to how easily they were perceived. If it plays a significant role, then the apparent completeness of subjects' descriptions of the pictures might not be a true indicator of what they had actually perceived but rather of what they perceived plus what they thought was likely to be there, given what they had perceived. Would an equally large array consisting of unrelated but familiar and meaningful objects be perceived as well? The experiments we did to try to answer this question, however, were unsuccessful. When large arrays of 6 unrelated objects were presented to subjects (an example appears in figure 7.4) they were unable to identify more than about 2.5 of them even under conditions of full attention. This was so despite the fact that subjects were only asked to pick out the 6 items from an array of 12 objects. The ease of encoding the familiar scenes clearly has a great deal to do with the fact that subjects were able to describe them with surprising adequacy under conditions of inattention. Because of the work others have done, we already know that context has a powerful influence on perception. (For example, it takes subjects more time to detect a target object in an unfamiliar environment, e.g., a fire hydrant on a kitchen counter, than in a familiar context, e.g., a fire hydrant on a sidewalk.) (See, for example, Biederman 1981; Palmer 1975.) Thus, it is not surprising that subjects fared far better with the familiar scenes.

Conclusion

The results reported in this chapter demonstrate that the size of the stimulus is a factor in the capture of attention. This seems intuitively correct because it seems inevitable that a very large object that more or less suddenly appears before us will be noticed. However, the size experiments do not finally answer the question of whether it is the retinal or phenomenal size of the stimulus that is the decisive factor.

Evidence also indicated that large, meaningful scenes are quite adequately perceived under conditions of inattention, whereas an equally large group of unrelated familiar objects are not. In both cases there is no inattentional blindness, which we attribute to the overall size of the stimulus.

In the next chapter we describe experiments that explored the fate of stimuli that are not detected under conditions of inattention. Do they disappear without a trace somewhere in the processing chain or are they actually encoded, even though not consciously perceived? To use the terminology suggested by Kihlstrom and his colleagues (Kihlstrom, Barnhardt, and Tataryn 1992), is there any evidence of implicit perception of stimuli to which subjects have been inattentionally blind? This issue is directly related to the question of the level of processing at which attention becomes engaged. If there is evidence that these unseen stimuli are encoded, it would suggest that they are processed deeply and that therefore it is plausible to propose that attention enters late, perhaps even after encoding has been completed.

Chapter 8

Inattentional Blindness and Implicit Perception

The Fate of Unseen Stimuli

An obvious question to ask about inattentional blindness is whether a critical stimulus presented under conditions of inattention of which the observer is unaware, nevertheless is registered and leaves behind some kind of viable memory. If so, our results demonstrate that such a memory is no more accessible by traditional tests of recall or recognition than is the percept itself. Nevertheless, there is now ample evidence in the literature that sensitive, indirect methods of testing often reveal that perceptions not consciously experienced seem to be encoded, and facilitate or inhibit subsequent perception when that same or a related stimulus object is subsequently presented to the observer. This phenomenon of unconscious perception has been referred to as implicit perception (Kihlstrom, Barnhardt, and Tataryn 1992). Examples range from instances of what is called "subliminal perception," that is, implicit perception that is based on subthreshold stimuli (Marcel 1983); to blindsight, the documented capacity of patients suffering from cortical damage causing blindness in a specifiable part of the visual field to localize or judge the presence or absence of objects presented within the blind field despite the fact that these observers report that they see nothing (see, for example, Weiskrantz 1986); to visual or unilateral neglect that is caused by damage to the posterior parietal cortex resulting in the failure to consciously perceive objects on the side opposite the lesion (Bisiach, Luzzatti, and Perani 1979); to cases of hysterical blindness; and to hypnotically induced instances of blindness (Kihlstrom, Barnhardt, and Tataryn 1992).

One procedure routinely used in exploring implicit perception is priming. In this procedure some stimulus that is either below threshold or shown under conditions in which it is not likely to be an object of attention is presented to an observer. Following this, the same or a related stimulus is shown to the subject and some response is required. If the subject's response reveals the influence of the previously presented stimulus, it is taken as evidence that implicit perception of that stimulus occurred. To cite several recent relevant experiments, Treisman and DeSchepper, 1996, DeSchepper and Treisman (1996; see also Tipper 1985) have shown negative priming using a method first devised by Rock and Gutman (1981). In the original experiment, overlapping, novel, red and green outlined figures were shown, a pair at a time in a rapid sequence, with the subject attending to either the red or green figure. In a subsequent recognition test the attended figures were recognized well above chance, but the unattended ones were not. DeSchepper and Treisman confirmed this result, but went on to use a priming method in which the unattended figure was presented on the next trial in a same-different task. They found an increased response time in these trials, implying that the unattended figure on the previous trial had been actively inhibited and that the inhibition carried over to the subsequent same-different trial. Therefore, at some level below conscious awareness, the unattended figure in the overlapping pair was perceived and its shape registered.

It is important to note that although subjects in these experiments may have had no conscious memory of having perceived the unattended figure in the figure pair, they certainly did detect its presence because the instructions they were following requested that they attend to the red (or green) rather than the green (or red) member of the pair, and these figures were overlapping. Had the subjects simply been asked whether there was a second figure present, there is little question that they would have responded that there had been. This difference clearly distinguishes the situation explored by Rock and Gutman *and* Treisman and DeSchepper, from inattentional blindness that occurs when subjects are completely unaware of the presence of the unattended, suprathreshold stimulus. Subjects who exhibit inattentional blindness, when asked if they are aware of anything else present on the screen while performing the distraction task, respond that there was nothing else there.

The recent research on implicit memory that is far more extensive than that on implicit perception parallels that on implicit perception and shows that memories can be present under certain conditions, but inaccessible by the traditional methods of explicit recall and recognition (Schacter 1987). The term *implicit memory* is used to refer to a memory that is revealed by the performance on some task when there is no deliberate intent to recall a past episode (Bowers and Schacter 1990). However, with the exception of amnesiacs who may have no conscious awareness of the episode that subsequently affects their performance, others who serve in implicit memory studies are generally aware of the past events when they occurred. Priming also has been widely used to study implicit memory both in normal subjects and in those suffering from brain damage resulting in amnesia (see Schacter 1987 for a review of some of this literature). Clearly, there is a close connection between implicit perception and implicit memory because evidence of implicit perception revealed by evidence of priming is necessarily based on an implicit memory.

The question about the fate of stimuli whose presence is undetected when viewed under conditions of inattention concerned us from the very beginning. However, we realized that our method of only one critical inattention trial did not lend itself to the most frequently used procedures for exploring this question. Typically implicit memory and perception studies rely on response time as the dependent variable, and response time procedures require a large number of trials and the averaging of the response times over many trials. We therefore sought some other method of probing for the presence of a trace of the critical stimulus that might indicate whether it had been registered and encoded, although not consciously perceived.

Stem Completion

The one method that had been used to explore the question of perception without awareness as well as implicit memory that does lend itself to our procedure is the method of stem completion (Roediger et al. 1992). This method, like all others used to explore the question of perception without awareness, is based on the assumption that if a stimulus that is not consciously perceived affects the subsequent performance of a task designed to reveal its effects, then this constitutes evidence that it has been implicitly perceived. Although this method has been most widely used to study implicit memory, it can also be used to study implicit perception, in which case, subjects are presented with a lexical stimulus under conditions that make its conscious perception unlikely, for example, an extremely brief and masked presentation. This stimulus is referred to as the *prime.* The presentation of the prime is followed by the presentation of a word stem composed of the first few letters of the priming word. This stimulus is called the *probe.* Subjects are asked to complete this word stem with the first or first several words that come to mind. For example, if the prime word were *Chart,* then subjects would be presented with *Cha.* If significantly more subjects offer *Chart* as one of their stem completion words than subjects who have not been presented with the prime, then the conclusion that the prime was unconsciously perceived is warranted. In order for this procedure to permit this inference, the prime must be chosen so that its stem can be completed by many other common English words. Moreover, the prime word must be among the most unlikely or infrequent of them, otherwise word frequency alone might account for its choice. On this criterion, Chart is an appropriate choice, since its stem *Cha* can be completed not only by *Chart*, but by *Chair, Change, Chap, Chafe, Champ, Chat, Chase, Chant, Charm,* and so on, and *Chart* occurs far less frequently in the language than some of the other possible stem completions.

With these criteria in mind, we designed an experiment using a stem completion task to evaluate whether a priming word presented under conditions of inattention affected a subsequent stem completion task in which the initial letters of the prime constituted the stem to be completed.[2] If evidence of a priming effect is obtained for subjects who are inattentionally blind to the prime word, it would indicate that the unseen word was registered and encoded below the level of conscious awareness. Thus, in the experiments to be described, the priming words served as the critical stimuli in our typical inattention paradigm in which the standard sized crosses served as the objects of the distraction task. The critical stimulus was presented at fixation on the third trial (the critical inattention trial), the sixth (the critical divided attention trial), and the ninth trials (the full attention trial). The crosses were centered in one of the four standard parafoveal locations 2.3 degrees from fixation and no masks were used.

Another difference between the method used in this experiment and that of our other experiments concerns the pacing of the trials prior to the critical trial. In the stem completion experiments the intervals between trials in each of the three conditions were automated, so that after the cross was presented for 200 msec. in one of the four possible locations around fixation, the screen became blank for 500 msec., during which time the subject had to report the longer line of the cross.[3] At the end of this reporting interval the fixation point automatically reappeared for 1500 msec., signaling the onset of the next trial. (In the standard experiments, the experimenter initiated the next trial by depressing the space bar on the computer keyboard. Thus subjects were under less pressure to respond quickly, although they usually did.) In order to make certain that the subjects would be able to use the timed interval between the disappearance of the cross and the reappearance of the fixation point marking the next trial, they were given an extra practice trial prior to the beginning of the actual experiment. On the third trial following the disappearance of the cross and the subjects' report of the longer cross arm, the subjects were questioned by the experimenter about whether they had seen anything else and if so what it had been. Following their answer to these questions, the experimenter initiated the screen presentation of the appropriate stem. Subjects were then asked to complete the three-letter word stem that appeared at the center of the screen with the first two English words that came to mind. Subjects knew nothing in advance about this aspect of the experiment, so this was their first exposure to a stem completion task. Because on this critical trial the experimenter controlled the time interval between the disappearance of the cross and critical stimulus and the appearance of the stem, the timing of the critical trial did not differ from other experiments. The stem remained on the screen until the subjects had finished the stem completion task.

Four different five-letter English words served as the critical stimuli or primes, each of which was among the least frequently occurring words that could complete its respective stem. The critical stimuli were *Flake, Prize, Short,* and *Grace.* The visual angle subtended by these words ranged from 1.1 to 1.3 degrees and a different prime was used in each of the three testing conditions, so if *Prize* were the critical inattention stimulus, then *Short* might have been the critical stimulus in the divided attention condition and *Grace* the critical stimulus in the full attention condition. The stems that the subjects were asked to complete were *Fla, Pri, Gra,* and *Sho.* A total of 80 subjects were tested, with 20 tested with each of the prime words.

A separate control experiment was run that consisted of asking people encountered in the halls of the New School Graduate Faculty building to complete one of the four stems used in the main experiment with the first two English words that came to mind. Each of the stems was displayed on an index card. Because these subjects had not participated in our experiment, they had no prior laboratory exposure to the primes, and their responses therefore provided the baseline against which we could assess the performance of our experimental subjects. If the subjects in the main experiment who were blind to the critical stimulus on the inattention trial offered the primes as stem completions significantly more often than these control subjects, it would provide evidence that the primes were tacitly or implicitly perceived, that is, perceived outside of awareness and encoded. Eighty subjects participated in the control experiment. Twenty were invited to complete each of the four primes with the first two words that occurred to them.

Although the most interesting results come from the subjects who were blind to the critical stimulus on the inattention trials, of interest as well are the stem completions of those subjects who reported seeing something new on the critical inattention trial but either were not able to describe what they saw or saw something other than what was there. Were these subjects to offer the prime as one of their stem completions significantly more often than the IB subjects, this would suggest that some conscious awareness is necessary for encoding and a subsequent priming effect to occur. Finally, it is of interest to compare the effect of priming for the inattentionally blind subjects with subjects who actu-

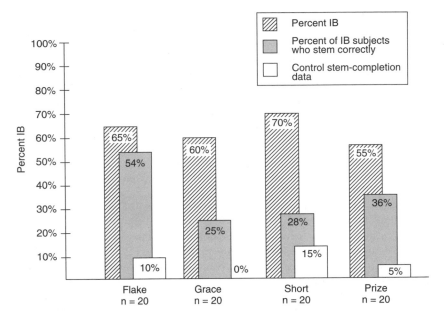

Figure 8.1
Summary of stem completion results (Flake, Grace, Short and Prize) with and without priming (control).

ally see and identify the prime. Do these subjects offer the primed word as one of their two stem completions? If they do not, it would be in line with other findings in the literature indicating the superiority of implicit effects over explicit effects under conditions in which subjects are unaware of the study or priming episode (see, for example Bowers and Schacter 1990).

The inattention results of the main experiment are summarized in figure 8.1. The results of the full attention condition demonstrate that subjects who consciously perceive the prime always offer it as one of their two stem completions. Only 3 of the 80 subjects failed to see the prime on the full attention trial and all 77 subjects who saw it offered it as one of their stem completions, establishing that priming occurs for the consciously perceived words.

The results of most importance are those from the inattention condition. Fifty of the 80 subjects were completely blind to the critical stimulus on the inattention trial, which amounts to an IB effect of 62.5%.[4] The question at issue is how many of these IB subjects offered the unidentified and undetected prime as one of their stem completions? The answer to this question provides positive evidence of priming. Of the 50 subjects who were blind to the prime, 18 (36%) offered it as one of their two stem completion words, whereas only 4 of the 80 (4%) control subjects offered a prime word as one of their two stem completions. This difference is highly significant (X^2 1 df = 23.0, p < .0001). Only 1 of the 22 subjects who saw and identified the critical stimulus on the inattention trial failed to offer the prime word as one of their stem completions. Only 6 subjects saw something but could not identify what it was on the critical inattention trial. Three of these subjects offered the prime word as one of their stem completions, a priming effect of 50%. Given the small number of cases, this result is not significantly different from the effect obtained with the IB subjects. In summary, these data present persuasive evidence of the processing, registration and encoding of the unseen and unidentified words presented under conditions of inattention.

Recognition Using Prime as Critical Stimuli

In order to further evaluate these priming results, we thought it was important to determine whether we could find any evidence that subjects who reported that they had not seen the critical stimulus in the inattention condition in fact might have seen the prime but simply failed to remember it or report it. Because recognition is a more sensitive index of memory than the free recall procedure that we used in the priming study, we decided to run one of our typical inattention experiments using the priming stimuli as the critical stimuli. Their presentation was followed by a forced choice task. Regardless of whether the subjects reported seeing anything new on the critical inattention trial, they were asked to choose what had been presented on that trial from an array of five possible words, 1 of which was the critical stimulus. (In order to avoid the possibility that the subjects might choose correctly because they had seen the first letter of the critical stimulus, all five choice words began with the same two initial letters.) We thought that if a significant number of subjects who reported seeing only the cross on the critical trial selected the correct word, it might mean that they had seen what was there and forgotten it, although this inference is by no means necessary because it is also possible that these subjects had only implicitly perceived it. The prior question, of course, is how to operationally distinguish between implicit and explicit perception which is now a subject of considerable discussion (for example, see Richardson-Klavehn, Gardner, and Java 1996). However, if one takes the sense of ownership or awareness as the primary, and most obvious criterion of explicit perception or explicit memory, then by this criterion IB subjects cannot have explicitly perceived the critical stimulus.

Forty new subjects were tested, 20 with *Flake* and 20 with *Short* as the critical stimulus. We repeated the procedure of the stem completion experiment and therefore used the paced procedure with no mask. In fact, this experiment was identical to the previous priming experiment except for the postpresentation procedure. Immediately following the reports of the longer line of the cross, and after answering questions about whether anything else had been seen, the forced choice array consisting of five common nouns, all of which began with the first two letters of the prime, was given to all subjects except those who spontaneously identified what they had seen.

Nineteen of the 40 subjects tested were blind to the critical stimulus on the inattention trial (IB = 47%), which does not differ significantly from the amount of blindness obtained in the main priming experiment. Of these 19 subjects, 9 (47%) chose the correct word in the recognition test. Thus, approximately the same percent of IB subjects chose the correct word in this experiment as offered the prime as a stem completions in the prior experiment.

This failure to find a difference in these two ways of testing for the perception of the critical stimuli that subjects report they have not seen may be viewed in one of two ways. It can be seen either as confirming the hypothesis suggested by the stem completion results of the prior experiment that inattentionally blind subjects implicitly but *not* explicitly perceive the prime stimulus, or, alternatively, that IB subjects actually do consciously perceive the critical stimulus, but quickly forget that they have done so. For the first inference to be true, it is necessary to assume that performance on both the stem completion and forced choice tests reflect implicit rather than explicit perception, whereas for the latter to be true it is necessary to assume that these two testing procedures measure different kinds of perceptions.

These results generate another puzzle as well. Why do a significant number of IB subjects in this experiment choose the correct stimulus from the choice array, but in earlier experiments in which words such as *Time* or *House* served as the critical stimuli, IB subjects failed to do so? Moreover, in those experiments we interpreted this failure to mean that these critical stimuli had not been perceived. A possible answer lies in the differences in procedure in these experiments. In the earlier experiments in which we compared the fate of *Time* or *House* with that of the subject's own name, the stimulus arrays were always followed by a mask and trials were unpaced, whereas in the present experiment there were no masks and trials were paced. It therefore seemed possible that either the mask and/or the pacing of trials might be responsible for this difference. In order to determine whether this was so, we ran four additional experiments in which masks were used and trials were either paced or not, and probing was with either a forced

Table 8.1
Summary of results: paced/unpaced and mask/no mask.

Trial type	Probe	Number of subjects	Percent IB	Percent correct responses into Probe
Paced/mask	Choice array	20	55.0%	18.0%
Unpaced/mask	Choice array	40	50.0%	10.0%
Unpaced/no mask	Choice array	40	52.5%	52.0%
Unpaced/no mask	Stem-completion	40	42.5%	23.0%

choice array or a stem completion task. In every other respect the experiments were identical to the two experiments just described, entailing either stem completion or forced choice. These four experiments are schematically described in table 8.1. A total of 140 new subjects were tested.

The results are summarized in table 8.1 as well, and are consistent with the hypothesis that the mask is the agent responsible for the difference between the earlier results. The mask seems to eliminate the subject's ability to choose the prime from the choice array. When no mask is used (experiment 3) more than half the subjects are able to correctly select the prime stimulus from the choice array, whereas with a mask only between 10% and 18% are able to do so correctly (experiments 1 and 2). Note that when stem completion was the measure of priming and trials were unpaced and unmasked (experiment 4), significant evidence of priming was again obtained, thus duplicating the original results which derived from paced, unmasked trials.

The simplest explanation of these results is that asking subjects to pick out a stimulus that they believe they have not seen from a set of stimuli provides a measure of explicit perception, which is eliminated by a mask, whereas asking the subjects to perform a stem completion task provides an index of implicit perception, which is unaffected by the mask. On the assumption that this analysis is correct the fact that IB subjects offer the unseen prime as a stem completion is clear evidence that the prime was unconsciously perceived and encoded.

The evidence of unconscious priming by stimuli that subjects are blind to is consistent with the theory of late selection proposed earlier, because in order for these stimuli to affect stem completion they must be processed, at least graphemically or perceptually, and encoded into memory.[5] These data, combined with the data showing that one's name is perceived whereas a very slightly modified version of that name is frequently not, and a happy face icon is perceived whereas a sad face or scrambled face icon frequently is not, are strong convergent evidence of late selection and extensive processing.

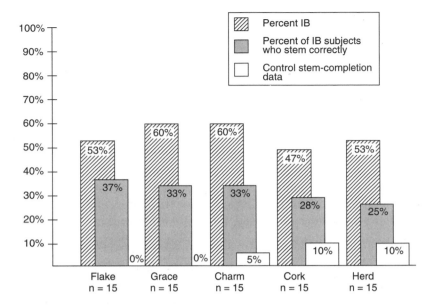

Figure 8.2
Summary of stem completion results (Flake, Grace, Charm, Cork, Herd).

Further Evidence of Implicit Priming

Because of the importance of the conclusion we wished to draw from the results of the priming experiment, we thought some additional confirmation of these results was in order. We therefore ran another priming experiment using the original priming procedure, that is, paced trials and no masks.

> Two of the prime words presented on the inattention trial were the same as those used earlier, *Grace* and *Flake*, and three new primes were added, *Cork* and *Herd* and *Charm*. Because two of the new prime words were composed of four rather than five letters, subjects presented with these words were given two- rather than three-letter stems to complete. Subjects presented with *Herd* on the critical inattention trial were asked to complete *He*, while subjects presented with *Cork* were asked to complete *Co*. Fifteen subjects were presented with each of the five words on the critical inattention trial so that a total of 75 new subjects were tested.

The results from this experiment are presented in figure 8.2. Forty-one of the 75 subjects tested failed to detect the presence of the critical stimulus on the inattention trial (IB = 56%). Of the 41 IB subjects, 13 (31.7%) gave the prime word as one of their two stem completion words. Of the 34 subjects who reported seeing something else on the critical inattention trial, 24 (71%) offered the prime as one of their stem completion words. We compared the 31.7% stem completion rate with the one obtained from a new control experiment in which we asked 60 people in the halls of the New School to tell us the two English words that completed one of the three new stems, *Cha, He,* or *Co.* Twenty subjects completed each of the three stems. Their rate of stem completion again was taken as the baseline rate against which the performance of the subjects shown the new primes in the main experiment were assessed. Only 5 of these 60 people (8%) offered one of the new target words as one of their two stem completions. (Two of 20 subjects offered *Herd,* 2 of 20 offered *Cork,* and 1 of 20 offered *Charm.*) If we now compare the baseline rate of stem completion with the frequency of stem completion obtained with those subjects who failed to detect the prime in the inattention condition, we again find significant evidence of unconscious priming.

These results duplicate and confirm the results from the first priming experiment. If we now combine the results of both priming experiments, which together involved 155 subjects, we find that there were 91 IB subjects, of whom 31 (34%) offered the prime as one of their stem completion words. (Of the 64 subjects who detected the presence of the critical stimulus on the inattention trial, 49 identified it correctly. There are too few subjects (15) to conclude anything about the performance of those who saw something but failed to correctly identify it.) These results provide strong evidence of a priming effect in those subjects who failed to detect the presence of the critical priming stimulus on the inattention trial. The combined results are summarized in figure 8.3.

Prime Outside Zone of Attention

Despite the strength of these findings we ran another lexical priming experiment in which the priming stimulus was located outside the zone of attention, even though most of the previous experiments that examined the effect of attentional zone on the phenomenon of inattentional blindness indicated that it had little effect when the critical stimulus was presented at fixation. This nevertheless seemed worth doing, because the evidence of priming weighs heavily in the proposed explanation of IB. Although we did not consider this a crucial experiment, we thought that if we continued to find evidence of priming in IB subjects despite the fact that the priming stimuli might now even be less likely to be detected, this would strengthen the evidence, from which we could conclude that undetected stimuli presented under conditions of inattention were processed and encoded.

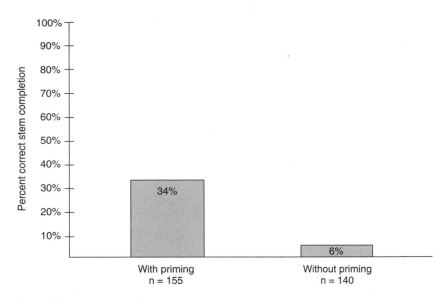

Figure 8.3
Summary of stem completion results (Flake, Grace, Prize, Charm, Short, Cork, Herd) with and without priming (control).

The method for presenting the critical stimulus outside the zone of attention was the same as the one used earlier. The smaller set of crosses served as the distraction stimuli. The location of these crosses was the same as in the first two priming experiments, namely, centered in one of the four parafoveal locations around fixation, and the critical priming stimulus was centered at fixation, as it had been in the two previous experiments. With the exception of the substitution of the smaller for the larger crosses as distraction stimuli, all other aspects of the stimuli and procedure remained the same as in that used in the two earlier priming experiments. Two previously tested priming words were used: *Short* and *Flake,* and 30 new subjects were tested, 15 of whom were presented with *Flake* as the critical priming stimulus on the inattention trial and 15 of whom were presented with *Short*.

Of the 30 subjects shown either *Short* or *Flake* on the inattention trial, 21 failed to detect its presence (IB = 70%) which represents some increase in IB over the prior priming experiments. Six of these IB subjects (28.5%) offered the critical stimulus as one of their two stem completion words. This is close to the rate of stem completion obtained in the previous two experiments. Of the 9 subjects who saw the critical stimulus, 3 correctly identified it, and 2 offered it as one of their stem completion words. Of the 6 subjects who saw something but could not identify what they saw, 2 (33%) offered the critical stimulus as one of their stem completions. It is of some interest to note that on the divided attention trial in which the prime was presented, 5 of the subjects also failed to detect its presence, and 3 of these subjects offered it as one of their stem completions.

Thus, even when the critical stimulus falls into a zone that may be *outside* the zone of attention, unconscious priming occurs, and it occurs just about as frequently as it does when the same stimulus falls within the zone of attention. It would seem that the combined results of all three priming studies, in which a total of 185 subjects were tested, provide solid evidence that the undetected priming stimuli are registered and encoded outside of awareness.

Although the evidence of priming revealed by the stem completion method provides clear proof that the lexical stimuli to which subjects are inattentionally blind may be registered and encoded, these data do not support the inference that unseen stimuli are semantically processed. Rather, evidence of priming derived from stem completion only demonstrates that these stimuli are encoded at a perceptual level of analysis. While it is of course possible that these stimuli also undergo semantic analysis prior to encoding, the fact that subjects offer words to which they were inattentionally blind as stem completion responses does not demonstrate this, because meaning plays no necessary role in the process of stem completion. Thus we persisted in trying to explore the possibility that IB stimuli are not only perceptually processed and encoded, but are also semantically processed prior to encoding. Our first attempts were unsuccessful, nevertheless, we include a brief account of them for the record before describing more fully the technique that did yield evidence of the semantic processing of IB stimuli.

Unsuccessful Methods[6]

One of the methods used to look for evidence of unconscious priming used ambiguous figures. It is well known that if one first shows an observer an unambiguous version of an ambiguous figure, when the ambiguous figure is shown subsequently, there is a past experience or set effect (Epstein and Rock 1960). The ambiguous figure is now likely to be perceived in the same way as the previous unambiguous one. So, for example, if one first presents an unambiguous drawing of a duck, and then presents Jastrow's (1900) ambiguous duck-rabbit figure, subjects will perceive it as a duck far more often than as a rabbit. Subjects first shown an unambiguous rabbit will have the opposite experience of the duck-rabbit figure.

We modified this method so that it could be used in our inattention paradigm by presenting an unambiguous drawing foveally or parafoveally on the critical inattention trial. Whether the subject detected something but could not make out the shape and recognize it, or whether the subject reported seeing nothing at all, we can ask whether the unambiguous drawing was nevertheless registered, perhaps even to the semantic level of recognition. If so, it should bias the interpretation of a subsequently shown ambiguous version of the same figure that was presented directly after the inattention trial ended and remained present until the subject responded. The subject was asked to tell us what the figure looked like. No masks were used.

We encountered various technical and other difficulties with this procedure but were finally able to overcome them and ran several experiments. We found no evidence of a priming effect, because the subjects did not select the primed version of the ambiguous figure more often than the opposite version. Among the other variations we tried were experiments in which the prime was a picture representing one meaning of an ambiguous word (e.g., *Tree*) and the test that followed was the ambiguous word (e.g., *Palm*). In another variation both the prime and the test consisted of words, for example the word *Tree* appeared on the inattention trial and was followed by the word *Palm*. The subject was then to interpret or define the word *Palm*. These variations also failed to yield a positive priming effect.

Our failure to find evidence of unconscious priming when the prime stimulus was a picture and the probe stimulus was a word may not be surprising, since studies of implicit memory reveal that words produce greater priming than pictures (Roediger III et al. 1992). Of course, this does not account for our failure to find evidence of priming when the prime stimulus was a word. The explanation of this failure, that is, the failure to find that, for example, presenting *Tree* as the critical inattention stimulus followed by the probe stimulus *Palm* potentiates the definition of *Palm* as a kind of tree rather than as a part of a hand, must lie elsewhere. It is possible that the failure of this kind of priming reflects the fact that the stem completion priming we did find is based on perceptual rather than semantic priming, but this is contradicted by the results of the next experiment.

Evidence of Semantic Priming

Unlike the stem completion method, none of the methods described in the previous section yielded evidence of priming, either perceptual or semantic. However, we ultimately devised a method that shared many of the features of the stem completion method and which not only provided evidence of priming, but of semantic priming as well.[7]

> As in the majority of the stem completion experiments, the interval separating trial one from trial two and trial two from trial three were automated. No mask was used and the critical stimulus that was presented on the third trial was one of the priming words used in the stem completion studies.[8] Following the critical trial, after subjects reported the longer arm of the cross and answered questions about whether they had seen anything else, an array of five pictures appeared on the screen and subjects were asked to chose one with no further explanation. One of the items pictorially represented the critical stimulus and the remaining four pictures were of objects whose names began with the first letters of the priming stimulus, so if the word *Flake* was the critical stimulus, one of the five pictures was of a snowflake and the other four were pictures of a flame, a flag, a flash (camera), and a flat (car tire). (See figure 8.4a & b.) We reasoned that if subjects who failed to see the critical stimulus on the inattention trial, that is, who were inattentionally blind, chose the picture that represented the object named by the critical stimulus significantly more often than a control group who had not participated in the experiment but simply were shown the five picture array and asked to choose a picture, this would be clear evidence of semantic priming, because choosing that particular picture necessarily indicates a semantic analysis of the priming word.

> Three critical stimuli were selected. They were the words *Prize, Flake* and *Cork,* all of which had served as stimuli in the prior stem completion studies. Twenty subjects were tested with each of the stimuli so that a total of 60 subjects participated in this study. As in the stem completion experiments both a divided and full attention condition, each with three trials, followed the inattention condition. These trials were identical to those in the inattention condition. As usual only the instructions to the observers were changed. An additional 60 subjects participated in the control version of this experiment in which they were simply shown one of the three-choice arrays of pictures (20 subjects were shown each array) and were asked to chose one of the pictures, again with no additional explanation. If IB subjects in the main experiment choose the relevant prime picture significantly more often than control subjects, this would be evidence of semantic priming.

The inattention results are summarized in figure 8.5. Of the 60 subjects participating in the main experiment 29 (48%) experienced inattentional blindness, with no differences in blindness among the three stimuli and with performance on the cross task consistent with that in the prior experiments (i.e., 70% correct on the critical inattention trial and 65% correct on the first inattention trial). Of the 29 subjects who

Figure 8.4a
Example of picture arrays for semantic priming experiment: prime Flake.

experienced blindness, 14 of them (48%) chose the picture that was
named by the critical stimulus to which they were inattentionally
blind. If we compare this outcome with the number of prime stimuli
chosen by the subjects who participated in the control experiment in
which they were simply shown one of the three choice arrays of pictures and asked to select one, we find that only 7 of these 60 subjects
(12%) selected a priming stimulus. This difference is highly significant
(X^2, $1df = 14.54$, p $< .001$) and seems to provide clear evidence of
semantic priming, because a stimulus that was not consciously perceived seems to have had a determining influence on the choice of the

Figure 8.4b
Example of picture arrays for semantic priming experiment: prime Cork.

picture made by a significant number of subjects. Of the 31 subjects who reported seeing something on the critical inattention trial and correctly identified it, 24 (77%) chose the picture of the named object from the choice array, which, of course, is what one might expect.

Results from the divided and full attention control conditions were predictable. Fourteen subjects failed to see the critical stimulus in the divided attention condition (23%). Six of these subjects (43%), selected the picture that the unseen word named, and these data provide additional evidence of semantic priming. Of the 36 subjects who saw the

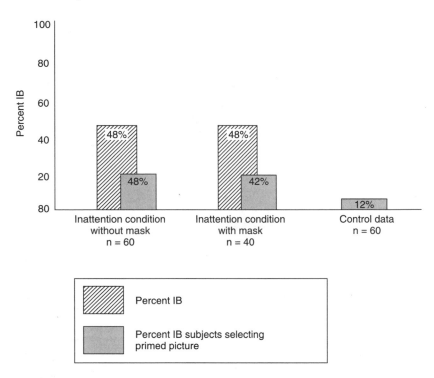

Figure 8.5
Summary of semantic priming results.

critical stimulus in the divided attention condition, 29 chose the named object (81%). Finally, all subjects saw and identified the critical stimulus in the full attention condition and all but one of them chose the named object from the choice array.

Semantic Priming with a Mask

Because in the semantic priming experiment no mask was used we elected to run another version using a mask in order to determine whether, as we have proposed, the mask would indeed have no effect on the priming, because the test of the priming was designed to provide an index of implicit rather than explicit perception. It is only explicit memory that we have argued is interrupted by the mask. The procedure and stimuli were identical to those of the previous experiment (the picture choice array was again given to the subject after the critical trial) with one exception. Every presentation of the stimulus array was followed by a mask. Forty new subjects were tested. Twenty were presented with the word *Flake* and 20 with *Short* as the critical inattention stimulus.

The inattention results from this experiment are also summarized in figure 8.5. Nine of the 20 subjects presented with *Flake* failed to see it (IB = 45%) but 3 of them chose the picture of a snowflake. Of the 11 subjects who reported seeing something else, 8 correctly identified it, and 3 reported seeing some word but did not know what it was. Ten of these 11 subjects chose the picture of a snowflake. Of the 20 subjects shown *Short* on the critical trial, 10 failed to see anything else (IB = 50%), and of these 10 subjects, 5 of them (50%) chose the picture of an electrical short circuit. Of the 10 subjects who reported seeing something else, 8 correctly identified it and the other two reported seeing some word they could not make out. Eight of these subjects chose the picture of the electrical short. If we combine these data, we find that inattentional blindness is 47.5%, and that 42% of the IB subjects chose the picture most closely related to the critical inattention stimulus. Thus here again there is robust evidence of semantic priming that not only replicates the previous finding but is also consistent with the proposal that masks do not interfere with implicit perception, at least in these displays.

The results reported in this chapter provide compelling evidence that stimuli that subjects fail to perceive under conditions of inattention are not filtered out at an early stage of processing, but rather seem to be fully processed and encoded at the semantic level. Thus they seem to support a late selection account of selective attention. This is consistent with the conclusion drawn from the experiments using one's own name and happy faces that stimuli presented under conditions of inattention, even if undetected, are extensively processed and encoded into memory. The fact that we were unable to demonstrate this using the ambiguity paradigm remains an unsolved problem, as does the question of why unconscious priming is somewhat, although not significantly, more evident in paced trials. This latter question is particularly mystifying given the fact that there are no pressures to respond quickly on the critical trial which is the trial which provides the evidence of unconscious priming.

Other Evidence

While finishing the manuscript for this book, another group of investigators reported research that produced results that also seem to demonstrate the implicit perception and encoding of stimuli not consciously perceived under conditions of inattention.[9] These results are not only consistent with the main results described in this chapter,

Noncritical trial:

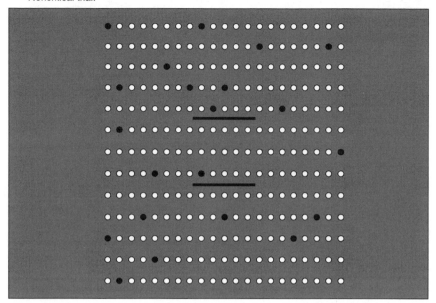

Figure 8.6a
Noncritical grouping display (Moore and Egeth 1997).

but also provide additional evidence of the extensive processing and encoding of stimuli that subjects do not experience when they are viewed under conditions of inattention. In this research the investigators (Moore and Egeth, 1997) used an ingenious method to examine grouping under conditions of inattention. Unlike our research on this issue described in chapter 2 that relied on the direct assessment of the perception of grouping under conditions of inattention, these investigators devised an indirect method that allowed them to assess the influence of grouping on the performance of a distraction task. In one of their experiments a pair of horizontal lines was presented against a background array of black and white dots that on critical trials were grouped so that they formed the inducing elements of either the Ponzo or Mueller Lyer illusions. (See figures 8.6a and 8.6b.)

Their procedure was modeled on our inattention method. The subjects' task, the distraction task, was to report which of two horizontal lines presented one above the other was the longer. These lines were surrounded by the dot arrays, which on the critical inattention trial and on other illusion-inducing trials were configured into the illusion-inducing patterns by virtue of similarity grouping. In all other trials the dot arrays were configured into random matrices of dots. The

Critical trial:

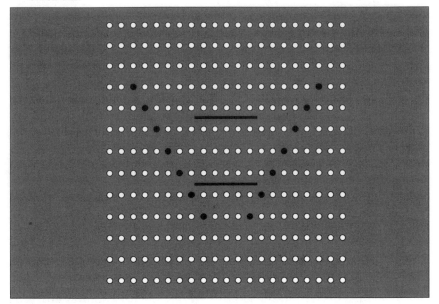

Figure 8.6b
Critical proximity grouping display (Moore and Egeth 1997).

arrays were displayed for 200 msec. and were followed by a masking array. After a series of practice trials, there was a block of 32 trials, which the investigators refer to as the *illusion block*. On 16 of these trials the dot matrix was randomly configured and one of the lines was longer than the other. On the remaining 16 trials the dot matrix was configured into the length illusion-inducing pattern, and the horizontal lines were the same length. Subjects were asked to perform the distraction task (deciding which line was longer) on every trial. These trials were followed by eight additional trials referred to as the *inattention block*. On the first three and the fifth and sixth of these trials the surrounding array was randomly configured and one of the horizontal lines was longer than the other. On the other trials the dot matrix was configured into the length illusion-inducing pattern and the horizontal lines were the same length. After the fourth and seventh trials subjects were not only asked which line was longer, they also were asked about the background pattern. The fourth trial is taken to be the critical inattention trial, the seventh trial is considered the divided attention trial and the eighth trial is considered the full attention, control trial because the subjects were told prior to this trial that they no longer had to do the line length task and only were to describe the background array.

Their reported results provide clear evidence of the influence of the illusion-inducing pattern on the subjects' reports of line length, even though subjects on the inattention trial were unable to describe or select the background pattern from a set of alternatives, and were unaware of the grouping of these background arrays. Thus, the illusion-inducing patterns, which only could have had an effect if they were grouped by virtue of similarity, significantly influenced subjects' reports of line length, even though subjects were unable to either describe or select these patterns from the appropriate recognition arrays.[10] These results seem to be evidence of the implicit perception and encoding of grouping in the absence of its conscious perception. They therefore are consistent with the stem completion data reported in this chapter and with our account of the processing of stimuli viewed under conditions of inattention. These results provide further evidence that stimuli presented under conditions of inattention that are not consciously perceived are, nevertheless, deeply processed and encoded, and can reveal their presence indirectly.

The Moore and Egeth results showing the implicit perception of grouping in the absence of any explicit percept also are consistent with the view that, under conditions of inattention, what captures attention and is therefore explicitly perceived is what is salient or meaningful to the observer. The fact that observers are unaware of the grouping under our standard testing conditions and in the experiment performed by Moore and Egeth strongly suggest that these kinds of grouping have no salience for subjects, which is why the fail to enter awareness. This is borne out by the research described in chapter 2 that explored whether subjects shown briefly displayed classical Gestalt grouping patterns identical to those used in our research on grouping under conditions of inattention would spontaneously report the grouping when all they had to do was look and describe what they saw. As the reader may recall, most subjects failed to spontaneously describe the grouping, again suggesting that it is not salient.

Conclusion

The experiments described in this chapter provide clear evidence of the implicit perception of stimuli to which subjects are inattentionally blind. Their importance lies in their relevance to our understanding of the nature of inattentional blindness. Had we been unable to find evidence of the implicit perception of stimuli subjects were unaware of seeing, it would have been more difficult to conclude that these stimuli are extensively processed. The fact that they are increases the plausibility of the hypothesis that attention is captured at a late stage of processing, and that it is the engagement of attention by an implicitly perceived stimulus that accounts for its explicit or conscious perception.

In the chapter 9 we review experiments that were designed to find the answers to two different questions, both of which were important in understanding the nature of inattentional blindness. The first question we attempted to answer is whether IB is caused by a failure to remember the critical stimulus under conditions of inattention, rather than by what we have been inclined to assume it is caused by, namely a failure to consciously perceive it. The other question explored is the role expectation plays in causing IB. Is it the fact that the subjects have an attentionally demanding task that causes IB, or is it rather the fact that they have no expectation that the critical stimulus will appear that is the source of the blindness, or is it both?

Chapter 9
The Role of Memory and Expectation[1]

Even with the strong evidence of unconscious priming presented in the preceding chapter, a question remains about the level of processing. A possible interpretation of many of our findings, such as the failure to achieve grouping, texture segregation, pop out, shape perception and, more generally, inattentional blindness, is that the subject has fleetingly perceived the critical stimulus, but fails to encode it, even into short-term memory. Thus a critical question is whether our results reflect a failure of memory or a failure of conscious perception.[2]

Failure of Perception or Failure of Memory?

This is a difficult question to resolve. Our method requires the passage of some short period of time before the subjects can respond to the question "Did you see anything else?" First, the subject is set to report on the length of the cross lines, and then our question must be stated and understood. Thus, a few seconds go by before the subject can answer the question, and during this period subjects must understand the instructions for a new and unexpected task. To some investigators familiar with this research, it is more plausible to believe that an object stimulating the retina (particularly in the foveal region) for an interval long enough to allow perception (as witness the results of all of our control trials) is briefly perceived, but not remembered, than to believe that it is not perceived at all.

One might think that the priming results of the stem completion experiments resolved the question about perception versus memory, because those results show that the undetected critical stimulus displayed on the inattention trial is indeed *perceived* (and must endure as a trace in some form to yield the appropriate stem completion). However, this reasoning misses the essential point, which is that the so-called perception that occurs is *not* conscious. The important fact is that the elimination of attention to the critical stimulus achieved by our method of presentation appears to eliminate conscious perception.

It therefore should follow that it also eliminates explicit memory as well. Nevertheless the question of whether IB could possibly be caused by a failure of short-term memory seemed important enough to warrant further investigation.

Several new methods were used to examine this issue. The first was essentially a failure, but it did lead to an unexpected and interesting result. In these experiments we sought to create a state of mind in the subjects that would lead them to spontaneously report the presence of the critical stimulus when it was presented on the inattention trial. This is, of course, treacherous, because the very essence of our method relies on the fact that subjects have no expectation that anything but the cross will be presented on these trials. In attempt to create the appropriate conditions, we divided the experimental procedure into two parts and told subjects that they were participating in two separate experiments. In the first version of this experiment we sequentially presented various colored shapes interspersed with letters of the alphabet shown in rapid succession, and trained subjects to report what shape was shown as accurately and as quickly as possible. While subjects fixated a central mark the shapes appeared parafoveally for 200 msec. and were followed by a colored mask. The subjects were told that they need not report if a letter was presented. On trials in which a shape was presented, a beep sounded as the signal for the subject to report. On trials in which a letter appeared, there was no beep.

In an attempt to improve upon this procedure, we altered it so that a shape was presented on each of twenty trials, but a beep sounded on only twelve. The subjects' task was to report the shape only on trials in which the shape was accompanied by the beep. In this way we hoped to have trained subjects to report the shape if they perceived one and a beep occurred. We then proceeded with the second experiment, which used the method employed throughout our research with one change.

> In this particular experiment when the critical shape stimulus was presented, it was accompanied by the beep. The cross was centered at fixation and appeared alone on the first three trials. On the fourth trial it was accompanied by the parafoveally located shape and the beep. The shape, of course, was the critical inattention stimulus. We hoped that now if subjects perceived the shape and heard the beep, they would spontaneously report it, thus eliminating the interval between its presentation and the time it took to ask the subjects whether they had seen anything else, which was the interval in which we thought forgetting might occur.

Unfortunately we found that no subject spontaneously reported a shape with the sound of the beep, despite the fact that many subjects did perceive the shape. They correctly reported it, but only when asked the question "Did you see anything else in that trial?" So in this respect the experiment was a failure. However, fewer subjects than usual exhibited IB, and a much higher percentage of subjects perceived the shape correctly on the inattention trial. This may be because exposure to the shapes in the first part of the experiment primed the shapes shown on the inattention trial and made them highly available, thus easier to encode and report, although we do not think so, given our earlier failed attempt to prime the grouping patterns (See chapter 2). An alternative explanation that seems more likely is that the early exposure to shapes led to an expectation, not necessarily conscious, that a shape might be presented during the second part of the procedure.

The second method we tried in our attempt to explore the question of memory versus perception was predicated on the assumption that if subjects perceived the critical stimulus on the inattention trial and were presented with another identical object immediately afterward that was slightly displaced from it, they would experience two objects, not one. Because the second object was to be presented directly after the 200 msec. inattention trial, we assumed that it would be consciously perceived. Moreover, because it appeared immediately after the first object, there would be no interval during which the first object had to be remembered. Assuming that the first object, that is, the critical stimulus, was perceived, then at the moment the second object appeared, the subject should experience either the presence of two objects or an apparent motion between them, because the conditions for apparent motion were met, that is, the first stimulus was present for 200 msec. and the second object was present for 250 msec. with no interstimulus interval. In fact, an interesting question is whether apparent motion can occur when one of two alternative objects stimulates the retina, but one of them is not consciously perceived, but of course, this question only arises if the first object is not consciously perceived, whereas our experiment was designed to test the possibility that it was.[3]

In one experiment based on this method, the first object that was the critical inattention stimulus was a small rectangle and was presented at fixation. The second object, an identical rectangle, was presented slightly displaced to the left or right by 0.72 degree, always opposite the side on which the cross had appeared. This second stimulus, which appeared as soon as the critical stimulus disappeared, remained on for 250 msec. In these experiments the cross was centered in one of the four parafoveal locations, and no mask was used. Except for the questioning of the subject concerning the number of objects perceived and whether motion was seen, the procedure was otherwise the same as in all previous experiments.

Of the 20 subjects who were tested, 10 reported seeing only one object on the inattention trial, but 2 of these described it as moving. Three subjects reported seeing two objects, 1 of whom described this as a motion experience. Seven subjects reported seeing nothing other than the cross, an IB effect of 35% that we assume pertains to the second object (as well as the first). Because the second object was visible for 250 msec. after the 200 msec. inattention trial ended, this failure to perceive it was completely unexpected and suggests that there is a perseveration of inattention. (Experiments that were designed to explore this unexpected finding are described in the next section of this chapter.) Of the 10 subjects who reported seeing only one object (minus the 2 who apparently did see two objects but reported this as the motion of one object), there were 8 who apparently did not see the first object, although there is no way to be entirely certain that it was the first and not the second object that was seen. If we add these 8 subjects to the group of 7 subjects who did not see either object, we have a total of 15 subjects, which means that only 5 subjects saw the critical stimulus. In other words, there seems to have been an IB effect of 75% for the critical stimulus, which is roughly what we have obtained in previous experiments. Therefore, it would seem that the results obtained using this new method also fail to support the interpretation that the IB effect in all our experiments is caused by a failure of immediate memory.

Results from the full attention control trial confirm the validity of our method because 8 subjects reported motion and 9 subjects reported seeing two objects. We do not know whether the 3 subjects who reported seeing only one object had seen the first or second, but whichever was the case, the important fact is that most subjects on the control trial reported perceiving two objects or one object moving, and this establishes that the method itself is valid. It is not very surprising that only about half of the subjects reported seeing motion, because it is known that a single half-cycle of an apparent motion display is not a very good stimulus for the experience of motion.

In a replication of this experiment, three different shapes were used as the critical stimulus. One was used for each of three separate groups of subjects. The second shape exposed was always the same as the first. In an effort to increase the probability that the second shape would be perceived, it was displayed for 800 msec. instead of the 250 msec. in the previous experiment. Otherwise, the procedure was the same. Eighteen subjects were tested.

The results were that only 3 subjects saw two objects and only 2 subjects reported seeing one object in motion. Altogether there were 5 subjects who apparently perceived the critical shape during the 200 msec. inattention trial. This of course means that 13 subjects did not, which translates into an IB effect of 72%, and thus there again is little evidence to support the *fleeting perception* hypothesis. Perhaps most surprising is the fact that 5 subjects did not see either object, so that there was startling 28% IB effect for the second object, despite the fact that it was visible for 800 msec. and appeared after the critical stimulus and cross had disappeared from the screen. Once again there seems to have been a perseveration of inattention that extends well beyond the 200 msec. critical trial interval.

A third method that we used to explore the memory or perception issue was a variation of the first. In this variation, we presented an object for 200 msec. *before* rather than after the inattention trial, so that we could be sure the subject would perceive it. This first object appeared at fixation and was the fixation mark enlarged to a rectangle. Now, if subjects perceive the second object, that is, the critical inattention stimulus, at the very moment it is presented, that is, *during* the inattention trial, they ought to experience either apparent motion or a second object that is identical to the first. As in the preceding experiments in which the added object appeared after the inattention trial, the direction of displacement of the second object that was now the critical inattention stimulus was always opposite the location of the parafoveally located cross. It therefore was presented slightly displaced to the left or right of fixation and consequently to the left or right of the first object. The second object that was the critical stimulus again was identical to the first.

Seventeen subjects were tested in this version of the experiment. Of these, 2 were disqualified because of what they reported on the control trial. One subject reported that the cross moved and the other reported neither motion nor two rectangles. Of the remaining 15 subjects, 10 failed to see either motion or a second object, an IB effect of 67%. Five subjects reported seeing motion but only 2 of these reported its direction correctly, so 3 of these subjects might be regarded as IB cases. On the control trial all 15 reported motion in the correct direction.

The results of this third attempt to find evidence that the critical stimulus is in fact consciously perceived despite subjects' inability to report it again fail to provide any such evidence. In fact, only 2 subjects correctly reported seeing motion on the inattention trial and no other subjects reported seeing two objects. Thus we conclude again using this new method that there is no evidence that supports the interpretation that subjects are perceiving the critical object on the inattention trial and not remembering doing so a few seconds later.

The Perseveration of IB

In two of the experiments described in the previous section in which the second stimulus object was presented after the critical trial, a significant number of observers failed to detect it, despite the fact that it remained visible for an additional 250 or 800 msec. This was quite surprising, particularly because the design of these experiments relied on the conscious perception of the second object to determine if the first object (the critical stimulus) was perceived. We reasoned, as we explained above, that if subjects perceived the critical inattention stimulus, they now either would report having seen two objects or the motion of a single object. Because in these two experiments the second object appeared after the inattention trial had ended, we believed there was presumably no further need for subjects to inhibit their attention to fixation which is of course, where the second object was presented. We therefore expected subjects would perceive the second stimulus object. Apparently, however, for some subjects, the state of inattention endured, and it was this effect that we thought merited further investigation.

In one experiment explicitly designed to explore this apparent perseveration of attention, we no longer presented two objects. Instead, the critical stimulus came on with the cross during the 200 msec. inattention trial, and simply remained on for an additional 500 msec. after the cross disappeared from the screen.

> The critical stimulus that was presented at fixation was either a black cross, a rectangle, or a triangle that subtended on average an angle of 0.75 degree. The standard set of crosses located in one of the four standard locations in the parafovea, served as the distraction stimuli. A mask appeared immediately after the 500 msec. had elapsed. In order to avoid the possibility that the subject's report of the longer line of the distraction cross would interfere with the perception of the critical stimulus that now remained visible, we asked subjects to delay their report of line length until after the mask appeared. This was done on all trials, not just the critical trial. Also in order to avoid the possibility that subjects would move their eyes during the long, 700 msec. interval in which the critical stimulus was visible, we reminded the subjects often and stressed the importance of maintaining their fixation. With the exception of these modifications, the procedure was otherwise our standard one. Whether or not subjects reported seeing the critical object, they were asked to select it from an recognition array after the display disappeared from

the screen and after they reported the longer line of the cross and responded to the question about whether they had seen anything other than the cross. Twenty subjects were tested, some of the whom were tested in the Berkeley laboratory, some at the San Francisco Exploratorium, and some at a home in which several college students were present.

Of the 20 subjects tested 16 (80%) failed to see the critical stimulus despite the fact that it was present for 200 msec. with the cross and 500 msec. more after the cross disappeared. (Only 3 subjects correctly identified the shape on this trial.) In contrast, all of the subjects detected the critical stimulus on the control trial, and 17 of them correctly identified its shape. This extremely frequent IB strikes us as an astonishing result, and we see no explanation of it other than that the state of inattention lingers on after the critical trial has ended.

A second experiment provided an even purer test of the perseveration effect. In the previous experiment, the critical stimulus came on *during* the 200 msec. inattention trial and remained on for 500 msec. after it ended. One reason for this procedure was to avoid an abrupt onset of the stimulus directly after the inattention trial, which might have captured the subject's attention. But in this second experiment we did just that, namely, no critical stimulus accompanied the cross during the inattention trial. Rather, the moment the cross disappeared, one of the three shapes was presented at fixation and remained visible for 500 msec., after which the mask appeared for 500 msec. The subjects were again asked to delay responding until after the mask appeared, and again were strongly encouraged to carefully maintain their fixation throughout the trial. A new group of 25 subjects were tested.

Eighteen of the 25 subjects (72%) failed to see the shape following the inattention trial, while in the control trial only one failed to do so, and all 25 subjects correctly identified the shape. Only 11 of the 25 subjects correctly identified the shape on the inattention trial. These results provide convincing evidence of the perseveration of inattention.

We have not yet tested the limits of this effect, that is, just how long it might last, but one experiment we did do suggests that the use of a mask is critical to the effect, because without it the effect essentially disappears. The relevant experiment was like the experiment described in the preceding paragraph except that no mask appeared after the 500 msec. interval, during which the shape was present. Instead a beep was sounded at the end of this interval, that is, when the shape disappeared, and this was the signal for the subjects to report the longer line of the cross. This beep sounded on every trial but on the first three trials it sounded immediately after the 200 msec. period in which the cross was presented. Subjects were told at the outset that they were to report the longer line of the cross when the beep sounded. Only 9 subjects were tested. Two of them (22%) failed to see the shape. And of the 5 subjects who saw the shape, only 2 failed to correctly identify it. Although this experiment involved only 9 subjects, it does strongly suggest that if the mask is absent, the perseveration effect does not occur. The reason for this is not clear, however, because in the prior experiment the 500 msec. interval—during which the shape was visible before the mask appeared—was surely long enough to permit whatever processing was necessary for the perception.

The results of these several experiments underscore in a new way the degree to which conscious perception is contingent on attention. Thus, if the state of inattention persists, which it seems to do well beyond the moment at which the cross that is the focus of attention disappears (perhaps until the observers have concluded that the trial is over, and it is time for them to report their perception of the longer cross line), many subjects fail to perceive a stimulus that appears abruptly at fixation and is present for 500 msec. This surprising perseveration of IB adds to the evidence of the importance of attention for conscious perception. We now turn to the ambiguity inherent in our method.

An Analysis of the Method: The Role of Expectation

Having explored the vexed question of whether the phenomenon of inattentional blindness is a failure of memory rather than a failure of perception, and concluded that it is, in fact, a genuine failure to consciously perceive, we turned to another question of equal importance in the interpretation of our findings. This question concerns an ambiguity not yet discussed in the method we have used to explore perception under conditions of inattention.

The ambiguity in the method used in all our experiments stems from the fact that it has two quite independent aspects. First, it engages subjects in an attention demanding task (the distraction task). Second, because the subject knows nothing about the possible appearance of an unrelated object (the critical stimulus) and does not expect one to appear, there is no intention to perceive it. Therefore it is possible that the occurrence of IB and the other failures of perception we have obtained may be due to either or both of these factors. In other words, these failures to perceive could be due either to the irrelevant, attentionally demanding task, to the absence of expectation or intention to see the critical stimulus, or to both. It is true that in the critical divided attention trial, about which we have said little thus far, the subjects do expect a stimulus object or pattern to occur, but they still must devote attention to the distraction task. That by and large IB no longer occurs and the perception of the critical stimulus is quite good in this condition might seem to suggest that it is the lack of expectation on the inattention trial that is crucial. However, that conclusion is not entirely warranted, because the expectation on the divided attention trials undoubtedly leads subjects to divide their attention between the distraction task and the rest of the display. In fact, in the method used in the New School laboratory, subjects are explicitly asked to continue to perform the distraction task, for example, to report the longer line of the cross *and* to report the presence of whatever else they perceive.

Lack of Expectation of When a Stimulus Will Appear

We sought to resolve this ambiguity in our method by experiments that attempted to isolate the lack of expectation for the critical stimulus while the subject is attending to the display but has no demanding other task to perform.

> In the first of these experiments, the subject fixated a small square and, after 6, 7, or 8 seconds, a beep sounded; after another second the beep and shape appeared, which in turn was followed by a black and white mask composed of small shapes that remained on for 500 msec. The shape was visible for 200 msec. and was presented in the parafovea in one of four possible locations used in many of our earlier experiments. The subject's task was to name the shape that appeared after the beep sounded. On the fourth of these trials the beep was eliminated and the fixation square was present for only 1 second. It was immediately followed by the shape that was present again for 200 msec. We considered this to be the critical trial, because we presumed that by this trial our subjects would be expecting the beep, and a few seconds after it sounded would be expecting a shape to appear. We therefore believed they would *not* be expecting a shape after only 1 second, particularly because no beep occurred. Note that the subjects' only task in this experiment was to remain fixated on the small square, and to report the shape that appeared following the sounding of the beep. Thus, attention was, in fact, directed to the task of discriminating shape. The subjects were asked following each trial which of six possible shapes they had seen. Nineteen subjects were tested.

Seventeen correctly reported the shape on the critical trial. So it would seem that lack of expectation and with it the lack of intention to perceive anything at a particular moment does not in itself prevent perception.

In the next experiment, subjects fixated a small black square that was surrounded by four large squares. Subjects were told to fixate the central mark and view the display for several seconds (4 to 9) after which a beep would sound and a second shape would be revealed where one of the large squares had been. Following that, the subjects were told a mask covering the screen would appear for .5 second. The subjects were asked to name the shape they perceived and indicate in which quadrant it appeared. After seven such trials and without any beep a shape was revealed 1 second after the trial began and remained on the screen for 200 msec. followed by the mask.

The result was again that 13 of 15 subjects correctly reported the shape and all 15 correctly reported its quadrant location. This experiment confirmed the result of the first with a slight variation of method. Again, it is fair to say that the subjects hardly expect the shape on the critical trial at the moment it appears. But this lack of expectation does not seem to eliminate perception.

In the next experiment the display was the same as in the previous experiment, but now the subjects were told that a shape would appear 30 seconds after a beep. However, instead, on the first and only trial, a shape was revealed in one of the four locations after only 1 second and without a beep. Of 9 subjects, 8 perceived the shape correctly and all 9 correctly identified the quadrant. So we have additional confirmation that lack of expectation, at least the lack of expectation of when something will appear, does not eliminate perception.

We then tried another method to attempt to deceive the subject as to when a shape would appear. In this procedure we used an alternation method entailing two tasks. The subjects were told that one task was to report whether two shapes that were to be presented simultaneously were the same or different. These two shapes were visible for 200 msec. and were located randomly in two of the four possible parafoveal locations. The subjects' other task was our frequently used cross task that required that subjects to tell us which line of the cross was longer. These tasks were alternated and subjects were told that they would begin with the shape task. So the sequence was as follows: shape, cross, shape, cross, shape, cross, shape, and so on. The eighth task then was supposed to be the line judgment and certainly that is what the subject expected. However, in fact it was the shape task (and for this trial the two shapes were always the same). The result was that, in spite of the lack of expectation, all 11 subjects reported the shape and the two quadrants correctly. So once again it is clear that when expectation is lacking as to when something will appear, it has no adverse effect on perception. In a general sense, across time, the subject does expect shapes to be presented and in this experiment attention is required for both tasks.

A Total Lack of Expectation of a Stimulus

However, in the next experiment we changed the method in an important respect. Now there was no mention of shape or of a beep that would precede a shape. Instead, subjects were told that we were investigating whether an afterimage could be established if they merely held their fixation constant on the display that would appear on the screen. The display was essentially the same one used in the previous two experiments, namely, four parafoveally located black squares symmetrically arranged in the four diagonal locations around the fixation mark. However, the cross itself was not presented. The importance of maintaining fixation was emphasized. After 5 seconds during which the display remained constant a shape replaced one of the four squares and was present for 200 msec. The result was that only 3 of 9 subjects perceived the correct shape. Six subjects correctly identified the quadrant. Three subjects did not perceive any shape at all, a 33% IB effect. Although the number of subjects was small, the trend was interesting. We tentatively interpreted it to mean that when there is no expectation at all that a shape will be presented, perception is adversely affected. In the previous experiments the subjects did expect to see a shape, but not at the moment it appears. Such a lack of expectation of *when* does not seem to affect the outcome. But lack of expectation of *what* does seem to matter. Because the subject merely had to fixate and had no task requiring attention, we do not regard the explanation given to subjects concerning afterimages as a task requiring attention.[4] This was not the case for the tasks requiring judgment of line length of the cross in all our other experiments. This experiment therefore seems to isolate expectation of what shape will appear and does seem to reveal its effect on conscious perception.

However, we followed up this experiment with one that, on the surface, seems to be very similar. Again, the subject was told that we were investigating whether subjects could form afterimages from repeated brief exposures. In this experiment, in addition to the four black squares, the cross was presented centered at fixation. Again the maintenance of fixation was stressed. The experiment then proceeded as usual, namely, there were separate trials, each beginning with fixation and followed by the entire pattern of cross and squares for 200 msec., which in turn was followed by the pattern mask. However, the subject had no task with respect to the cross other than to form an afterimage, which, as just noted, we do not regard as a task requiring attention, or at least much attention. Although the subject was attending, all the subject had to do was to continue fixating. On the fourth trial a shape was presented in one of the quadrants, replacing a square.

The result of this procedure was different than that of the previous experiment that also entailed afterimage instructions. Of 15 subjects, only 1 was inattentionally blind. Of the remaining 14 who saw something additional, 10 correctly reported the shape and all were aware of the quadrant in which the shape replaced a square. In a control trial that was also included, the subjects were told they did not have to form an afterimage and were to simply look passively at the display when it came on. We do not regard these instructions as making any difference, but the fact that the control trial follows the inattention trial that included a recognition test is likely to have led the subjects to expect a shape to replace a square. As we might expect, all 15 subjects saw something and 14 reported the correct shape.

Why is this result different than the previous one (assuming that the 9 subjects in that experiment are sufficient to reveal a trend)? We believe the difference is that in this experiment the subject knows exactly that the entire stimulus pattern will appear and when it will appear, whereas in the previous experiment in which there was really only the one trial lasting 5 sec., and the shape replaced a square for the last 200 msec., the subject had no idea that anything would appear or change and certainly no knowledge of when a change would occur. Perhaps the procedure of presenting the pattern repeatedly for a brief moment does cause the subject to attend to it more actively, even though there is no real task to perform. The subject realizes that the brief flashes are the occasions on which he or she will form an afterimage, so this knowledge may trigger some kind of expectation.[5] In the previous experiment that would not be the case. Another possible reason for the different outcomes of these last two experiments could be that the requirement to fixate for 5 sec. is more taxing and therefore more attentionally demanding than the task of fixating for a period of only 200 msec., although we have not yet been able to find any evidence that the degree of difficulty of the distraction task differentially affects IB. Unhappily, we are at a loss to explain the result of this experiment and recognize the inadequacy of these speculations.[6]

Because the difference between the results of the last two experiments puzzled us, the last experiment was repeated with one change. Instead of the four black squares, only the cross appeared on each trial. The shape appeared on the fourth trial parafoveally, in one of the quadrants, and in one of the locations where a square had appeared in the previous experiments. Here again, of the 14 subjects tested, only 2 subjects reported seeing nothing additional, an IB effect of 14%. The remaining 12 subjects perceived the shape correctly, so this result parallels the previous one using offset instead of onset. Once more we are at a loss to explain these results.

Subsequent Replications and Variations

This is where the matter stood over a considerable amount of time, during which we went on to investigate other aspects of our inattention project. However, the inconclusiveness of the results and our speculations about them drew us back to this problem about expectation. We decided to reopen the investigation with new experimenters and new variations. The first experiment we performed was a repetition of the only one that had given positive results in the entire previous series in the sense of indicating an effect of lack of expectation, namely, the one entailing a single trial of 5 seconds. There was good reason to repeat this experiment because it had only involved the testing of 9 subjects. There were, however, some minor differences in the procedure we now introduced.

> In the repetition, 18 subjects were run. The procedure consisted of instructing the subject that we were investigating the formation of afterimages and therefore that the subject was to maintain fixation on a central mark for 5 sec. and would be viewing a cross figure. In the previous experiment, four squares were used instead of a cross as the pattern for which the subject believes he or she is to form an afterimage. During the last 200 msec. of the 5 sec. period, with no prior alerting of the subject, a shape appeared parafoveally. This was the only other difference in the new procedure because in the initial experiment, a shape replaced a square. The parafoveal location was the same as that used in most of our investigation of the effects of inattention, namely 2.3 degrees from the center of the cross and the fixation mark in one of the quadrants along a virtual line bisecting the 90 degree angle of that quadrant. Following this 5 sec. trial, the trial was rerun in a control trial because now the subject was expecting a shape to appear, if not because he or she had seen it on the inattention trial, then because of the questioning and forced guessing required after that trial. The shape appeared randomly in one of the other quadrants on this trial.

The results confirmed the earlier finding. Of the 18 subjects, 8 failed to see the shape, an IB effect of 44%. Of the 10 subjects who reported seeing something else, only 5 selected the correct shape in the recognition test. Thus only 5 of the 18 subjects perceived the shape and perceived it correctly. By contrast, on the control trial, all subjects were aware that something additional was present, that is, 0% IB, and all but 1 subject selected the correct shape in the recognition test. This is fairly solid evidence that the lack of expectation alone, without the additional factor of attention to another task, can cause IB and poor shape perception.

To be sure that the crucial difference in yielding positive results was the 5 sec. single exposure versus the repeated 200 msec. exposures, we also repeated one of the other earlier experiments. In that experiment, it will be recalled, the subject was told that the study concerned the ability to form an afterimage from repeated brief exposures. The cross appeared centered on the fixation mark for 200 msec. on the first three trials. On the fourth, a shape appeared in one of the quadrants. Of the 18 new subjects tested only 2 failed to see something additional, an IB effect of 11% although of the other 16 subjects, only 9 selected the correct shape in the recognition test. So we here confirm the earlier finding that the repeated trials method seems not to lead to the same degree of IB as does the single longer exposure method. However, it is interesting to note that, even with this repeated trials method, although it is true that very little IB occurs, the perception of shape is none too good. Thus one might conclude that some of the failure of shape perception in our earliest experiments (see chapter 3) can occur just from lack of expectation, even without the focusing of attention on a difficult distracting task. In the control condition of the present experiment there was no IB and virtually every subject perceived the shape correctly.

The Critical Stimulus at Fixation

The earlier set of experiments described in this chapter attempting to isolate expectation—or rather the lack of it—as a factor in research on inattention were performed before we had discovered that IB will occur for foveally presented stimuli. But now that we had returned to the question about lack of expectation, and because we now did know about the even greater IB occurring for fixated rather than peripheral stimuli, we naturally decided to investigate the effect of lack of expectation on foveally presented objects.

We performed two experiments with the critical shape stimulus presented at fixation. In the first of these we repeated the method of several 200 msec. trials because it had failed to show much of an effect of lack of expectation. The question raised was whether reversing the location of the cross and the shape would make any difference. Therefore the procedure was exactly like that described above for 200 msec. duration trials in which the subject received afterimage instructions rather than length judgments with respect to the cross. However, the cross was now centered in one of the four possible parafoveal locations and the shape that appeared on the fourth trial was located where the fixation mark had been. The subjects were told to keep their eyes on the fixation mark and not to move them to where the cross appeared on each trial.

The result was a considerable increase in IB. Of the 18 subjects tested, 9 failed to see anything else, an IB effect of 50%. Of those 9 who did not exhibit IB, all perceived the shape correctly. This latter fact suggests, once again, that when the unexpected shape is presented to the foveal region, and the subjects do see it, that there is a much greater likelihood that they will perceive it accurately than when it is presented parafoveally. A plausible explanation, as we have suggested before, is that acuity is better for the foveal location. Because subjects usually have no difficulty identifying the critical object in the control trial, whether foveal or parafoveal, we have tended to overlook the possibility of a difference in acuity. It seems possible then that the lessened acuity in the parafoveal region is sufficient for object identification with attention, but not without it.

There is a problem raised by the results of this experiment. Although we presented the critical shape at the fovea because of the success we had in many previous experiments with such foveal location there is one reason not to expect it here. It will be recalled that our explanation of the greater IB at the fovea has been that the subject actively suppresses or inhibits information in this region because the cross to which he or she must attend is parafoveal and is expected to be parafoveal on every trial. But in the present experiment there is no task associated with the cross, only the need to develop an afterimage of it. So we need to ask whether there is any strong reason to inhibit the foveal region, that is, the region at fixation? If there is, why? If there is not, why are we achieving such a high rate of IB, something we failed to achieve in an otherwise identical procedure except that the critical shape was presented parafoveally? We do not know the answer to this question, although one possibility is that the cross that is the principle focus of the attempt to create an afterimage is parafoveal, and so the subjects are in fact attending to it. Because it is parafoveal an effort is required, and this effort may lead to the inhibition of attention to the area around fixation that only contains a very small fixation mark, the consequence of which may be the increase in IB.

In the last experiment we performed on the role of lack of expectation, we reverted to the 5 sec. exposure period with the critical shape stimulus appearing during the last 200 msec. We had already shown that this procedure leads to appreciable IB. The only difference was that now the cross was located in one of the four parafoveal locations and the shape appeared at fixation on the fourth trial. The result was that of 18 subjects, 10 failed to see the shape, an IB of 56%. Of the remaining 8 subjects, 5 were able to perceive the correct shape. In the control condition all 18 subjects perceived the shape and identified it correctly.

In summary of the last group of four experiments (two with the expected shape shown parafoveally and two with it shown foveally) we achieved an IB averaging 50% on three of them and a smaller IB of only 11% on one of them. That one experimental result, however, is one we should have expected because it closely duplicated the procedure used in many early experiments in which a parafoveal object was presented on the critical trial. Because in those cases there were two factors at work that might have led to IB—namely close attention to a difficult cross task and lack of expectation—whereas in the present experiment, only one such factor was isolated—namely lack of expectation—there is every reason to expect better conscious perception and less IB in this experiment than in the others in this series or in many earlier experiments for that matter.

Conclusion

The experiments described in this chapter concerned two issues relevant to the understanding of the nature of inattentional blindness. The first set of experiments attempted to resolve the question of whether inattentional blindness was a failure of memory rather than of conscious perception. The results of these experiments argue for the latter and are consistent with at least one set of results described earlier. These are the results of the experiment in which the only task subjects were given during the interval in which the critical stimulus was displayed was to move their eyes from one marked location to another, that is, to saccade between marked locations. The fact that the frequency of IB was high in this situation also appears to be consistent with the conclusion that IB is a true failure of perception. However, even if the combined results of these experiments had less strongly supported this conclusion, we do not believe this would have made the fact of inattentional blindness any the less important. The reason for this is that even if there were stronger grounds for believing that memory failure was responsible for IB, the fact that subjects had no conscious memory of perceiving a suprathreshold familiar stimulus frequently located at fixation and displayed for 200 msec. and sometimes longer would still have been surprising and of theoretical importance while perception of the few stimuli detected under conditions of inattention endures? Why should memory of these objects be so fleeting? We ask this question particularly because the evidence of priming by these stimuli described in chapter 8 points to the fact that implicit memories of these objects exist. This being the case, the question that would need to be answered is, why, if these objects were consciously perceived, is the memory of them unavailable?

The main conclusion that would seem warranted from the second group of experiments described in this chapter, which were designed to examine the role of expectation in IB, is that under the right condi-

tions, lack of expectation is a sufficient condition to yield IB. It is difficult to isolate the other factor inherent in our method—attention to a
difficult task—in such a way that expectation is allowed or present.
The divided attention trial that was included in many of our experiments perhaps comes closest to creating such a condition. In that condition, the subjects are attending to the line judgment task and are
expecting some new object to appear along with the cross. However,
as we said at the beginning of this chapter, the subjects' degree of
attention to the cross may not remain constant.

A plausible conclusion about our method is that there are two factors
operating that together or in interaction create a condition of no voluntary or anticipatory attention to the critical stimulus. Perception can
then only occur if it is attracted by the stimulus.

Before trying to sum up what we think all of our research might
mean we turn in chapter 10 to a series of preliminary experiments that
tried to examine whether the inability to perceive without attention
is peculiar to vision or is a more general characteristic of sensory
systems.

Chapter 10

Inattentional Deafness and Tactile Insensitivity

Throughout this book the focus has been on the effects of inattention on visual perception. However, as the research progressed and we became increasingly aware of the profound effect of inattention on seeing, we began to wonder whether the effects we were finding in vision might be paralleled in other sensory modalities, and although this question never became central, it did lead to certain amount of preliminary empirical investigation and some delving into what seemed as if it might be relevant literature. Of course, we were already familiar with the work on selective attention in audition that had convincingly demonstrated subjects' inability to report the contents of a message spoken into their unattended ear during a dichotic listening task. However, although subjects placed in these situations could report only gross features of the message spoken into the unattended ear, for example, whether the voice was that of a male or a female, there seemed to be no reports of auditory deafness, that is, reports that subjects were completely unaware of the presence of sound stimulation to the unattended ear. Only evidence of complete auditory deafness produced by inattention to the auditory stimulus would seem to qualify as a proper analogue in audition to inattentional blindness in vision.

The analogue in the tactile modality would seem to be a total unawareness of above-threshold tactile stimulation under conditions of inattention. We found no discussion of this in the literature either, although in the next chapter we do review some of the reports of hypnotically induced analgesia and other instances of pain insensitivity that might be related to inattention, as well as reports of hypnotically induced blindness which also might be related to attention.

Auditory Deafness

The first questions we set out to answer were whether subjects would fail to detect the presence of an above-threshold, fully audible tone when their attention was focused on another auditory task and whether they would fail to perceive the grouping of a series of tones based on their temporal proximity just as they failed to perceive the grouping of visual elements based on their spatial proximity. Because the attempts to study auditory grouping based on temporal proximity were the first auditory experiments we attempted, the fact that they seemed to yield evidence of attentionally induced deafness led us to temporarily set this line of research aside and instead to first look for unequivocal evidence of inattentional deafness.

Because these experiments[1] concerned audition rather than vision, both new equipment for delivering the stimulation and a new distraction task were needed. The distraction task we settled upon at first required that subjects listen to a recorded string of five letters. Each letter was linearly compressed to about 50% of its normal length (average duration about 250 msec.). The compressed letters were then spliced together to create a continuous five-letter string devoid of any gaps or pauses. The letter strings were prepared using a Turtle Beach Wave SE wave form editor running on 486 DX computer. The stimuli were recorded on digital audio tape and were played for the subject by means of a Sony Digital Auditory Tape player through a set of Sony stereo headphones. Each letter string was preceded by a warning or cue tone that signaled that the letter string was about to be played. The cue tone was a synthesizer-generated and digitally edited sample of a vibraphone, 1,000 msec. in duration corresponding to middle C on the piano keyboard (frequency 261.3 Hz).

The subject's task (the distraction task) was two-fold. Subjects were asked to press the left button of the mouse that rested on a table before them as soon as they heard the letter *A* in the letter string, and they were also asked to write down, in the proper sequence, the five-letter string they had heard as soon as the last letter was played. (The letters used in the letter strings were chosen from among the letters O, A, L, Q, X, R, Y. Five different combinations were prepared.) The letter strings were presented monaurally to either the left or right ear. On the fourth trial, the critical stimulus was presented to the ear opposite the ear receiving the letter string. The critical stimulus, also synthesizer-generated and digitally edited, was a clarinet tone 200 msec. in duration that was equivalent to an A above middle C (frequency of 440.00 Hz). It was synchronized with the last letter in the letter string. As soon as the subjects completed the distraction task, they were asked whether they had heard anything that had not been present on the previous three trials. If they had, they were asked what it was and in which ear it had been. Any positive answer to this question was taken as evidence of a subject's ability to detect the critical auditory stimulus under conditions of inattention. A fifth trial followed. On this trial a different letter string was played and again the critical stimulus tone was presented to the ear opposite the one receiving the letter string, but subjects now were asked to ignore the letter string and only to report anything else they heard. This was the full attention control trial.

The intensity level of the critical stimulus varied between groups of subjects. For 25 subjects it was 30 decibels lower than the letter strings. For 20 subjects it was 20 decibels lower, for 10 subjects it was 10 decibels lower, and for 15 subjects the critical stimulus was played at the same intensity level as the letter string. A total of 51 subjects were tested, 17 of whom were male and 34 of whom were female. Only data from subjects who reported and correctly located the origin of the critical stimulus on the control trial were included in the study.[2]

Figure 10.1 summarizes the results from the four different testing conditions (i.e., the four different decibel levels). Even though at the lowest intensity level (-30 dB) no subject detected the critical stimulus tone, this cannot be attributed to the intensity of the critical stimulus because all the subjects detected and identified the same tone embedded in an identical aural scene in the control condition. Because the physical features of all the stimuli were identical in both the inattention and the full attention conditions, we can reasonably conclude that the presence or absence of attention accounts for the difference between detection and deafness.

In subsequent experiments we progressively increased the relative intensity of the critical stimulus tone in 10 dB increments. As figure 10.1 indicates, it was not until the tone was set equal to the level of the distraction task that a significant number of subjects began to perceive it. In that case 10 of the 15 subjects (67%) when probed reported hearing something, but only 5 of these 10 subjects correctly identified the tone and its location in the ear opposite the letter sequence. We suspect that asking the question "Did you hear anything other than the sequence of letters during this last trial?" may have led many subjects to respond "yes." So if we assume that only those subjects who were able to correctly locate or say something appropriate about the quality of the tone actually heard it, then the level of inattentional deafness, even at this high level of intensity, increases from 33% to 67%.[3]

Several conclusions can be drawn from these results. The first is that inattention is not only responsible for a failure to detect a visual stimulus, it is also responsible for the failure to hear an above-threshold auditory stimulus. Therefore this aspect of attention, or rather, inattention, is not unique to vision. The second conclusion these results support is that as the intensity of the critical inattention stimulus increases, the chances that it will capture attention increase. Thus intensity seems to play the role in audition that size plays in vision.

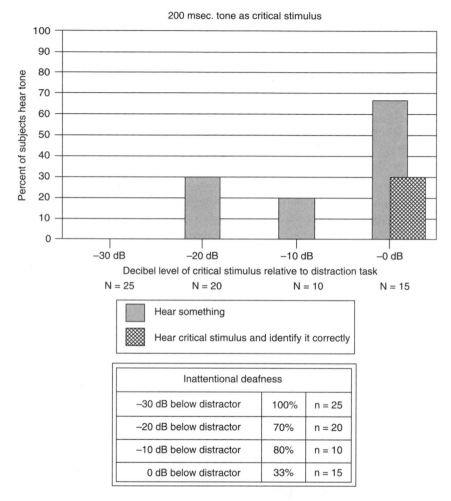

Figure 10.1
Graph of results of inattentional deafness experiments.

Auditory Grouping

In addition to exploring inattentional auditory deafness, we sought to explore the perception of auditory grouping under conditions of inattention in an effort to determine whether it, like visual grouping, also would fail to occur. The distraction task was revised so that it would be less reliant on memory and provide a clear measure of shadowing success. Again we avoided a distraction task that required any audible response.

A series of numbers from one to nine randomly arranged provided the distraction stimulus. The subject's task was to shadow these numbers using the number line on a computer keyboard, that is, the subjects were asked to track the numbers they heard (which were delivered to either the left or right ear) using the number keys on a standard computer keyboard.[4] This not only was an on-line task that ended as soon as the number string terminated (which meant that questions about hearing the critical stimulus could be asked as soon as the trial ended), but also entailed a silent shadowing response that was extremely easy to score because the computer kept track of the subject's responses. It should be noted that silent shadowing, unlike the more commonly used audible shadowing, eliminates any masking of the shadowed stimuli by the shadowing responses.

A digital audio tape was prepared using audio data edited on the Macintosh Audio workstation. The tape consisted of five individual trials, four experimental and one control. Every trial consisted of a preparatory cue tone immediately followed by a randomized sequence of 10 single-digit numbers, each of which were compressed to a length of 250 msec. The numbers were presented in one audio channel only, while the other channel contained a patterned sequence of audio beats recorded at -20 dB relative to the number sequence. On the first three trials there was a steady pattern of evenly spaced single beats. On the fourth (critical) trial the beats were grouped into a staccato pattern of three beats followed by a rest, followed by three more beats and a rest, and so on. On the fifth (control) trial the same triplet beat pattern was repeated.

The subjects sat in front of a standard computer keyboard wearing headphones and were told that they were participating in a reaction time experiment. We explained to them that they would hear a random sequence of digits and that their task was press the corresponding number key on the top row of the keyboard as quickly and as accurately as possible in response to each digit heard. No mention was made of the beats. After the fourth (critical) trial, subjects were asked whether they had heard anything other than the numbers. If a positive response was given, they were asked to describe what they heard and to indicate its location, that is, whether it was on the same channel as the digits or on a different channel. They were also asked whether they heard any other sounds on the prior three trials and, if so, they were asked to describe them as well.

Subjects were then asked to listen to another trial, this time without doing the keyboard task. This was the full attention control trial. Immediately following the end of the number sequence, subjects were again asked whether they heard anything other than the numbers and if so they were asked to describe what they heard and locate it. Finally, the subjects were asked if the sounds they had just heard were present on any of the previous trials. Twenty subjects participated in this experiment.

The subjects performance on the number tracking, distraction task varied between 45% and 70% correct across the four trials with the lowest accuracy rate on the fourth (critical) trial. Thus there was some drop in performance accuracy on the critical inattention trial, but no significant difference in performance between the third and fourth trials (x^2, 1 df = 1.62). This suggests that whatever was causing the decline in performance, it was not likely to have been the introduction of the critical stimulus sequence. As can be seen in figure 10.2a there was clear evidence not only of the failure to hear the grouping, but of inattentional deafness as well. Of the 20 subjects tested, only 7 reported hearing anything other than the number sequence, and of these subjects only 3 correctly located what they heard in the opposite ear. Thus 65% of the subjects showed inattentional deafness and no subject correctly identified the pattern of beats. In contrast all of the 20 subjects heard the beats on the full attention control trial, and only 1 of these subjects failed to identify the pattern as consisting of triplet of

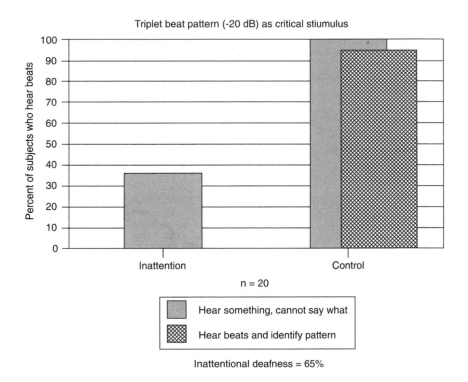

Figure 10.2a
Auditory grouping I.

beats. (The 1 subject who failed to correctly identify the pattern referred to it as one with a polyrhythm.)

The results of this experiment thus provide clear evidence not only of inattentional deafness using an on-line distraction task (thus confirming the results of the earlier experiments) but also confirm the results found with visual grouping under conditions of inattention. Neither auditory nor visual grouping by proximity is perceived under conditions of inattention. These results attest to the generality of the effects of inattention on perception.

Reversing the Order of the Inattention and Control Trials

In an effort to increase the likelihood that the pattern of tones would be heard, and if heard, that their grouping might also be described, we decided to reverse the order of the experimental and control trials as we had done when studying visual grouping even though in that instance it had no facilitating effect. The reasoning here was the same as it had been earlier, namely to prime or alert subjects to the critical stimulus pattern.

> The control trials that now came first consisted of a random sequence of 10 numbers (each 400 msec. in length) presented monaurally (i.e., in one ear only). A steady pattern of beats (actually a digital sample of a bass drum) was presented in the other channel concurrently with the numbers. On the third of these trials, the beats were grouped into a triplet pattern (three beats spaced 50 msec. apart) followed by a 650 msec. space followed by another group of beats, and so on. The subjects were asked to describe what they heard.
>
> Following these three control trials, the subjects were given a new set of instructions. They were told that they were to shadow the numbers they heard on the computer keyboard. There were four trials in the inattention condition instead of the typical three, in order to give subjects an opportunity to master the number tracking task. On the first three of these trials the beats in the unattended ear were evenly spaced while on the fourth they were grouped into the critical triplet pattern. Following the critical trial subjects were immediately asked whether they had heard anything other than the numbers and were again asked to describe it and locate it.

The results are summarized in figure 10.2b. On the control trials all of the 15 subjects correctly identified the critical stimuli as beats, correctly reported whether they were steady or triplets, and correctly located them in the ear opposite the one in which the numbers were heard. Thus it is clear that the beats were clearly audible and the grouping perceptible with attention. The results from the inattention

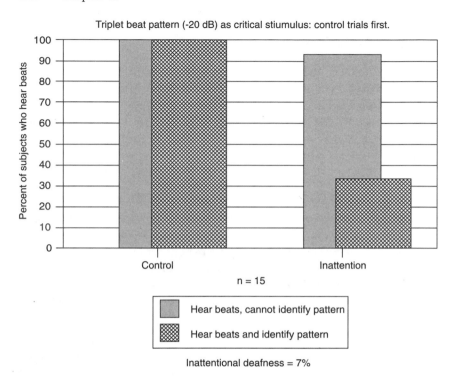

Figure 10.2b
Auditory grouping II.

trials suggest that reversing the order of trials did seem to have some effect. On the critical inattention trial 14 of the 15 subjects (93%) reported hearing the beats and 11 of these subjects correctly located them in the opposite ear. We attribute this significant increase in the number of subjects perceiving the beats on the unattended channel to the fact that subjects were alerted to their presence on the preliminary control trials and so were more likely to expect that they would again accompany the number sequences. However, despite the fact that most of the subjects now perceived the elements making up the grouping pattern, only 5 of the 14 subjects who heard them succeeded in correctly describing their grouping. These results therefore again mirror those obtained in the visual grouping experiments where most subjects also failed to perceive the grouping despite the fact that they perceived the elements making up these patterns. Thus the evidence supports the conclusion that grouping is not consciously perceived without attention.

Touch[5]

Having found evidence of inattentional deafness, we attempted to explore the possibility that inattention might also lead to a failure to perceive an above threshold tactile stimulus. The question we wished to try to answer was whether subjects would fail to detect the fact that they had been touched by something, if the touch event occurred while they were attending to some other tactile task.

Once again a new distraction task and critical stimulus were needed. The distraction task selected was one in which the subjects were asked to identify a letter which was drawn on their forearm by one of the experimenters.

> When the subjects arrived in the laboratory, the nature of the task was explained to them. We then asked the subjects if we could place cuffs on both their left and right forearms. These cuffs each had a square opening, 3.72 cm on a side, which they were told was the area in which the letters would be written. The cuffs were adjusted so that the window exposed an area above the wrist on the underside of the forearm. At this point the experimenter drew the letter *B* in the aperture in full view of the subject. A small, blunt-nosed plastic stylus was used to draw the letters. Subjects were asked if they were comfortable with the pressure of the stylus and if they could identify the letter. If the subject complained about the stylus pressure or failed to identify the letter *B* the experimenter repeated the demonstration, if necessary with reduced pressure to the skin. No subject failed to identify the letter by the second demonstration. At this point subjects were asked to put their arms through the openings in a large vertical screen that rested on a table in front of them that prevented them from seeing either their own or the experimenter's arms. They were asked to rest their arms on the table with palm sides up allowing access to the openings in the cuffs. Subjects were told that every letter, like the demonstration letter, would be written so that it faced the subject, that is, it was in the proper orientation for reading. Actual trials now began. The writing of each letter took approximately 0.2 sec. Letters were drawn on either the left or right forearm and this varied from trial to trial. If the subjects indicated they could not identify the letter that was drawn, they were asked to select it from a choice sheet which contained a series of 11 letters, one of which was the correct one, (S, V, J, T, W, N, O, L, M, Z, C). These were the group of letters used in the distraction task. On the third trial, a droplet of room-temperature water was applied by means of a hand-held eye dropper to the forearm through the window in the cuff on the arm opposite the one on which the letter was being written. Following this trial, the critical inattention trial, subjects were asked if they felt anything different on this trial, and if so where and what. The responses to these questions served as the index of inattentional tactile insensitivity. These trials were

then followed by a second triad of trials, the divided attention trials. They were identical to the first trials, that is, letters were drawn on the forearm and on the third of these trials the critical droplet of water stimulus was again presented. Prior to the divided attention trial, subjects were asked to report the letter as well as anything else they felt. The final trials were the full attention control trials. The critical stimulus was again presented on the third trial, but on these trials subjects were told to ignore the letter writing on their arm and simply report anything else they felt. Fifteen subjects were tested.

The subjects did quite well in identifying the letters. On the first trial 73% correctly identified the letter drawn and on the second and third trials 87% did so. Thus the level of difficulty of the distraction task was comparable to the cross task used in the visual experiments. Only 6 of the subjects (40%) reported feeling anything other than the pressure caused by the drawing of the letter following the critical trial, whereas 13 of the 15 subjects (87%) did so on the full attention, control trial. Eleven of the subjects (73%) reported the critical stimulus on the divided attention trial. Since 9 subjects (60%) failed to detect the drop of water to their arm on the critical inattention trial, this would seem to be evidence of inattentional tactile insensitivity and analogous to the effect of inattention on visual perception. However, given the rather crude equipment and procedure, these results are at best only suggestive. We attempted two other experiments to explore the effects of inattention on touch sensitivity, but neither experiment was less crude than the experiment just described.

The next experiment was a version of the first touch experiment except that a new critical stimulus was introduced. Instead of a droplet of water, the critical stimulus was a puff of air to the forearm that was delivered to the arm opposite that on which a letter that the subject had to identify was being drawn. The air puff was produced by manually squeezing the bulb of an infant nasal aspirator during the period in which the letter was being written.

Instead of three triads of trials, there were six trials in both the inattention and divided attention conditions and two trials in the full attention control condition. The critical puff of air stimulus was presented on the last trial in each of the three conditions. Following the critical inattention trial, subjects were asked if they had felt anything other than the drawing of the letter. In the inattention and full attention conditions letters were drawn on the subject's right arm and the critical stimulus was delivered to the left arm. Arms were reversed for the divided attention condition. Ten subjects were tested.

Subjects performed less well on the distraction task than they had in the previous experiment. On the critical inattention trial only 40%

of the subjects correctly identified the letter written on their arm. This might have been because the letter G—which was the letter presented on this trial—was more difficult to decipher than, for example, the letter R, which 80% of the subjects identified correctly on trial three. Of more interest is the fact that only 1 of the 10 subjects reported feeling the critical stimulus in the inattention condition and thus inattentional tactile insensitivity was 90%. Fifty percent of the subjects reported the puff of air on the critical divided attention trial and all but 1 (90%) did so and the full attention control trial. Thus these results also suggest that inattention can eliminate the conscious experience of an above-threshold tactile stimulus. This insensitivity may be a partial analogue of the frequently reported anecdotal experience of unawareness of severe pain under conditions of high stress, like those that occur in times of war.

Conclusion

The preliminary findings reported in this chapter suggest that there is neither tactile nor auditory perception in the absence of attention. This is not only consistent with the affect of inattention on visual perception, but also seems to conform to our everyday experiences in which while extremely absorbed in something we are sometimes deaf to sounds and fail to respond to a touch. Of course, more rigorous experiments must be done before any firm conclusions can be drawn. However, if these preliminary findings are confirmed, it would be interesting to look at the question of whether evidence of unconscious perception can also be found in these sensory modalities.

In the last chapter we review the results of our research and attempt to provide a general account of them.

Chapter 11
Some Conclusions

Attention and Conscious Perception

The preceding chapters have described what we did and what we found in our exploration of the effects of inattention on perception. Although the research will surely continue beyond the writing of this book in an attempt to answer the many remaining questions, we have learned enough to draw some tentative conclusions. Having started with what appeared to be the self-evident assumption—that some percept, if only a minimal one, must exist prior to the engagement of attention, because attention requires an object—we arrived at what seems to be exactly the opposite conclusion. Our results drew us ineluctably to the view that there is no conscious perception at all in the absence of attention and therefore no perceptual object can exist preattentively. This, on the face of it, seems impossible.

The contradiction between what we assumed at the outset and what we came to believe is more apparent than real, however, and rests on what we mean by the term *perception*. If we take perception to refer to the *conscious awareness* of some object or event, as we did at the beginning of this project, then indeed there is a contradiction between the assumption we began with and the conclusion we have been led to. But, if we extend the meaning of the term *perception* to include the *unconscious encoding of sensory stimulation*, the contradiction dissolves. In other words, once the distinction between explicit or conscious perception and implicit or unconscious perception is drawn, the apparent contradiction disappears. It is not that no perceptual object can exist preattentively, but only that no conscious perceptual object can do so. Our results have led us to the conclusion that there is no explicit perceptual object prior to the engagement of attention, and that the object to which attention is directed or by which it is captured is an object of implicit—not explicit or conscious—perception.[1]

We have not rejected the idea that attention demands an object, nor that it must exist prior to the engagement of attention, for this seems to be dictated by the inherently intentional nature of attention. Rather, what we have rejected is the idea that the object of attention is one that is consciously perceived. We now believe that the perceptual object to which attention is directed exists at the level of implicit, unconscious perception, and only if attention is engaged by this object does it become an object of conscious perception. Moreover, the object to which attention is directed is not a single feature, but is a complex and meaningful object or scene.

Attentional Capture

If attention is necessary for perception, then an object presented under conditions of inattention necessarily must capture attention to be perceived. It therefore follows that anything increasing the likelihood that an object will capture attention should increase the likelihood that the object will be detected. (*Detection* refers to the conscious awareness of the presence of some object.) One such factor is the position of the object relative to the spatial focus of attention. If, like Posner (1980), we think of spatial attention metaphorically as a spotlight, then an object falling within its beam should be less likely to remain "in the dark" (be unilluminated), and therefore should be more likely to be consciously perceived. In contrast, any stimulus located outside the zone of attention should be less likely to capture attention and consequently should be less likely to be consciously perceived. This proposition was strongly supported by data from many experiments including those in which varying amounts of IB were obtained as a function of the relative size of the distraction stimulus and its location relative to the critical inattention stimulus (chapter 4).

Inhibition of Attention

The close causal connection between attentional capture and conscious perception is also revealed by all the findings demonstrating that anything that causes attention to be inhibited at the location in which the critical stimulus appears predictably increases the likelihood of IB.

Meaningfulness and Attention

Not only did we find that the location of an object affects the probability of its capturing attention and therefore of being detected under conditions of inattention, we also found that other factors play an important role in this process. The most important of these is the meaningfulness or signal value of the stimulus. Thus, one's own name almost always will be seen under conditions of inattention while some very familiar words will not be.

That meaning should play this role is surprising only if you hold the belief that simple, low-level features of stimuli are perceived preattentively and therefore provide the basis for the capture of attention that is essential to the construction of objects from preattentively perceived features (Treisman and Gelade 1980). If, however, high-level, complex stimuli are unconsciously perceived without attention (i.e., preattentively), then it seems virtually self-evident that stimuli that are highly meaningful or important are far more likely to capture attention than meaningless or unimportant ones. Once again, to quote William James: "A faint tap per se is not an interesting sound; it may well escape being discriminated from the general rumor of the world. But when it is a signal, as that of a lover on the window-pane, it will hardly go unperceived" (1981, 395).

Early and Late Selection

As we have already stated, if nothing is seen without attention then factors that maximize attentional capture should increase the probability that an object will be perceived under conditions of inattention. This conclusion is well supported by the data. An obvious next question is when in the sequence of events leading to conscious perception is attention likely to be captured. This question was explored in chapter 7. In principle, there seem to be three possible answers, all of which have been proposed and defended by one or another investigator over the last 30 years. Either attention is captured early by the products of a low-level analysis of the input (e.g., Broadbent 1958), later, after some or all of the processing is complete (e.g., Deutsch and Deutsch 1963; Logan 1988), or attention is captured either at an early *or* late stage of processing, depending on some specifiable other factor(s) (e.g., Treisman and DeSchepper 1994; Lavie and Tsal 1994).

Late Selection

Without restating all the reasons why we were led to the conclusion that capture is likely to occur later rather than earlier (see chapters 5 and 6), we recall that very small modifications in meaningful stimuli that were found to capture attention and therefore to be seen under conditions of inattention caused these stimuli to go undetected. We take this to mean that prior to the capture of attention, the processing of at least all the formal perceptual qualities, including the organization of the input, must be complete and this necessarily implicates late rather than early selection. Furthermore, the fact that stimulus meaning seems to play a role in the capture of attention seems to implicate a high level of stimulus processing and late selection.

Familiarity

Had we succeeded in finding unequivocal evidence of the role of familiarity in the capture of attention, it would have been possible to minimize reliance on the notion of meaningfulness, or salience and late selection as an explanatory concept. However, as the data reported in chapter 6 reveal, we failed to do so, even though we consistently found that words that are low in meaningfulness but are among the most frequent in the language generated less IB than their less familiar but more meaningful counterparts. *The,* was detected by more subjects than *Tie* and *And* was detected by more subjects than *Ant.* However, neither of these differences were statistically significant, even though in the first case (*The* versus *Tie*) the data derive from the testing of 130 subjects and the second derives from the testing of 40 subjects. It is of some interest to note however, that a comparison of the overall frequency of detection arrived at by combining the results obtained with the two familiar words (69%) with those obtained by combining the results from testing with the two less frequently encountered words (43%) does yield a significant difference ($x^2 \, df1 = 8 \, p < .01$) suggesting that familiarity may play some, even if not central role in the capture of attention. Were this so, it would require some modification of our interpretation. However, whether it is remains to be determined.

Availability

Despite our failure to find unequivocal evidence of the role of familiarity in the capture of attention, the suggestion that it may play some role led to speculation about how it might operate. One possible way of accounting for it might be in terms of availability. There is considerable evidence that the various contents of mind (i.e., contents stored in memory) are more or less available, and are more or less easily accessed, and that there are many factors that can govern their availability. Among them are the strength of an item or the association between items, recency, and saliency (in the sense we have been using the term, for example, to account for the perception of one's own name). Priming clearly increases availability. In fact, making something highly available is close to a definition of priming. It also may be that words in general are more available than other mental contents such as the representations of object and shapes, although why this might be so is by no means obvious. Given our experimental paradigm in which a stimulus is presented without voluntary or anticipatory attention to it, whether it is perceived and recognized might have something to do with its availability. Certainly this is true of recognition per se. For pure perception, (i.e., perception of object properties such as shape, size, color, depth, and so forth), one would think that, to the extent that such perceptions are bottom-up, the availability of a mental content or trace would be irrelevant. Generally that is true. However, given the nature of our experimental procedure, the critical stimulus is registered and, judging by our results of priming of stem completion, as well as the Moore and Egeth (1997) report suggesting the implicit perception of grouping under conditions of inattention, it is deeply processed and encoded.

The question then is whether it will break through into conscious awareness. At this point, availability may be relevant. If so, salient items, very familiar items, words as compared to images of objects, their recency of encounter, and possibly other factors that play a significant role in the outcome may do so because of their availability. Therefore, it is at least worth considering whether availability might be the superordinate factor that determines whether a stimulus is consciously perceived when it is presented under conditions of inattention.

There are, however, several reasons for doubting that the concept of availability can account for these data. First, in several experiments that are relevant to the question of whether recency reduces IB, the evidence clearly indicated that it usually did not. Although the effects of recency were not systematically explored, several experiments did examine whether presenting the critical stimulus to the subjects prior to the inattention trials decreased the frequency of IB for that stimulus. With one possible exception, the amount of IB obtained following the repeated exposure to the critical stimulus was not less than the amount of IB for the same stimulus when the subjects were given no prior exposure to it. In other words, there was no effect of recency, and therefore no evidence that the availability of an encoded stimulus plays a significant independent role in IB. Similarly, preexposure to the grouping patterns that were then presented under conditions of inattention produced no increase in the perception of grouping.

The second reason for doubting whether the concept of availability is to be preferred over that of meaningfulness or salience as an explanation for why a stimulus is consciously perceived when it occurs under conditions of inattention is that there is no clear reason why meaningful words should be more available than highly familiar shapes. For this reason any advantage that might appear to be gained by substituting the one concept for the other may be more apparent than real.

What Is Meaningful?

There are also problems, however, with the idea that meaningfulness governs whether a stimulus will be consciously perceived under conditions of inattention. First, there is at least one case in which it is not clear that the version of a stimulus that captures attention and is perceived under conditions of inattention is more meaningful than the versions that do not. One troublesome case is the happy face icon. As we reported in chapter 6, there is clear evidence that it is very likely to be perceived under conditions of inattention, whereas the neutral and sad face icons are not. The problem here is that it is far from clear that the happy face carries any more meaning than either of the other two versions.

Second, IB was never complete even in experiments in which the critical stimulus was relatively meaningless, for example, when it was a simple geometric shape. Thus, either it is necessary to argue that these cases of perception under conditions of inattention are due to some idiosyncratic meaning the stimulus may have for the observer, which is both circular and unlikely, or other stimulus attributes must play a role in the capture of attention. Of course, in experiments in which the critical stimulus is located within the zone of attention, the fact that it is seen even though it is relatively meaningless is probably due to its location. The more difficult cases are those in which a relatively meaningless stimulus located outside the zone of attention is perceived, but these cases are far less frequent, and once they are distinguished from cases of false positive reports discussed later in this chapter, their number decreases even further. Nevertheless, insofar as there are true cases of the perception of "meaningless" stimuli located outside the zone of attention under conditions of inattention, some factor(s) other than meaningfulness must be at play. Although availability per se does not seem likely to be one of them, familiarity which increases availability might be, since there is some, albeit weak, evidence of its role.

Priming

To return to the proposal that attentional selection occurs later rather than earlier in the course of processing sensory input, additional and persuasive support comes from the evidence of priming by stimuli to which subjects are inattentionally blind reviewed in chapter 8. The clearest evidence that attentional selection is late and occurs at the level of semantic analysis is that inattentionally blind subjects choose a picture from an array representing the unseen word significantly more often than those not presented or primed with it. This would not have occurred unless the unseen word had been implicitly perceived and its meaning encoded.

The demonstration of semantic priming by stimuli that were not consciously perceived is not only evidence for a late selection theory of selective attention, it is also evidence that raises questions about the view that implicit perception is limited to the formal aspects of stimuli. This view is clearly expressed in the following quotation.

> Subliminal perception appears to be analytically limited, in that there are restrictions on the amount of processing subliminal stimuli can receive (Greenwald 1992), and on the amount of information that can be extracted from them. . . . Subliminal priming is often limited to repetition effects, which can be mediated by perceptual rather than semantic representations (Dorfman, Shames and Kihlstrom 1996, 262).

Of course, the reader will recall that not all our attempts to find evidence of priming by unseen stimuli were successful, and we do not yet know why. Additionally, a long series of experiments on priming reported in chapter 8 yielded results that, although consistent with the view that unconscious priming occurred, are also consistent with the growing sense that the distinction between implicit and explicit memory or perception may not be as clear as it previously had seemed to be. On the face of it, the distinction between conscious and unconscious perception seems deceptively straightforward. A perception is considered unconscious if a subject reports no awareness of it but there is indirect evidence that it occurred, and conscious if subjects can recall or recognize it. In our experiments evidence of implicit perception was afforded by stem completions or picture choices following presentation of words as primes. Evidence of conscious perception was provided first and foremost by subjective reports of having seen the stimulus in question, but we also considered correct responses on recognition tests that were announced to contain the unseen critical stimulus as evidence as well. So if after giving a negative response to the question about whether they had seen anything other than the distraction stimulus, subjects nevertheless selected the correct stimulus from the choice array that they were told included the stimulus that had been there, this too was counted as evidence of explicit rather than implicit perception. On the other hand, if inattentionally blind observers selected a picture that correctly depicted a verbal critical stimulus from a choice array without being told that this array included a version of what had been presented (they were simply asked to choose one item from an array without being given a reason to do so) this was counted as evidence of unconscious perception.

The troubling aspect of this is that this seemingly small difference in procedure in this case is the basis for distinguishing conscious from unconscious perception. But although this is troubling, a look at the summary of results presented in table 11.1 appears to support this distinction as long as we continue to assume that the presence of a mask interrupts explicit perception without affecting implicit perception. The table reveals that the frequency of stem completion or of choosing the appropriate picture (both assumed to be indicators of implicit perception) is clearly unaffected by the mask. In contrast, selection from a choice array that subjects are told includes the unseen stimulus (assumed to be an indicator of explicit perception) drops from an average frequency of 49.5% to an average of 14% when a mask is introduced. However, whether or not this analysis of the priming results is correct, there seems to be no question that high-level priming by unseen stimuli occurs. Therefore, there is substantial reason to believe that stimuli that are not consciously perceived are deeply processed and encoded, and this is consistent with a late selection model of attention.

It is more than a little puzzling that so much of what is not consciously perceived is nevertheless deeply processed and encoded—as seems clear from the proliferating evidence. Were everything in our visual fields to be stored in memory, the result would be almost unimaginable clutter, so it seems likely that there must be some limits on what stimuli can leave enduring traces. Perhaps only those objects that fall within a certain area of the retina close to the fovea are deeply processed and stored. Perhaps there are other limiting criteria and what they are ought to become a subject for future research. But even with limits, the sheer quantity of information not directly accessible

Table 11.1
Summary of results obtained with and without a mask testing with stem completion, picture array and word recognition array.

Mask	Stem completion (implicit index)	Picture choice (implicit index)	Word choice (explicit index)
Present	36%	42%	14%
Absent	29%	48%	50%

and not previously consciously perceived that seems to be maintained in memory is still far too large not to subserve some important adaptive purpose. One possible purpose it may serve is to guide motor responding that would be consistent with the view (repeatedly proposed) that there are two visual systems (Trevarthan 1968; Schneider 1969; Ungerleider and Mishkin, 1982; Goodale and Milner, 1992; Milner and Goodale, 1995). For example Milner and Goodale (1995) propose that one of these two systems is concerned with perceptual representation whereas the other is concerned with visuomotor control. A piece of supporting evidence for this view derives from the finding that eye movements are not governed by the consciously perceived position or motion of a stimulus but rather by its retinally defined location or motion which is not consciously perceived when the two are discrepant (e.g. Wong and Mack, 1981; Bridgeman, Kirch, and Sperling, 1981). If not consciously perceived yet deeply processed and encoded input were to be implicated in the control of motor behavior, its presence and its quantity would be far less puzzling.

Early Selection and Stimulus Size

Even though much of the evidence we have accumulated is consistent with an account of attention that places its engagement late in the processing hierarchy, we did find one exception. This is the evidence confirming that the size of a visual stimulus and the loudness of an auditory one affect their detectability under conditions of inattention. Of course, had we found clear evidence that the postconstancy aspect rather than the retinal aspect of stimulus size was the responsible agent here (we did not investigate the analogous question concerning loudness), this too would have been more consistent with a late selection model of attention, and would have made the explanatory story simpler. In fact, however, the results of the relevant experiment were somewhat equivocal and seemed to reveal the influence of *both* the retinal and postconstancy aspects of stimulus size although the weight of the evidence pointed toward the importance of retinal size.[2] In addition, we have clear evidence that the presence of large displays of multiple elements such as the displays used in the experiments on grouping, pop out, and large realistic scenes also are invariably detected under conditions of inattention even though grouping and pop out are not. It therefore seems that in addition to the meaning and possible familiarity of a stimulus, its size or the number of elements it contains and the area they cover or the loudness of an auditory stimulus also may affect its perception under conditions of inattention.

To the extent that it is the retinal size of these multielement displays and the retinal size of a stimulus that subtends a visual angle larger than about 1 degree that is responsible for their detection under conditions of inattention, attentional selection would appear to occur early rather than late. However, even if, in the end, it turns out to be retinal size that is the decisive factor in the capture of attention, it might be possible to argue as we suggested earlier that this too is an instance in which meaning determines perception. This possibility arises from the fact that it is retinal size alone that is responsible for the perception of looming, that is, the perception that a stimulus that is rapidly increasing in retinal size is approaching, even though the available distance information indicates that its position is unchanged. Because even very young infants respond with fear and displeasure to a looming stimulus (Bower 1967) it seems possible that we may be genetically programmed to treat retinal size as important and as something to which attention should be directed.

However, if this is not the case, then there seems to be evidence of both early and late selection which suggest that the point at which attention is engaged may not be irreversibly set, but may be variable and depend on the nature of the stimulus.[3] If there is a single inattention stimulus and it is large, or it is a multielement display covering a large area, it will capture attention and probably do so at an early processing stage. If, however, the critical stimulus is neither large nor covers a large part of the viewing area, unconscious processing may proceed to a higher level, and this level must be sufficiently late to permit complete perceptual processing and, it would seem, the assessment of meaning as well. For these stimuli the possibility of capture by attention arises only later and seems to be determined by the meaningfulness of the stimulus.

Another Problem

This analysis, which is not distinguished by its simplicity, entails a puzzle. If a large object or display is seen under conditions of inattention (which happens, according to our analysis, because its size captures attention) why do we fail to perceive grouping, pop out, or shape in these displays? Once attention is captured it might seem reasonable to expect that other aspects of the stimulus would be perceived as well. However, the empirical evidence clearly indicates that this does not happen. Perhaps the reason is that, although the size or extent of a stimulus has the power to capture attention, its other attributes do not and are therefore not available to conscious perception. If we were to assume that these other aspects of the stimuli have no particular salience or meaning to the observer and by themselves would fail to capture attention, then our analysis would predict that they would not be consciously seen. On this analysis, the reason why grouping, for example, may not be consciously perceived, even though subjects perceive the presence of the stimuli making up the grouping pattern, is because the grouping is not particularly meaningful. If conscious perception is limited to stimuli with high signal value under conditions of inattention, then this could explain why, even though the presence of the grouping stimulus is detected, its grouping is not consciously perceived. This would imply that the capture of attention is not an all-or-none phenomenon, and that some properties of a stimulus can capture attention without bringing along other properties of the same stimulus.

This analysis is borne out by the results of the research reported by Moore and Egeth (1997), which is described in some detail at the close of chapter 8. These researchers found clear evidence of the *implicit* perception of grouping under conditions of inattention resembling ours, even though subjects had no conscious perception of it.

The view that only what has salience and meaning to an observer is likely to be consciously perceived under conditions of inattention also is consistent with the findings described in chapter 7 that, when large, complex, and meaningful stimuli serve as the critical stimuli under conditions of inattention, their presence is not only detected, but their contents are identified as well. When the critical stimuli were photographs of real scenes (see figures 7.2 and 7.3), subjects not only invariably detected them, which was predictable from their size alone, but generally were able to describe them as well. If, as we have argued, the size of these stimuli accounts for the fact that they are invariably detected under conditions of inattention, the fact that they are representations of meaningful scenes probably accounts for why much of their content generally is explicitly perceived.

Evidence of False Positive Responses

It seems clear that the weight of the accumulated evidence points to the importance of stimulus meaning and salience in the capture of attention. However, there remains at least one other troubling aspect of our results not yet discussed that might be viewed as counterevidence to the proposition that stimuli presented under conditions of inattention are processed and encoded, but only those which are highly meaningful or salient pass from the level of implicit to that of explicit perception. In many of our experiments we regularly encountered instances in which following the critical inattention trial subjects reported having seen something that they had not seen on previous trials, but were completely unable to indicate either where or what it had been. We did not classify these responses as evidence of inattentional blindness because we thought it was possible that these subjects actually might have detected the presence of the critical stimulus even though they could in no way describe it. If these responses actually are instances of detection without identification, that is, of perceiving that something is there without perceiving what or where it is, they present a problem.

Were these anomalous instances to be true instances of detection without identification, they would appear to demonstrate that in some cases the mere presence of a stimulus, independent of its meaning, succeeds in capturing attention. In other words, were these responses true instances of detection without identification, they would seem to stand as evidence that some stimuli may capture attention for reasons other than their importance to the observer, and therefore may do so at some earlier stage before much processing has occurred.[4]

There is, however, another way of viewing these troubling cases. It is at least possible that these cases are not evidence of detection at all, but rather are instances of false positive responses. That is, in answer to the experimenter's question following the critical inattention trial about whether anything had been seen other than the distraction stimulus, some observers might have answered "yes" on the assumption that there must have been something else present or we would not have asked about it. Thus to avoid appearing either dumb or blind, these subjects may have answered yes to our question even though they actually had not seen anything else. If this were to turn out to be the correct interpretation of these responses, then, of course, they should not have been classified as cases of detection without awareness, but rather as additional cases of inattentional blindness, and this reclassification would have at least two important consequences. First, it would increase our estimates of the frequency of inattentional blindness and indicate that the phenomenon is even more pervasive than our reporting of the data throughout this book has indicated. Second, were these responses found to be false positives, one potential source of evidence standing against the proposed account of perception under conditions of inattention would be eliminated.

Because of the important theoretical implications of these cases, it was imperative to try to determine which account of them was correct. Were they really cases of pure detection under conditions of inattention or of inattentional blindness masquerading as detection without identification? Fortunately, there was a fairly straightforward procedure available for investigating this question. By obtaining an estimate of the frequency with which subjects are likely to report that they had seen something new on the critical inattention trial when *no* critical stimulus is actually presented, we can obtain an estimate of the frequency of false positive responses, which then can be used to interpret the cases of detection without identification that occurred in experiments in which a critical stimulus actually had been present.

It seemed safe to assume that if we were to obtain significant evidence of false positive responses under these conditions, and if the frequency of these responses was not different from the frequency with which subjects reported detecting something without being able to either locate or identify it in any way in our standard experiments involving the actual presentation of a critical stimulus, then there would be valid grounds for reclassifying these responses as cases of IB rather than of anomalous cases of detection without identification. We therefore set about determining the base rate of false positive responses when no critical stimulus is presented.

The experiments we did were versions of our standard inattention experiment except that on the critical trial no critical stimulus was presented along with the distraction stimulus. In the first of these experiments[5] 24 subjects were tested. The standard crosses served as the distraction stimuli and were centered at fixation. Following the fourth trial which, in the standard Berkeley version of our experiments, would have been the critical inattention trial, as soon as the subjects had reported the longer arm of the cross they were asked whether they had seen anything other than the cross and if so, where and what it was. Six of the subjects (25%) reported that they had seen something else, although, not surprisingly, they could not say what it was. In contrast, on the full attention control trial in which an actual critical stimulus (a small black square) was presented in one of the four standard locations within a quadrant of the cross centered at fixation, all subjects reported seeing it.[6]

In the next experiment,[7] in which 20 subjects were tested, the procedure was identical to the procedure used in the New School laboratory, that is, in each of the three testing conditions—inattention, divided and full attention—there were three trials, but unlike the standard experiments, no critical stimulus was presented in any condition. Nevertheless, following the third trial in each condition, subjects were asked if they had seen anything other than the distraction stimulus. The standard cross task was used with one of the standard set of larger crosses centered at fixation serving as the distraction stimulus. This allowed us to assess the frequency of false positive responses when subjects were actually told to look for and report anything other than the cross that they saw.

Seven of the subjects reported seeing something other than the cross following the third trial in the inattention condition (35%) and 4 of these subjects were unable to say anything about what they had seen. Of the 3 remaining subjects in this group, one reported seeing a red dot but could not locate it. One claimed to have seen the letter p, and one reported seeing something in the upper right side of the screen. Obviously nothing had been present that corresponded to these descriptions. Interestingly, 6 subjects even reported seeing something in addition to the cross on the critical divided attention trial, and the same number did so on following the third trial in the full attention control condition as well. The fact that there were almost the same number of false positive responses in all three conditions seems strong evidence of the tendency on the part of some of the subjects to give a positive answer to the experimenter's question about whether anything besides the cross was seen even when this question was not posed until *after* the critical trial, as it was in the trial corresponding to the critical inattention trial. Thus, at least when the distraction crosses are presented at fixation, reports of what looked like cases of *pure detection* (reports of having seen something which were unaccompanied by correct information about either location or identification) in our standard experiments were more likely to have been actual instances of inattentional blindness masquerading as cases of pure detection.

Because a substantial number of the experiments in which cases of detection without identification occurred were experiments in which the distraction crosses were presented in the parafovea and the critical stimulus had been presented at fixation, it seemed important to evaluate the frequency of false positive responding in this condition as well. Thus, in every trial in the final experiment in this series one of the larger set of crosses was centered in one of the four typical parafoveal locations around fixation and again, no critical stimulus was presented on any trial. Another group of 20 subjects were tested.

Four subjects reported having seen something other than the cross on what would have been the last trial of the inattention and divided attention conditions (20%) and 5 of the subjects (25%) reported doing so following the third trial on the full attention control trial, although understandably none of the subjects in any of the conditions could say much about what they had seen.[8] These three experiments thus provide clear evidence of a tendency on the part of roughly 25% of the subjects to give false positive responses, and suggests that the reports of pure detection that occurred in our standard inattention experiment should be reclassified as additional instances of IB. This, of course, means that we have consistently underestimated the amount of IB that we obtained because cases of pure detection occurred in most of our standard experiments, although rarely in experiments in which a meaningful stimulus such as a happy face or the subject's own name served as the critical stimulus.[9] Clear evidence of a tendency to give false positive responses eliminates the need to provide some other account of what seemed to be cases of detection without identification since these anomalous instances now only seem to be additional cases of IB.

Preattentive Perception

If, as we believe, nothing is explicitly perceived without attention, then all the processes that enable perception to occur (including grouping and constancy operations) must operate without the benefit of attention. This rules out the possibility of conscious preattentive perception and is at odds with the claim that these kinds of perceptions do occur (e.g., Treisman 1980; Julesz 1984). However, it does not necessarily conflict with the related claim that some aspects of visual search are based on parallel while others are based on sequential processing, even though this distinction has been understood to be synonymous with the distinction between preattentive and attentive perception. (See, for example, Treisman and Gelade 1980.) Nevertheless, all the work on visual search that has shown that rapid search is by no means restricted to search for so-called single primitive features[10] with which our own finding that one's name pops out is completely consistent, undermines the usefulness of this distinction. An argument to this effect is persuasively made by Nakayama and Joseph in an article that adopts a view virtually identical to the one presented here, namely that "almost all of what we consider to be vision cannot occur without attention" (1997, 8). They continue:

> Early vision theories of visual search have suggested two types of vision, the one not requiring attention and responsible for "parallel" visual search, the other requiring attention and mediating more deliberate serial search. So far we have presented three reasons to reject this early vision metaphor. First, the number of primitive features emerging is too large. With such a list, it becomes difficult to imagine how all such patterns, including letters of the alphabet, are reproduced in all positions at all spatial scales in early cortical maps. Second, there is psychological

evidence that we do not respond to elementary features at all in rapid vision, that visual search works on a representation that is of higher order. Visual search has no access to those putative earlier representations. Third, we have provided evidence that even the easiest, so-called "parallel" visual tasks require attention (15).

Although the claim that there is no perception without attention has no logically necessary consequences for the claim that visual processing is either parallel or sequential, it does deny the claim that visual search operates in the absence of attention and denies the possibility of preattentive perception. Moreover, our data has not only led us to reject the concept of preattentive vision and preattentive search, but has also led us to reject the related notion that its products form the basis for the engagement of focused attention. Rather, the argument made here is that attention is not only necessary for perception but its engagement is a function of the meaning of the stimulus. On this view conscious perception is by definition a top-down process.

We have one last comment about the question of why most of the stimuli that have been found to pop out in visual search experiments are not seen under conditions of inattention. One possible reason for this lies in the role of attention in these different paradigms. In visual search experiments the observers are always asked to look for a particular target, which immediately bestows importance on it and turns it into the object of attention. In contrast, in inattention experiments the only object of attention designated by the instructions to the observers is the distraction stimulus, so if anything other than the distraction stimulus is to be consciously perceived, it must capture attention, assuming, as we do, that attention is necessary for perception. Thus it makes sense that the target in search experiments will be seen because it is the object of attention, whereas only those objects capable of capturing attention will be seen in inattention experiments.

Attention: Voluntary and Captured

It undoubtedly seems odd that throughout this book, which concerns the ways in which inattention affects perception, we have offered no general definition of attention. Rather, we have proceeded as if the meaning of the term was transparent which, of course, it is not, even though James wrote in a now famous passage that "Everyone knows what attention is. It is the taking possession of the mind in clear and vivid form of one out of what seem several simultaneously possible objects or trains of thought" (381). Instead we have relied on an operational definition of *inattention*. For a subject to qualify as inattentive to a particular visual stimulus, that subject must be looking in the general area in which it appears, but must have no expectation that it will appear nor any intention regarding it. (Research described in chapter 9 suggests that this absence of expectation and intention alone may be sufficient conditions for a state of inattention. Therefore, it may not be necessary for the subject's attention to be engaged by some other attentionally demanding task, although when it is there is a greater probability that the anticipated stimulus in question will not be explicitly perceived.)[11]

If the state of inattention to something is defined as the state that occurs when there is no expectation and intention toward a particular object, it follows that a state of attention exists when intention and expectation are directed to that object, at least if we are referring to a state of voluntary attention, now also referred to as *endogenous* attention, which is characterized by a preexisting state of intention and expectation towards the object. The state of voluntary attention is one in which one has issued instructions to oneself to process some object or event. For example, in listening or reading, the self-directed instruction is to follow the meaning of a sequence of words. Voluntary attention is not only the instruction to process, but the act of doing it as well.

This characterization, however, does not cover instances of captured attention, also referred to as states of *exogenous* attention. By their very nature, these are states in which there is neither the expectation of, nor preexisting intention toward a particular object or event. So, although inattention is the polar opposite of voluntary attention, captured attention lies somewhere in between. In the case of captured attention, expectation is absent, and if an intention is aroused it is aroused after, rather than before the stimulus has become an object of attention.

Earlier we speculated that conscious perception based on captured attention may differ qualitatively from perception associated with voluntary attention, and although the work reported in this book is not directly relevant to this issue, there is some suggestion that this may be the case. For example, Ethan Newby working in the Rock laboratory at Berkeley found that the precision with which subjects localize a stimulus is greater when that stimulus is presented under conditions of full attention than when it is presented under conditions of inattention and captures attention.

If voluntary attention entails intention and expectation and captured attention does not, there must be some process they both share that qualifies them as attentional states. One shared characteristic is that both modes of attention bestow priority with respect to conscious perception. Objects or events that engage our attention are those present in awareness. It is as if attention, whether voluntary or involuntary, provides the certification that permits an implicit percept to pass through the barrier separating implicit from explicit perception.

Other Categories of Attention

There, of course, are other ways of categorizing modes of attention. For example the term *selective attention* refers to its filtering aspect that serves to reduce the enormous amount of information impinging on the senses at any given moment and without which we would suffer continuously from sensory information overload. The term *selective attention* by definition therefore assumes that attention is a limited resource that cannot be directed to all possible input at any one time. This aspect of attention has been the most thoroughly studied and the literature concerned with it is extremely large. It is the research on selective attention that gave rise to the theories of early and late selection and to which research on inattention is most closely related.

Another way of categorizing attention is in terms of the distinction between spatial attention and object-based attention (Baylis and Driver 1992; Duncan 1984). The spatial aspect of attention has been documented by evidence showing that observers are more likely to detect, identify, or more quickly perceive a stimulus located in an area to which attention is directed. This aspect of attention is clearly relevant to our findings showing that under conditions of inattention a stimulus located within the zone of attention is more likely to be seen than one outside that region.

Object-based attention refers to the fact that observers are faster to respond if their task involves comparing features that are present in one object rather than two even when the spatial relations between these features are identical in the one and two object displays. We briefly considered whether the object-based aspect of attention might account for the cases in which a stimulus outside the zone of attention is perceived under conditions of inattention, but these cases seemed more easily explained in terms of the meaningfulness or salience of the stimulus.

Attention as Perception

If nothing is consciously perceived without attention, are conscious perception and attention the same? Are the processes responsible for conscious perception the same processes we designate as attention? If so, then voluntary attention, entailing as it does intention and expectation, might be construed as a kind of highlighting operation which amplifies certain perceptual processes. Captured attention might differ only in the degree of amplification and thus not as predictably yield conscious perception. The speculation that attention acts to highlight relevant stimulus information is consistent with the position maintained by LaBerge that

> Attention is expressed by the relative enhancement of information flow in particular pathways relative to the flow in surrounding pathways. A structure of the brain that produces a modulation of information flow is conjectured to be the thalamocortical circuit, which is found at virtually every area of the cerebral cortex. During the moments when the activity in a cortical area that specializes in a perception . . . is elevated sufficiently by the thalamocortical circuit that perception . . . fills the mind. Being "mindful" of a particular process is not just a spectator activity: Mindfulness, or attentional processing, shapes the way that mental activity proceeds (1995, 221–222).

Unfortunately, although the proposal that conscious perception and attention refer to identical processes has the advantage of simplicity, it is discredited on several grounds. First, it would appear to lead to the false conclusion that there can be no attention without perception. This conclusion seems false on both experiential and empirical grounds. It is not an uncommon experience to be looking for something or keenly awaiting its appearance in the absence of perceiving it, for example, waiting in silence in the dark for the phone to ring. Both the looking for and the awaiting are part of what we mean by attention in our ordinary language, but in cases such as these the looking for is not associated with any perception. In its most extreme form, anticipatory attention even may generate a perception in the absence of any sensory input, which again would seem to distinguish perception from attention. James echoes this not unfamiliar experience when he writes: "When watching for the distant clock to strike, our mind is so filled with its image that at every moment we think we hear the longed-for or dreaded sound. So of an awaited footstep" (1981, 419).

The empirical grounds for rejecting the proposal that perception and attention are one parallel those based on ordinary subjective experience. In addition, laboratory studies of vigilance provide another example of the distinction between attention and perception. These studies demonstrate an observer's ability to monitor one particular region of blank space, which results in the more rapid or more sensitive detection of a stimulus in that location. Although the consequence of the vigilance may be a lower detection threshold and a more rapid perception of the target, if no event occurs, there will be no perception. In other words, one can be vigilant without actually perceiving, implying that perception and attention are distinct processes. A state of vigilance may precede but does not necessitate perception. One can remain vigilant for some period of time without perceiving anything at all if there is nothing there to be perceived.

Still another quite simple-minded reason for rejecting the notion that perception and attention are one is that the objects of attention need not be perceptual at all. We can and do attend to ideas and feelings and, in fact can attend so completely or exclusively to them that we may fail to perceive events occurring in our immediate environment. How can perception and attention be one if we can attend without perceiving and can attend to nonperceptual objects?

Finally there now seems to be accumulating evidence of an anatomically separate attentional system. Posner, one of the investigators who has explored this system writes, "First there exists an attentional system of the brain that is at least somewhat anatomically separate from various data-processing systems. By *data-processing systems,* we mean those that can be activated passively by input or output" (Posner 1995). In other words, this means that there are structures in the brain that "seem to be specific to attention rather than being primarily involved in other forms of processing" (Posner 1995, 616).

Other Modes of Perception Without Attention

We have seen that the conclusion that nothing is perceived without attention, extends to sensory modalities other than vision. Although our inquiry into the role of attention in audition and touch were of a very preliminary nature, the results nevertheless attest to the centrality of attention in these modalities as well. In the case of audition, a clearly audible tone was not detected by a significant group of subjects when they were engaged in a task that required them to pay attention to a message delivered to the other ear. Not only did we find auditory deafness to a single tone but in an exploration of the perception of auditory grouping under conditions of inattention, we also found significant deafness (65%) to a repeated sequence of tones, which on the critical trial were grouped into triplets. In this case not only was grouping not perceived, but the repeated tones making up the grouping patterns also failed to be detected under conditions of inattention, although both the tones and the grouping were perceived with attention. The fact that auditory deafness also occurs under conditions of inattention when the distraction task occupying the subject's attention is visual rather than auditory further suggests that the effects of attention on perception are not modality bound.

Visual Neglect: A Clinical Analogue to IB

The centrality of attention to perception is also evident in various disorders of perception. The clearest example is unilateral visual neglect, which is frequently associated with damage to the right parietal cortex. Patients suffering from visual neglect fail to orient toward stimuli present on the contralesional side of space (i.e., on the left) and may appear completely blind to objects or parts of objects that are located to the left, opposite the side of the injury, even though there is no sensory impairment.[12] These patients can easily be distinguished from those demonstrating neglect who have suffered unilateral lesions that have destroyed their primary visual cortex. Unlike the unilateral neglect patients, these patients demonstrate clear hemianopia and suffer from a sensory deficit in the field opposite the lesion. In contrast, unilateral visual neglect is not associated with any visual sensory deficit and instead is considered a disorder of visual attention. This is clear from the fact that neglect patients will orient toward and report a *single* object regardless of whether it is on the left or the right, that is, regardless of whether it is the field opposite the lesion or on the same side as the lesion, making it clear that their deficit is not sensory. (Hemianopic patients, in contrast, will neither orient toward nor report seeing an object in the field opposite the lesion even if it is the only object in the visual field.) If two identical objects are shown to a unilateral neglect patient, one to the left and one to the right, they appear to be blind to the object on the left (on the side opposite the lesion). This phenomenon is referred to as *extinction*. If the two objects are different, extinction may not occur, that is, the patient may see both objects. If, however, the objects are different examples of the same thing, for example, a plastic and metal fork, the one on the contralesional side may not be seen (Farah, Monheit, and Wallace 1991; Rafal and Robertson 1995, 625–627; Gazzaniga, 1995). These symptoms have been explained in terms of a deficit in the attentional system.

Balint's syndrome[13] is another clinical instance of a severe visual attentional deficit that is associated with bilateral lesions of the posterior parietal lobes or the parieto-occipital junction (Farah 1990; Rafal and Robertson 1995; Rafal, in press). These patients are only able to see one object at a time and suffer from a severe narrowing of visual attention. Both unilateral neglect and Balint's syndrome provide additional grounds for rejecting the view that perception and attention are one, as well as for accepting the proposition that attention is necessary for perception.

It seems just possible that inattentional blindness may be an experimentally induced analogue of unilateral visual neglect because both neglect and IB are caused by a failure to attend to a particular stimulus. The parallel between unilateral neglect and IB, in fact, is striking. Just as the apparent blindness in unilateral neglect seems to be caused by the failure to attend to some object, IB also is caused by the failure to attend to a stimulus. Just as there is evidence of the deep processing and encoding of stimuli to which subjects are inattentionally blind (see chapter 8), so there is evidence that this is true of stimuli suffering extinction in neglect patients (Marshall and Halligan 1988; Baylis, Driver, and Rafal 1993; Ladavas, Paladini, and Cubelli 1993; Berti and Rizzolatti 1992). This has been demonstrated by documenting priming by stimuli suffering extinction in patients with visual neglect (Mattingly, Davis, and Driver 1997) that is similar to the priming found for stimuli suffering inattentional blindness. This also appears to be true of the objects that Balint's syndrome patients fail to see (Coslett and Saffran 1991). In both cases (IB and visual neglect), there is evidence that stimuli not consciously perceived will produce priming. The fact that experimentally produced inattention has consequences not unlike those caused by deficits of attention associated with cortical damage not only lends greater credibility to the phenomenon of IB, but also suggests that the study of IB may lead to a better understanding of the nature of the attentional deficit associated with neglect.

Finally it is of some interest to note that researchers studying unilateral neglect seem not to question the reality of the apparent blindness that is an earmark of the condition, whereas a frequently asked questions about IB is whether it actually is an instance of apparent blindness or only a failure of memory. The parallel between IB and neglect therefore provides another reason for rejecting the possibility that IB is caused by a failure of memory.

Hypnosis

Other evidence of the importance of attention for perception may be found in various hypnotically induced perceptual insensitivities (see Kihlstrom 1985). For example, as a result of suggestion hypnotized subjects may report that they do not see some object that is squarely within their visual field, a phenomenon referred to as *hypnotic blindness* (Bryant and McConkey 1989; 1990). Bryant and McConkey provide evidence suggesting that the hypnotic blindness may require that attention be allocated to the supposedly unseen input. Here attention may be serving to inhibit rather than to enable perception and is supposed to be responsible for maintaining the supposed blindness. Thus, in their experiment when stimulus information was present that had to be suppressed, their hypnotized subjects took longer to respond on some secondary task they were required to perform.

Insofar as hypnosis involves the manipulation of attention, it too provides an example of the importance of attention to conscious perception. Thus inattentional blindness would appear to be one of a number of well-documented phenomena that support the conclusion that there is no perception without attention.

Implicit Perception

Not only does IB seem to have a clear relationship to visual neglect and perhaps hypnotically-induced blindness, but the evidence of priming by stimuli suffering IB also connects it to the growing evidence that many stimuli that are not consciously perceived for other reasons nevertheless produce priming. In the previous section on visual neglect it already was noted that stimuli not seen because of neglect produce priming. There now is also evidence that a word presented during an attentional blink produces priming (Luck, Vogel, and Shapiro 1996). The term *attentional blink* refers to the failure to detect a target item that occurs within 100–600 msec. after a target is detected when a series of stimuli are presented in rapid succession. This phenomenon is also attributed to a failure of attention (Raymond, Shapiro, and Arnell 1992; Shapiro 1994). There is also evidence that stimuli not perceived because they are suppressed due to binocular rivalry produce semantic priming (Zimba and Blake 1983), and there is considerable evidence that stimuli that are not perceived because they are presented subliminally produce priming. (For example, Marcel 1983; Greenwald, Klinger, and Liu 1989; Greenwald 1992.) And in the New School laboratory we have obtained evidence (Silverman and Mack 1997) that one row of letters in a 3 × 3 matrix presented briefly (50 msec.) that is not cued for recall nevertheless prime a subsequently viewed letter array, even though it has long been believed that the stimuli in the uncued rows of such displays are evanescent and fade very quickly from iconic memory (Sperling 1960). The procedure typically used in iconic memory experiments entails briefly presenting a matrix of stimuli and following them with a cue, often auditory, that signals which row of a 3 × 3 or 4 × 4 matrix the subject is meant to report. The cued stimuli that benefit from attention to the iconic image are generally reported more or less correctly and were believed to be encoded, whereas the other stimuli that do not benefit from attention were thought to decay rapidly. However, our results indicate that this is not the case, and that these other stimuli, which subjects can neither recall nor otherwise recognize, can prime and in this respect are related to the priming by IB stimuli.

All these many different avenues of evidence to which IB stimuli must be added, point to a theory of perception that must allow for the deep processing of a great deal of visual input that is not generally available to consciousness. It is not clear that any theory of perception can yet easily accommodate this accumulating evidence.

Some Implications

The fact that the absence of attention causes apparent blindness, deafness, and numbness and perhaps even insensitivity to extreme pain is the basis for our claim that attention is necessary for conscious perception. It is a claim that is strongly supported by our results and is the major conclusion we draw from this research. It is a conclusion that has strong implications for contemporary theories of perception, particularly those that distinguish between preattentive and attentive perception or between low level and high level vision. If all conscious perception entails attention then no conscious percept can be either preattentive or low level.

However, although our findings suggest major revisions in theories of perception, they are not only consistent with our everyday experiences, but echo our past as well. The phenomenon we have called inattentional blindness is one that appears to have been observed and commented upon by philosophers long ago but has never before been systematically investigated nor even acknowledged by contemporary psychologists. We must once again revert to James who, in *The Principles of Psychology* (1981), cites the experiences and comments of others like Archimedes and Pascal to the effect that deep attentional absorption can lead to insensitivity to even the severest pain.[15] Even Aristotle discussed the profound affects caused by the absorption of attention.[16]

> Another question respecting sense perception is as follows. Assuming, as is natural, that of two movements the stronger always tends to exclude the weaker, is it possible or not that one should be able to perceive two objects simultaneously in the same individual time? The above assumption explains why persons do not perceive what is brought before their eyes, if they are at the time in deep thought, or in a fright, or listening to some loud noise (lines 447:11–14).

Notes

Chapter 1

1. The term constancy refers to a pervasive perceptual phenomenon characterized by the fact that our perceptions remain constant despite wide variations in the retinal image. For example, as we and the objects in our environment move, the distances to objects change, and this change causes a correlative change in the sizes of the images of objects on our retinas. (There is an inverse relationship between image size and distance.) However, these changes in retinal image size (visual angle) are usually not reflected in our perceptions of size, which tend to remain constant. The same achievement of constancy occurs for other object properties such as shape, direction, stability, and lightness of surfaces, despite continual changes in the proximal image representation of these properties.
2. See also Rock et al. (1992b) on grouping by similarity of perceived lightness rather than of registered intensity (or luminance) and Sekular and Palmer (1992) on grouping by similarity of perceived shape rather than on the shape of the elements on the retina. Moreover, other findings on the perception of shape that are clearly related to perceptual organization have shown that the perception of shape requires attention (see Rock, Schauer, and Halper 1976; Rock and Gutman 1981).
3. Variations from this general method are always noted in the text.
4. The dimensions of the various crosses serving as distraction stimuli in the Berkeley lab were as follows: each cross was randomly selected from the following four possible lengths: 3.6 cm (2.7 degrees), 4.4 cm (3.3 degrees), 5.2 cm (3.9 degrees), and 6.0 cm (4.5 degrees). In The New School lab one of the following crosses was used on each trial: 4.9 cm (3.7 degrees) by 4.1 cm (3.1 degrees), 4.3 cm (3.2 degrees) by 4.9 cm (3.7 degrees), 5.1 cm (3.8 degrees) by 4.9 cm (3.7 degrees), and 4.7 (3.5 degrees) by 5.1 cm (3.8 degrees).
5. Although some subjects may have moved their eyes during the 200 msec., this should not affect the meaning of the results, as will be clear subsequently.
6. We later explored the frequency of false positive responses elicited by asking observers whether they had seen anything that had not been present previously. The results are described in chapter 11.
7. To our surprise we found subjects failing to spontaneously report grouping by similarity of lightness or proximity even with full attention in the control trials of several experiments. This matter will be discussed more fully in chapter 2.
8. This view was questioned by the research results.
9. Some might maintain that attention is confined to the contours of the attended object, that is, it is directed only to the cross itself (LaBerge and Brown 1989). However, results from experiments explored in later chapters argue against this.

10. There is now accumulating evidence indicating that a *change* in a stimulus is frequently not perceived (Rensink, O'Regan, and Clark 1997; Pashler 1988; Levin and Simons, in press) which may be another reason why many subjects failed to perceive the critical stimulus.

11. Chapter 7 addresses the question of whether it is the phenomenal or retinal size of the stimulus that is primarily responsible for the capture of attention under conditions of inattention.

12. The fact that certain stimulus attributes like flicker and abrupt onset, which have been found to capture attention in other experimental paradigms (Jonides and Yantis 1988; Yantis and Jonides, 1990; Yantis 1993), failed to overcome IB in our studies complicates any explanation in terms of early selection.

13. The question of whether evidence of stem completion is grounds for inferring semantic processing or only what Bowers and Schacter (1990) refers to as "presemantic perceptual representation" is difficult to resolve and will be discussed.

14. By this definition attention is *necessary* for conscious perception.

Chapter 2

1. Unless otherwise noted, all the experiments described in this chapter were performed in the New School laboratory.

2. The reader is referred to this article for more details about the procedure and results and about the specific experiments performed.

3. The finding that texture segregation is not perceived without attention is supported by results reported by Ben-Av, Sagi, and Braun 1992.

4. The effect of the mask was not always predictable. Sometimes it made a difference and sometimes it did not. We note when it did not matter. This issue is discussed in chapter 3, pp. 68–70; 72–74.

5. Amodal completion describes the perception of a partially occluded object as complete. An example of this phenomenon is the perception of a complete circle when it is partially occluded by a superimposed rectangle. Because the image of the complete circle does not exist on the retina, the reasonable assumption is that the perception of amodal completion relies on processes occurring late in the analysis of the sensory input.

6. The research on common fate was done as the honor's M.A. research project by Willann Stone at the New School for Social Research in 1993.

7. This research is summarized in Chapter 3.

8. See also Spelke, Gutheil & Van de Walle (1995) showing the importance of common fate in infants.

9. The fact that only 15% of the subjects reported perceiving a difference when the difference was based on coherent versus random motion is puzzling, because it is well below chance assuming that the probability of guessing that there was an odd quadrant of motion was equal to guessing that there was not. Perhaps the reason for the infrequency of guessing that there was an odd quadrant is attributable to the fact that the coherent versus random motion difference was very difficult to detect so that subjects simply did not perceive any difference and therefore reported they did not.

10. The experiments on color pop out were performed and analyzed by Christopher Linnett (1996) as part of his doctoral dissertation in the laboratory at the University of California, Berkeley.

11. This, however, might not be surprising because one of the characteristics of pop out is the failure to perceive target location.

12. This experiment was just like those described earlier that explored the perception of the motion of a single moving element in an array of stationary elements. In those experiments also no pattern was present with the cross prior to the critical trial.

13. This result differed from the result obtained in exploring motion pop out in which only 41% of the subjects reported perceiving motion.

14. It is puzzling to consider why there is frequent pop out in the present experiment when the array surrounding the cross only appears on the critical trial and so much less pop out under similar conditions when the target is defined by motion. Perhaps the present experiment in which the target is defined by two dimensions of difference—shape and color—produces stronger pop out than one in which the target is only defined by one dimension of difference as in the motion pop out experiments.

15. If as Northdurft (1992) and others have suggested, grouping, texture segregation and pop out are based on the detection of local discontinuities rather than on grouping of elements by similarity, then it would be incorrect to say that these perceptual failures occur because grouping is not achieved without attention. Rather, if all these perceptual experiences are based on the perception of local discontinuities, then it follows that it is these discontinuities which are not perceived without attention and that therefore account for the failure to perceive pop out, texture segregation, and grouping under conditions of inattention.

16. Later research reported in subsequent chapters led to the hypothesis that, for the most part, only salient or highly meaningful stimuli capture attention when presented under conditions of inattention, and only those stimuli are consciously perceived. If this is true, then the failure to consciously perceive grouping or pop out could be due to their lack of salience or meaningfulness when they are not actively searched for. This issue will be discussed again.

Chapter 3

1. Many of the experiments described in this chapter were performed at the Berkeley laboratory by Christopher Linnett and Tony Ro with the assistance of Diane Beck. Berkeley students volunteered as subjects.

2. In chapter 6 experiments are described that demonstrate the effect of size on the capture of attention. The finding that a critical stimulus array that covers a fairly large area like the numerosity, grouping, and pop out displays are likely to capture attention is consistent with the finding that larger arrays are likely to do so as well.

3. These experiments were done by Williann Stone at the New School for Social Research and were reported at the 1992 meeting of the Psychonomic Society.

4. This change was made in order to meet the conditions necessary for the achievement of stroboscopic motion with a 3.4 degree step size.

5. Because short range apparent motion is considered by many to be a sensory phenomenon, and long range apparent motion is considered to be a perception based on cognitive inferential processes, this might be thought to account for why short range apparent motion (or an approximation of short range motion) is more likely to be perceived under conditions of inattention. However, the explanation of our findings presented in the last chapter makes this seem unlikely.

6. That those subjects who reported seeing something else on the critical trial were able to identify it distinguishes these results from those obtained when the critical shape stimulus was located in the parafovea. Subsequent experiments led us to wonder if this may have been due to an acuity difference between fovea and parafovea, even though subjects identified the shapes in the control condition when they were

in the parafovea. If this were so, it would suggest a connection between acuity and attention.

7. A series of experiments virtually identical to these on the role of a mask and on the presentation of the critical stimulus at fixation were performed at the New School laboratory, with somewhat different results. In particular there was less IB. However, some investigation of this difference led us to conclude that the difference was due to a difference in the masks used, and when this difference was eliminated the results from the two laboratories became consistent. Moreover, the many subsequent experiments in which the critical stimulus was presented at fixation consistently produced high degrees of IB. We therefore have chosen not to describe these New School experiments and simply wish to note the discrepancy.

8. The question of whether the diffusion of attention is relevant to the relatively smaller amounts of IB when the critical stimulus is presented in the parafovea in a quadrant of the cross centered at fixation rather than when the cross is centered in the parafovea and the critical stimulus is presented at fixation is examined in Chapter 4 where evidence is presented to support the diffusion of attention hypothesis.

9. This experiment was suggested, designed, and programmed by Tony Ro, in the Berkeley laboratory.

10. This explanation was first suggested to us by Margaret Wilson.

11. The failure to find pop out of either color or motion despite the fact that under conditions of inattention a moving or colored stimulus is likely to be seen when presented in a empty field in the parafovea suggests that conspicuity is a factor in the capture of attention. It would appear that embedding the critical stimulus in a multi-element array makes it less conspicuous and therefore less likely to be perceived without attention.

12. Harris Ingle and Daniel Kuang performed the experiments on conspicuity in the Berkeley laboratory.

Chapter 4

1. In the previous chapter we raised the possibility that the region to which attention is directed may be more narrowly defined by the locus of points along the contours of the cross rather than the virtual ellipse defined by its arms. However, the results of an experiment described later in this chapter, which directly addressed this issue, ruled this out.

2. These experiments were performed by Willann Stone at the New School.

3. This latter result indicates a certain degree of imprecision in the perception of location because all subjects were precisely correct in the divided and full attention conditions. This finding is supported by experiments designed to investigate the precision of localization under conditions of inattention done in the Berkeley laboratory by Ethan Newby.

4. Were we to take the *attention as spotlight* metaphor literally then the zone of attention might more aptly be described as a circular area surrounding the attended stimulus. It would then follow that a stimulus falling within the circular area immediately surrounding the rectangle, but outside of it, would still be within the zone of attention. However, this issue is not relevant to the experiments we did because stimuli we defined as outside the zone of attention were always outside the rectangle and outside the circular area immediately surrounding it.

5. These experiments were done at the New School by Willann Stone.

6. Because the subjects were told prior to each trial on which side of fixation the rectangle would appear, there is a possibility that the subjects might have moved their

eyes away from the fixation point toward where the rectangle was expected. Had this happened, it would have brought fixation closer to the critical stimulus, which then might account for any decrease in IB. In order to minimize the chance that this would occur, on every trial the experimenter made a point of stressing the importance of maintaining fixation.

7. The reader is reminded that these parameters yielded apparent motion perception under conditions of inattention in our earlier experiments on motion (see chapter 3, p. 62–67).

8. Recently reported findings indicating that subjects fail to notice change even if they are looking for it if it does not occur in the objects of interest within a scene suggest that it is very unlikely that subjects will notice change in what have been irrelevant stimuli when they are not actually looking for it (Rensink, O'Regan, and Clark 1997; Levin and Simons, in press).

9. If on trials in which subjects were guessing there were an equal probability of their reporting having seen something other than the rectangle and not reporting having seen something else, then the fact that 90% of the subjects reported not seeing anything else becomes puzzling because it is greater than what could be expected by chance. However, there is no reason to believe that these are equally probable responses when subjects do not perceive anything else and are fairly sure that nothing else was there, which is what we believe was the case and what it means to suffer IB.

10. When this experiment was repeated without a mask, 3 of the 10 subjects (30%) tested reported seeing the outside dot move and correctly identified the direction of its motion. Thus, IB was 70%. These results confirm the results obtained from the 10 subjects tested with a mask as well as the results of the experiment reported previously indicating that the mask has a modest effect. (See also the discussion of the effectiveness of the mask chapter 3, p. 72–74).

11. The finding that only 58% of the subjects perceived the odd quadrant on the critical inattention trial, despite the fact that subjects were actively searching for it, argues even more strongly against the view that texture segregation based on orientation differences is a preattentive percept.

12. These experiments were performed by Teresa Hartmann at the New School.

13. These experiments were carried out at the Berkeley Laboratory by Quinn Hume.

14. Because the frequency of correct reports in the two task experiments was about the same as in the single distraction task experiments, it may be that doubling the task did not significantly increase the attentional load and consequently failed to cause an increase in IB.

15. The experiments described in this section were carried out by Teresa Hartmann at the New School.

16. Another experiment not reported in this chapter lends additional support to this conclusion. In one of the experiments in which 20 subjects participated, the cross was located in the parafovea, and on the critical trial, the critical stimulus appeared at its center, that is, at the center of the attentional field but 2.0 degrees from fixation. In another experiment with 20 subjects the cross was centered at fixation and the critical stimulus was again at its center, that is, it was both at the center of attention and at fixation. In both cases only 1 of the 20 subjects failed to detect the presence of the critical stimulus in the inattention condition (IB = 5%) suggesting that what is important is the position of the critical stimulus relative to the focus of attention and *not* its position relative to fixation. (Fifteen of the 19 subjects (79%) who detected the presence of the critical stimulus when it was at fixation identified it correctly, whereas only 8 of the 19 subjects who detected it when it was in the periphery did so.

17. Contrary to what intuitively might seem the case, evidence has been reported (Kowler et al. 1995) showing that the execution of saccadic eye movements require attention.

18. The amount of IB obtained is comparable to the IB for the identical critical stimulus obtained using the standard crosses located in the parafovea with the critical stimulus at fixation (see experiment described in chapter 3).

19. The IB found in this experiment cannot be attributed to saccadic suppression. First, if saccadic suppression was the cause of the blindness, it should have been present in the divided attention condition as well. Second, the time course of suppression is shorter than the 700 msec. duration of the critical stimulus and during part of this 700 msec. the eyes were stationary.

Chapter 5

1. All the experiments described in this chapter were carried out in the New School laboratory with the collaboration of Jonathan Katz, Teresa Hartmann, and Sarah Hahn.

2. When lexical stimuli were used, whether as the critical stimulus or the distraction stimulus, the first letter of each word was always capitalized.

3. Although an early selection theory may be able to account for the recognition of a highly familiar stimulus such as one's name with the assumption of a low recognition threshold, it seems less able to account for why the presence of words as familiar as *Time* or *House* go undetected. The coarse information that permits the recognition of one's own name ought to lead at least to the detection of the presence of these other stimuli, even if there is insufficient information available for their identification.

4. Although this roughly summarized account of the early selection theory seems to explain the failure to recognize most stimuli on the unattended channel, it is not clear why, according to this theory, the presence of these stimuli is not detected, because the coarse information that survives the early filter should be sufficient for this purpose.

5. An additional 10 subjects were tested with the standard mask following each trial. The effect of the mask here was profound. IB went from 30% to 90%. Only 1 of the subjects reported seeing something else on the critical inattention trial. That 1 subject correctly reported her name. The profound effect of the mask with a 100 msec. stimulus presentation contrasts sharply with its negligible effect when the stimulus is present for 200 msec. This may be due to the fact that processing may be complete in 200 msec., whereas it may not be after only 100 msec. Thus, in this latter case, processing is interrupted, whereas in the former case it is not.

6. If the subjects are divided into those whose names had five letters (average visual angle, 1.5 degrees), of which there were 12, and those with three- or four-letter names (average visual angle, 1.1 degrees, only one subject had a three-letter name), we find that only 33% of the subjects with five-letter names were blind, whereas all 8 of the subjects with three- or four-letter names were blind. This suggests that the angular size of the name might be a factor when the spelling of one's name is slightly modified. This would be consistent with the finding that increasing the size of a geometrical stimulus increases the probability of its detection under conditions of inattention.

7. These results by no means unequivocally demonstrate that it is the meaning of the stimulus that captures attention. The results are equally consistent with the hypothesis that it is the graphemic or perceptual character of the stimulus that is the basis

for the capture of attention and the perception of one's own name. Were this the case, it also would be consistent with the fact that modifying the name by switching a vowel significantly reduces the likelihood that it will be perceived without attention. This question will be discussed at greater length in Chapter 8.

8. Another experiment in this series that examined the affect of modifying the form of the subject's name was done in which the subject's name was presented vertically. Fifteen subjects were tested. On the critical trial in the inattention condition, the name appeared at fixation with the first letter(s) immediately above and the last letter(s) immediately below the center of fixation. In the divided and full attention conditions, the subject's name written vertically was again the critical stimulus. Another group of 15 subjects were tested with someone else's name written vertically as the critical stimulus in all three conditions. Both versions of this experiment yielded little IB. Nevertheless, very few subjects in either version were able to identify the critical stimulus, which was also true in both the divided and full attention control conditions. We therefore concluded that words written vertically are extremely difficult to read and therefore no theory should predict that they will be identified without attention.

9. This experiment was suggested by Howard Egeth.

10. The question of whether familiarity plays a role in the capture of attention under conditions of inattention and therefore might account for the "own name effect" is explored in the next chapter.

11. The stimuli were presented on the display screen of a MAC SEII computer which was 76 cm from the subject's face. Subjects rested their chins in a chin rest to help them stabilize their fixation and the center of the screen was marked. The experiment was run using the program, V-search/Color, version 3.3 designed by R. Rensink and J. T. Enns.

12. Exactly what a failure to find the predicted asymmetry effect would mean is difficult to assess because it is not clear that the asymmetry effect reliably occurs in the many instances of pop out that have been reported. For that reason there may be no strong reason to believe that the processes underlying the search for one's own name are necessarily unique.

Chapter 6

1. All the experiments described in this chapter were run in the New School laboratory, most of them by Teresa Hartmann. Sara Hahn also ran some of the experiments described in this chapter.

2. Of the 3 subjects who were (inattentionally) blind, only 1 chose the happy face.

3. Although the difference between the frequency of IB for an upside down face is greater than that for a scrambled face (70% versus 44%), this difference is not significant (X^2, $df 1 = 1.93$ p. $< .20$).

4. One subject in the inattention condition reported seeing *the end* and another reported seeing *end*. The fact that this happened in the divided attention condition as well, where two subjects reported seeing *end* and one reported seeing *the end* may be a surprising version of the proofreader's error. Perhaps we see the word *The* almost completely isolated from other words primarily when it is attached to the word *end*, as it often is in the movies or in children's stories.

5. Over the course of this research it became clear that lexical stimuli, whether *The, Tie, Time, House* or names, on the whole, were seen more frequently under conditions of inattention than simple geometric shapes like circles, diamonds, and rectangles. This might be a consequence of the importance of meaning in the capture of

attention, because words are, by definition, meaningful, whereas simple geometric shapes are not. If this inference were correct, then a familiar and meaningful shape like a heart or a swastika ought to behave like a word under conditions of inattention. The validity of this inference is assessed later in this chapter.

6. To repeat what has been suggested earlier, the fact that we repeatedly find no increase in IB for a critical stimulus located outside the zone of attention when it is presented at fixation (the reader is referred to experiments with the subject's own name or the happy face where, under similar conditions, similar results were obtained) suggests that the postulated inhibition of attention in the region around fixation may be sufficiently effective to preclude any other inhibitory effect.

7. The frequency of occurrence of *Pear* is considerably higher than that of *Rape* (Kucera and Francis 1967), which means that if *Rape* is seen significantly more often than *Pear* under conditions of inattention, it not only cannot be attributed to its greater familiarity, but would be additional evidence against the speculation that familiarity alone contributes to the capture of attention.

8. No differences occurred in the divided and full attention conditions, nor in the accuracy with which subjects reported the longer line of the cross.

9. X^2 of 3.84 is necessary for significance at the .05 level.

10. Our looming stimulus only grew from 0.1 degree to 0.6 degree, which may explain why it did not attract attention. When we tested subjects with a stimulus which grew from 0.1 degree to 1.1 degrees in the same 200 msec. interval, 9 of the 10 subjects reported seeing either a looming or a stationary disc, but the fact that most subjects report seeing a disc when it is stationary and subtends an angle of 1.1 degrees prevents the conclusion that it is the looming that captures attention.

11. This series of experiments was carried out in the New School laboratory by Rista Luna and Jack Hoppenstand.

Chapter 7

1. Size constancy may also be based on the relationship between a stimulus and its surroundings.

2. A pilot experiment yielded similar results and thus strengthens these findings. Twenty subjects were tested with the larger stimulus at the greater viewing distance and only 7 of them detected its presence (IB = 65%). In contrast, when the same stimulus was at the closer viewing distance, only of 3 of the 10 subjects tested failed to detect it (IB = 30%). We also found that when we compared the amount of IB for the two stimuli subtending a visual angle of 0.6 degree—the larger stimulus at the greater distance against the smaller stimulus at the closer distance—IB was approximately the same.

3. The fact that one's own name that may subtend a visual angle of only 0.6 degree (e.g. Sue, or a happy face icon, the diameter of which is also only 0.6 degree, are seen under conditions of inattention) is evidence of the power of these stimuli to attract attention despite their angular size.

4. A reconsideration of the possible role of retinal or phenomenal size in IB appears in the last chapter.

5. These experiments were carried out in the Berkeley laboratory by Harris Ingle and Dan Kuang.

Chapter 8

1. The term *unconscious perception* may seem to some readers to be an oxymoron, since the term *perception* in ordinary English is generally defined as "awareness of objects

directly through the senses; consciousness" (Webster's New Riverside University Dictionary, 1988). What we mean by the short hand expression *unconscious perception* is that some sensory stimulus has been registered and encoded even though it has not been perceived or its presence detected.

2. All the lexical priming experiments were designed and carried out by Teresa Hartmann in the New School laboratory.

3. Although this automation of the trial sequence was initiated for the sake of convenience rather than from any theoretical considerations, it turned out not to significantly alter the results. In subsequent experiments we found that if the standard unpaced sequence of trials were used, there was slightly less IB, but the percent of the IB subjects who stem completed with the prime was not significantly different.

4. The robust IB effect occurred despite the fact that the critical stimuli subtended visual angles of between 1.0 and 1.3 degrees and the presentations were *not* masked.

5. The results of the stem completion experiment do not necessarily support an inference about semantic processing, because stem completion consistent with the prime requires only that the graphemes making up the word be processed and encoded.

6. The experiments described in this section were done in the Rock laboratory at Berkeley.

7. This research was designed and executed by Teresa Hartmann in the New School laboratory. It was her ingenuity and perseverance that is responsible for our successful attempt to document semantic priming.

8. We persisted in using this method because we had already established that priming measured by stem completion is unaffected by either the mask or by the pacing of trials.

9. This research was brought to the attention of one of us (AM) by Diane Beck.

10. These data indicating that similarity grouping is implicitly but not explicitly perceived is completely consistent with the findings reported in chapter 2 that demonstrate that none of the kinds of grouping explored—texture segregation, proximity or similarity grouping, and grouping by common fate—are consciously perceived under conditions of inattention. Furthermore, the Moore and Egeth results suggest that despite the failure to consciously perceive these kinds of grouping under conditions of inattention, the requisite organizational processes operate and their outcomes are implicitly perceived.

Chapter 9

1. The experiments described in this chapter were performed by Chris Linnet, Tony Ro, Harris Ingle, and Daniel Kuang in the Berkeley laboratory.

2. The results of the experiment described in chapter 4 in which executing saccades between sequentially displayed targets served as the distraction task also argues against an account of IB in terms of a failure of short-term memory.

3. Apparent motion has been reported when one of the two apparent motion stimuli is not perceived due to binocular rivalry suppression (Weisenfelder and Blake 1991). This would seem to mean that apparent motion can be perceived even when only one of the motion stimuli is visible, which raises a question about why subjects in our experiments failed to perceive it.

4. Of course, one might argue that having to maintain fixation on a particular location does require attention. However, even if it does, it would seem to require very little. Moreover, it is difficult to imagine any less demanding task that would keep the subjects fixated on the correct location which, of course, was essential because otherwise subjects might be looking in the wrong place when the critical stimulus appears.

5. A version of this experiment was done in the New School laboratory and produced very similar results, that is, virtually no IB for the critical stimulus.
6. It is tempting to attribute the difference in results to the difficulty observers are reported to experience when asked to search for a change between two successively presented pictures (Rensink, O'Regan, and Clark, 1997), but the fact that the observers are more likely to perceive the shape when the array is presented successively for 200 msec. than when it is continuously present and the critical shape replaces one of the continuously present small squares in the concluding 200 msec. makes this unlikely. The results reported by Rensink, O'Regan, and Clark would seem to predict the opposite outcome. Of course, an important difference between their procedure and ours is that in their experiments subjects were actively searching for a change in complex scenes.

Chapter 10

1. All the auditory inattention experiments were designed and executed by Jack Hoppenstand in the New School laboratory.
2. Very few subjects (4) were excluded from the study for failure to hear the tone with full attention.
3. An experiment examining the rate of false positive responding under conditions of inattention described in chapter 11 persuaded us that the reports of subjects who could neither locate nor in any way identify what they thought they heard belonged in the false positive category.
4. This task was suggested by Professor William Hirst, a colleague at the New School for Social Research.
5. All the touch experiments were done in the New School laboratory.

Chapter 11

1. The distinction between explicit and implicit perception is clearly described and discussed by Kihlstrom and his collaborators (Kihlstrom, Barnhardt, and Tataryn, 1992).
2. Evidence suggesting that, in the absence of attention, distance information is not taken into account in the explicit representation of objects (Epstein and Lovitts 1985) provides an additional reason for concluding that it may be retinal and not perceived size that accounts for detection under conditions of inattention, because perceived size is generally dependent on distance information.
3. We are not the first to propose a variable entry point for selective attention. Others have suggested that whether attentional selection occurs early or late is a function of perceptual load (Lavie and Tsal 1994). When the load is light, selection is late. When it is high, selection is early. Although the evidence marshaled in support of this analysis is considerable, the analysis does not seem to account for our results. The finding that retinal size that is processed early may play a role in stimulus detectability under conditions of inattention is not associated with an increase in perceptual load, nor is the finding that stimulus meaning can determine detectability associated with a decrease in load. Moreover, the one experiment expressly designed to manipulate perceptual load (chapter 4), produced no evidence of any effect on IB. The dimension of perceptual load simply does not seem to be relevant, because in all cases perceptual load is constant and by the definition offered by Lavie and Tsal must be considered low.
4. This issue also arises in the cases in which the size of a stimulus is responsible for its capture of attention. In that case the suggestion was made that the other aspects

of the stimuli are not consciously perceived because they are not highly meaningful. But in the cases now under discussion, it is not the size of the stimulus that is the basis for its capture of attention, so if these stimuli are in fact detected under conditions of inattention, the question is why.

5. This experiment was done by Ethan Newby at Berkeley.

6. In many of the experiments run at Berkeley, subjects were asked to provide a confidence rating for their reports of having seen something other than the distraction cross, which they did by assigning the number one, two, or three to their report, with three indicating virtual certainty and one indicating great uncertainty. The mean confidence rating for the false positive responses in the full attention condition was 2.33 whereas for the negative responses it was 1.61. Paradoxically this suggests that the subjects were surer about having seen something when there was nothing there than they were when something was there.

7. The remaining experiments investigating false positive responding were carried out by Teresa Hartmann at the New School for Social Research.

8. It is of some interest to note that although the number of subjects making false positive responses was nearly the same in each of the three conditions both in this and the previous experiment, these were not always the same subjects.

9. It perhaps should be noted that in our standard experiments subjects were almost invariably able to at least locate if not describe the critical stimulus on the critical divided attention trial and every subject was able to do both on the full attention control trial.

10. For example see, He and Nakayama 1992; Enns and Rensink 1990; Nakayama and Silverman 1986; Wang, Cavanagh, and Green 1994.

11. To repeat a point made earlier, if maintaining fixation or executing saccades between marked targets are considered tasks requiring attention which, at least in the case of saccades has been shown to be so (Kowler et al. 1995), then we have failed to establish that no attentional task is necessary to insure a state of inattention to some stimulus. However, it would appear to be virtually impossible to create conditions in which absolutely *no* mental activity is occurring in the observer, consequently requiring only that the subjects maintain fixation on a point directly in front of them may be the least demanding task possible.

12. The phenomenon of visual neglect has been extensively studied and this research has produced a substantial literature. The reader is referred to the following references for additional information: Bisiach 1993; Bisiach, Luzzatti, and Perani 1979; Rafal, 1994; Rafal and Robertson 1995; Rafal, in press.)

13. Farah (1990) refers to this as *dorsal simultanagnosia*. The underlying impairment in dorsal simultanagnosia appears to be a disorder of visual attention so severe that unattended objects are not seen at all (1990, 16).

14. If this is in fact the case, it should be possible to find evidence of negative priming, which is revealed by a subsequent increase in reaction time to a previously presented and ignored or in this case, repressed stimulus (see, for example, Tipper 1985).

15. Leibniz wrote, "Besides, there are hundreds of indicators leading us to conclude that at every moment there is in us an infinity of perceptions, unaccompanied by awareness or reflection" (1981, passage 53).

16. We are grateful to William Prinzmetal for leading us to this passage in Aristotle.

References

Aristotle 1984. *The Complete Works of Aristotle, Volume 1.* J. Barnes, ed. J. J. Beare, trans. Princeton, N.J.: Princeton University Press.

Atkinson, J., Francis, M., and Campbell, F. 1976. The dependence of the visual numerosity limit on orientation, colour, and grouping in the stimulus. *Perception* 5: 335–342.

Baylis, G., and Driver, J. 1992. Visual parsing and response competition: The effect of grouping factor. *Perception and Psychophysics* 51: 145–162.

Baylis, G., Driver, J., and Rafal, R. 1993. Visual extinction and stimulus repetition. *Journal of Cognitive Neurosciences* 5: 453–466.

Beck, J. 1966. Effect of orientation and of shape similarity on perceptual grouping. *Perception and Psychophysics* 1: 300–302.

Beck, J. 1972. Similarity grouping and peripheral discriminability under uncertainty. *American Journal of Psychology* 85: 1–19.

Beck, J. 1982. Textural segmentation. In J. Beck, ed. *Organization and Representation in Perception.* Hillsdale, N.J.: Lawrence Erlbaum Associates, pp. 285–317.

Berti, A., and Rizzolatti, G. 1992. Visual processing without awareness: Evidence from bilateral neglect. *Journal of Cognitive Neuroscience* 4: 345–351.

Ben-Av, M., Sagi, D., and Braun, J. 1992. Visual attention and perceptual grouping. *Perception and Psychophysics* 52: 277–294.

Biederman, I. 1981. On the semantes of a glance at a scene. In M. Kubovy and J. Pomerantz, eds. *Perceptual Organization.* Hillsdale, N.J.: Lawrence Erlbaum Associates.

Bisiach, E. 1993. Mental representation in unilateral neglect and related disorders: The Twentieth Bartlett Memorial Lecture. *Quarterly Journal of Experimental Psychology: Human Experimental Psychology* 46: 435–561.

Bisiach, E., Luzzatti, C., and Perani, D. 1979. Unilateral neglect, representational schema and reality. *Brain* 102: 757–765.

Bower, T. 1967. The development of object permanence: Some studies of existence constancy. *Perception and Psychophysics* 2: 416–418.

Bowers, J., and Schacter, D. 1990. Implicit memory and test awareness. *Journal of Experimental Psychology* 16: 404–416.

Braun, J., and Sagi, D. 1990. Vision outside the focus of attention. *Perception and Psychophysics* 48: 45–58.

Bridgeman, B., Kirch, M., and Sperling, A. 1981. Segregation of cognitive and motor aspects of visual function using induced motion. *Perception and Psychophysics* 29: 336–342.

Broadbent, D. E. 1958. *Perception and Communication.* London: Pergamon Press.

Bruce, V. 1988. *Recognizing Faces.* Hillsdale, N.J.: Lawrence Erlbaum Associates.

Bryant, R., and McConkey, K. 1989. Hypnotic blindness: Awareness and attribution. *Journal of Abnormal Psychology* 98: 443–447.

Bryant, R., and McConkey, K. 1990. Hypnotic blindness and the relevance of attention. *Australian Journal of Psychology* 42: 237–296.

Butler, L., and McKelvie, S. 1985. Processing of form: Further evidence for the necessity of attention. *Perceptual and Motor Skills* 61: 215–221.

Cherry, E. C. 1953. Some experiments on the recognition of speech, with one and two ears. *Journal of the Acoustical Society of America* 25: 975–979.

Coslett, H. B., and Saffran, E. 1991. Simultanagnosia. To see but not two see. *Brain* 113: 1523–1545.

DeSchepper, B., and Treisman, A. 1996. Visual memory for novel shapes: Implicit coding without attention. *Journal of Experimental Psychology: Learning, Memory, and Cognition* 22: 27–47.

Deutsch, J., and Deutsch, D. 1963. Attention: Some theoretical consideration. *Psychological Review* 87: 272–300.

Dorfman, J., Shames, A., and Kihlstrom, J. F. 1996. Intuition, incubation, insight: Implicit cognition in problem solving. In G. Underwood, ed. *Implicit Cognition*. Oxford: Oxford University Press.

Driver, J., and Baylis, G. 1989. Movement and visual attention: The spotlight metaphor breaks down. *Journal of Experimental Psychology: Human Perception and Performance* 15: 448–456.

Duncan, 1984. Selective attention and the organization of visual information. *Journal of Experimental Psychology: General* 113: 501–517.

Egeth, H., Jonides, J., and Wall, S. 1972. Parallel processing of multi-element displays. *Cognitive Psychology* 3: 674–698.

Enns, J., and Rensink, R. 1990. Sensitivity to three-dimensional orientation in visual research. *Psychological Science* 1: 323–326.

Epstein, W., and Lovitts 1985. Automatic and attentional components in perception of shape-at-a-slant. *Journal of Experimental Psychology: Human Perception and Performance* 16: 11, 355–366.

Epstein, W., and Rock, I. 1960. Perceptual set as an artifact of recency. *American Journal of Psychology* 73: 314–328.

Eriksen, C. W., and Murphy, T. D. 1987. Movement of attentional focus across the visual field: A critical look at the evidence. *Perception and Psychophysics* 42: 299–305.

Farah, M. 1990. *Visual Agnosia*. Cambridge, Mass.: MIT Press.

Farah, M., Monheit, M., and Wallace, M. 1991. Unconscious perception of "extinguished" visual stimuli: reassessing the evidence. *Neuroscience* 29: 949–958.

Folk, C. L., Remington, R. W., and Wright, J. H. 1994. The structure of attentional control: Contingent attentional capture by apparent motion, abrupt onset, and color. *Journal of Experimental Psychology* 20: 317–329.

Gazzaniga, M. S. 1995. *The Cognitive Neurosciences*. Cambridge, Mass.: MIT Press.

Goodale, M. A., and Milner, A. D. 1992. Separate visual pathways for perception and action. *Trends in Neuroscience* 15: 20, 25.

Greenwald 1992. New look three: Unconscious cognition reclaimed. *American Psychologist* 47: 766–779.

Greenwald, A. G., Klinger, M. R., and Liu, T. J. 1989. Unconscious processing of dichoptically masked words. *Memory and Cognition* 17: 35–47.

He, Z., and Nakayama, K. 1992. Surfaces versus feature in visual search. *Nature* 359: 231–233.

James, W. 1981. *Principles of Psychology*. Cambridge, Mass.: Harvard University Press.

Jastrow, J. 1900. *Fact and Fable in Psychology*. Boston, Mass.: Houghton Mifflin Company.

Johansson, G. 1950. *Configurations in Event Perception*. Uppsala: Almqvist and Wiksell.

Jonides, J., and Gleitman, H. 1972. A conceptual category effect in visual search: O as letter or as digit. *Perception and Psychophysics* 12: 457–460.

Jonides, J., and Yantis, S. 1988. Uniqueness of abrupt visual onset in capturing attention. *Perception and Psychophysics.* 43: 203–206.

Julesz, B. 1980. Spatial nonlinearities in the instantaneous perception of textures and with identical powers. In C. Longuet Higgins and N. Sutherland, eds. *The Psychology of Vision: Philosophical Transactions of the Royal Society.* London 290: 83–94.

Julesz, B. 1981. Textons: The elements of texture perception and their interactions. *Nature* 290: 91–97.

Julesz, B. 1984. Toward an automatic theory of preattentive vision. In G. M. Edelman, W. E. Gall, and W. M. Cownan, eds. *Dynamic Aspects of Neocortical Function* New York: Neurosciences Research Foundation, pp. 585–612.

Kahneman, D. 1973. *Attention and Effort.* Englewood Cliffs, N.J.: Prentice-Hall.

Kihlstrom, J. 1985. Hypnosis. *Annual Review of Psychology* 36: 385–418.

Kihlstrom, J., Barnhardt, T., and Tataryn, D. 1992. Implicit perception. In R. F. Bornstein, and T. Pittman, eds. *Perception Without Awareness: Cognitive, Clinical, and Social Perspectives.* New York: Guilford Publications.

Kleffner, D., and Ramachandran, R. 1990. On the perception of shape from shading. *Perception and Psychophysics* 52: 18–36.

Köhler, W., and Adams, P. 1958. Perception and attention. *American Journal of Psychology* 71: 489–503.

Kowler, E., Anderson, E., Dosher, B., and Blaser, E. 1995. The role of attention in programming saccades. *Vision Research* 35: 1897–1916.

Kucera, H., and Francis, W. 1967. *Computational Analysis of Present Day American English.* Providence, R.I.: Brown University Press.

LaBerge, D. 1995. *Attentional Processing: The Brain's Art of Mindfulness.* Cambridge, Mass.: Harvard University Press.

LaBerge, D., and Brown, V. 1989. Theory of attentional operations. *Psychological Review* 96: 101–124.

Ladavas, E., Paladini, R., and Cubelli, R. 1993. Implicit associative priming in patients with visual neglect. *Neuropsychologia* 31: 1307–1320.

Lavie, N., and Tsal, Y. 1994. Perceptual load as a major determinant of the locus of selection in visual attention. *Perception and Psychophysics* 56: 183–197.

Leibniz, G. 1981. *New Essays on Human Understanding.* (P. Remnant and J. Bennett, ed. and trans. Cambridge, England: Cambridge University Press.

Levin, D. T., and Simons, D. J. In press. Failure to detect changes in attended objects in motion pictures. *Psychonomic Bulletin and Review.*

Linnett, C. M. 1996. Perception without attention: Redefining preattentive processing. Ph.D. dissertation, University of California at Berkeley.

Logan, G. 1988. Towards an instance of automatization. *Psychological Review* 95: 492–527.

Luck, S., Vogel, E., and Shapiro, K. 1996. Word meanings can be accessed but not reported during the attentional blink. *Nature* 383: 616–618.

Mack, A., Rock, I., Stone, W., Gotham, H., Linnett, C., and Ro, T. 1991. The perception of motion without attention. Psychonomics Meeting, San Francisco.

Mack, A., Tang, B., Tuma, R., Kahn, S., and Rock, I. 1992. Perceptual organization and attention. *Cognitive Psychology* 24: 475–501.

Marcel, A. 1983. Conscious and unconscious perception: Experiments on visual masking and word recognition. *Cognitive Psychology* 15: 197–237.

Marshall, J., and Halligan, P. 1988. Blindsight and insight in visual-spatial neglect. *Nature* 336: 766–767.

Mattingley, J. B., Davis, G., and Driver, J. 1997. Preattentive filling-in of visual surfaces in parietal extinction. *Science* 275: 671–674.

Milner, A. D., and Goodale, M. A. 1995. *The Visual Brain in Action.* Oxford: Oxford University Press.

Moore, C., and Egeth, H. 1997. Perception without attention: Evidence of grouping under conditions of inattention. *Journal of Experimental Psychology: Human Perception and Performance* 23: 339–352.

Moray, N. 1959. Attention and Dichotic Listening: Affective cues and the influence of instructions. *Quarterly Journal of Experimental Psychology* 11: 56–60.

Nakayama, K., and Silverman, G. 1986. Serial and parallel processing of visual feature conjunctions. *Nature* 320: 264–265.

Nakayama, K., and Joseph, J. 1997. In R. Parasuraman, ed. Attention, pattern recognition, and popout in visual search. *The Attentive Brain*. Cambridge, Mass.: MIT Press.

Neisser, U. 1967. *Cognitive Psychology*. New York: Appleton-Century-Crofts.

Nothdurft, H. C. 1992. Feature analysis and the role of similarity in preattentive vision. *Perception and Psychophysics* 52: 365–375.

Nothdurft, H. C. 1993. Faces and facial expressions do not pop out. *Perception* 22: 1287–1298.

Olsen, R., and Attneave, F. 1970. What variables produce similarity grouping? *American Journal of Psychology* 83: 1–21.

Palmer, S. 1975. Visual perception and world knowledge: Notes on a model of sensory cognitive interaction. In D. Rummelhart, eds. *Explorations in Cognition*. New York: Freeman Press.

Palmer, S., Neff, J., and Beck, D. 1996. Late influence on perceptual grouping: Amodal completion. *Psychonomic Bulletin and Review* 3: 75–80.

Palmer, S., and Rock, I. 1994. Rethinking perceptual organization: The role of uniform connectedness. *Psychonomic Bulletin and Review* 1: 29–55.

Pashler, H. 1988. Cross-dimensional interaction and texture segregation. *Perception and Psychophysics* 43: 307–318.

Perrett, D., Smith, P., Potter, D., Mistlin, A., Head, A., Milner, A., and Jeeves, M. 1985. Neurons response to faces in the temporal cortex: Studies of functional organization, sensitivity to identity and relation to perception. *Human Neurobiology* 3: 197–208.

Posner, M. 1978. *Chronometric Explanations of Attention*. Hillsdale, N.J.: Lawrence Erlbaum Associates.

Posner, M. 1980. Orienting of attention. *Quarterly Journal of Experimental Psychology* 32: 3–25.

Posner, M. 1995. Attention in cognitive neuroscience: An overview. In M. Gazzaniga, ed. *The Cognitive Neurosciences*. Cambridge, Mass.: MIT Press.

Posner, M., and Roger, M. 1978. Chronometric analysis of abstraction and cognition. In W. K. Estes, ed. *Handbook of Learning and Cognitive Processes*. Hillsdale, N.J.: Lawrence Erlbaum Associates.

Purcell, D., and Stewart, A. 1986. The face detection effect. *Bulletin of the Psychonomic Society* 24: 118–120.

Rafal, R. 1994. Neglect. *Current Opinion in Neurobiology* 4: 231–236.

Rafal, R. In press. Neglect. In R. Parasuraman, ed. *The Attentive Brain*. Cambridge, Mass.: MIT Press.

Rafal, R. 1997. Balint's Syndrome. T. E. Feinberg and M. J. Farah, eds. *Behavioral Neurology and Neuropsychology*. New York: McGraw Hill.

Rafal, R., and Robertson, L. 1995. The neurology of visual attention. In M. Gazzaniga, ed. *The Cognitive Neurosciences*. Cambridge, Mass.: MIT Press.

Raymond, J., Shapiro, K., and Arneall, K. 1992. Temporary supression of visual processing in and RSVP task: An attentional blink? *Journal of Experimental Psychology: Human Perception and Performance* 18: 849–860.

Reicher, G. M., Snyder, C. R., and Richards, J. T. 1976. Familiarity of background characters in visual scanning. *Journal of Experimental Psychology: Human Perception and Performance* 2: 522–530.

Rensink, R. A., O'Regan, J. K., and Clark, J. J. 1997. To see or not to see: The need for attention to perceive changes in scenes. *Investigative Ophthalmology and Visual Science* 37: s213.

Richardson-Klavehn, A., Gardiner, J., and Java, R. 1996. Memory: Task dissociation and dissociation of consciousness. In G. Underwood, eds. *Implicit Cognition* Oxford: Oxford University Press, pp. 85–158.

Rock, I. 1974. *Orientation and Form.* New York: Academic Press.

Rock, I., and Brosgole, L. 1964. Grouping based on phenomenal proximity. *Journal of Experimental Psychology* 67: 531–538.

Rock, I., and Gutman, D. 1981. The effect of inattention on form perception. *Journal of Experimental Psychology: Human Perception and Performance* 7: 275–285.

Rock, I., Linnett, C., Grant, P., and Mack, A. 1992a. Perception without attention: Results of a new method. *Cognitive Psychology* 24: 502–534.

Rock, I., Nijhawan, R., Palmer, S., and Tudor, L. 1992b. Grouping based on phenomenal similarity of achromatic color. *Perception* 21: 779–789.

Rock, I., Schauer, R., and Halper, F. 1976. Form perception without attention. *Quarterly Journal of Experimental Psychology* 28: 429–440.

Roediger, H., Weldon, M., Stadler, M., Michael, L., and Riegler, G. 1992. Direct comparison of two implicit memory tests: Word fragments and word stem completion. *Journal of Experimental Psychology: Learning, Memory, and Cognition* 18: 1251–1269.

Roll, E. 1984. Neurons in the cortex of the temporal lobe and in the amygdala of the monkey with selective for faces. *Human Neurobiology* 76: 249–271.

Schacter, D. L. 1987. Implicit memory. *Journal of Experimental Psychology: Learning, Memory and Cognition* 13: 501–518.

Schneider, G. E. 1969. Two visual systems: Brain mechanisms for localization and discrimination are dissociated by tectal and cortical lesions. *Science* 163: 895–902.

Searle, J. 1992. *Rediscovering of the Mind.* Cambridge, Mass.: MIT Press.

Sekular, A. B., and Palmer, S. E. 1992. Perception of partly occluded objects: A microgenetic analysis. *Journal of Experimental Psychology: General* 121: 95–11.

Shapiro, K. 1994. The attentional Blink: The brain's Eyeblink. *Current Directions in Psychological Science* 3: 86–89.

Silverman, M., Mack, A., and Hoppendstand, J. 1997. Priming by iconic images. *ARVO Abstracts: Investigative Ophthalmology and Visual Science* 38: s963.

Spelke, E. S., Gutheil, G., and Van de Walle 1995. The development of object perception. In D. Oshserson, ed. *Invitation to Cognitive Science, 2nd edition, volume 2: Visual Cognition.* Cambridge, Mass.: MIT Press.

Sperling, G. 1960. The information available in brief visual presentations. *Psychological Monographs: General and Applied* 74.

Theeuwes, J. 1991. Exogenous and endogenous control of attention: The effects of visual onsets and offsets. *Perception and Psychophysics* 49: 83–90.

Theeuwes, J. 1992. Perceptual selectivity for color and form. *Perception and Psychophysics* 51: 599–606.

Tipper, S. 1985. The negative priming effect: Inhibitory priming of ignored objects. *Quarterly Journal of Experimental Psychology* 37: 571–590.

Treisman, A. 1969. Strategies and models of selective attention. *Psychological Review* 76: 282–299.

Treisman, A. 1982. Perceptual grouping and attention in visual search for features and objects. *Journal of Experimental Psychology: Human Perception and Performance* 8: 194–214.

Treisman, A. 1985. Preattentive processing in vision. *Computer Vision, Graphics and Image Processing* 31: 156–177.

Treisman, A. 1986. Features and objects in visual processing. *Scientific America* 255: 114b–125.

Treisman, A. 1988. Features and objects: The Fourteenth Bartlett Memorial Lecture. *Quarterly Journal of Experimental Psychology* 40: 201–237.

Treisman, A., and DeShepper, B. 1996. Objects, tokens, attention, and visual memory. In T. Inui and J. McClelland, eds. *Attention and Performance XVI: Information Integration in Perception and Communication.* Cambridge, Mass.: MIT Press.

Treisman, A., and DeSchepper, B. 1994. Objects, tokens, attention and visual memory. Paper presented at Attention and Performance Conference, Kyoto, Japan.

Treisman, A., and Gelade, G. 1980. A feature-integration theory of attention. *Cognitive Psychology* 112: 97–136.

Treisman, A., and Gormican, S. 1988. Feature analysis in early vision: Evidence from search asymmetries. *Psychological Review* 95: 15–48.

Treisman, A., and Souther, J. 1985. Search asymmetry: A diagnostic for preattentive processing of separate features. *Journal of Experimental Psychology: General* 114: 285–310.

Trevarthan, C. B. 1968. Two mechanisms of vision in primates. *Psychological Forschung* 31: 299–337.

Ungerleider, L. G., and Mishkin, M. 1982. Two cortical visual systems. In D. J. Ingle and R. J. W. Mansfield, eds. *Analysis of Visual Behavior.* Cambridge, Mass.: MIT Press.

Wang, Q., Cavanagh, P., and Green, M. 1994. Familiarity cued pop out in visual search. *Perception and Psychophysics* 56: 495–500.

Weisenfelder, H., and Blake, R. 1991. Apparent motion can survive binocular rivalry suppression. *Vision Research* 31: 1589–1599.

Weiskrantz, L. 1986. *Blindsight: A case study and implications.* Oxford: Oxford University Press.

Wertheimer, M. 1923. *Untersuchungen zur lehre von der gestalt.* (Principles of perceptual organization) *Psychologische Forschung* 4: 301–350.

Wolfe, J., Cave, K., and Franzel, S. 1989. Guided search: An alternative to the feature integration model for visual search. *Journal of Experimental Psychology: Human Perception and Performance* 15: 419–433.

Wong, E., and Mack, A. 1981. Saccadic programming and perceived location. *Acta Psychologica* 48: 123–131.

Yantis, S. 1993. Stimulus attentional capture and attentional control settings. *Journal of Experimental Psychology: Human Perception and Performance* 19: 676–681.

Yantis, S., and Jonides, J. 1990. Abrupt onsets and selective attention: Voluntary versus automatic allocation. *Quarterly Journal of Experimental Psychology* 28: 429–440.

Zimba, K., and Blake, R. 1983. Binocular rivalry and semantic processing: Out of sight, out of mind. *Journal of Experimental Psychology, Human Perception and Performance* 9: 807–815.

Index